MAGIC, MYTH AND MEDICINE

Other books by the same author

EXTERNAL DISEASES OF THE EYE

THE OCULAR FUNDUS IN DIAGNOSIS AND TREATMENT

A TREATISE ON CATARACT

SURGERY OF THE EYE, NOSE AND THROAT

EYE, EAR, NOSE AND THROAT TREATMENT

ADENOIDS AND KINDRED PERILS OF SCHOOL LIFE

Magic, Myth and Medicine

BY DONALD T. ATKINSON

SC.D., M.D., LL.D., F.A.C.S., F.I.C.S.

FOREWORD BY DR. MAX THOREK

FOUNDER, INTERNATIONAL COLLEGE OF SURGEONS

CLEVELAND AND NEW YORK

THE WORLD PUBLISHING COMPANY

Library of Congress Catalog Card Number: 56-5306

2HC456

 Manufactured in the United States of America.

Designed by Abe Lerner

DEDICATED TO MY WIFE *Wanda Wiley Atkinson*

WHOSE ENCOURAGEMENT AND CO-OPERATION

HAVE DONE MUCH TO HELP MAKE THIS BOOK POSSIBLE

Contents

Foreword

Any book about the medical profession, whether it is a novel, a biography, an informative treatise in popular form, or, as in the case of Dr. Atkinson's *Magic, Myth and Medicine,* a history of the healer's art from the dawn of science to the present hour, is sure to be well and widely read. When the scholar's wisdom is combined with the storyteller's art, the result is fascination—a fascination no less magic, in its way, than the primitive arts with which Dr. Atkinson deals so ably.

The average lay person still regards the physician or the surgeon as a man set apart, a modern miracle worker; and this is understandable, for without the great background of the long hard struggle toward truth and without the immense bulk of accumulated special knowledge that goes into the making of a doctor, it would be difficult, indeed, not to regard him so. To focus a slowly moving spotlight on medicine down the centuries, as Dr. Atkinson does, is to dispel the misapprehension and dissolve the myth. Here the reader will find most of the great names in medicine, from Aesculapius to the giants of today.

And he will find them human as well as humane; fighting, struggling, studying, experimenting, inventing, and conferring. He will find none who accomplished his miracles in any other way than through hard work and patience. Hippocrates, Galen, Paracelsus, Paré, Vesalius, Semmelweis, Laënnec, Harvey, Mackenzie, Ehrlich—all these and many other names have become immortal, but those who bore them were all too sadly mortal. They are gone. To read of their problems and how they strove to solve them is an experience that has revived hope and vigor in many a doctor in a disheartened hour. It can hardly do less for those who are not doctors, but who share with the physician an ardent concern for the welfare of all mankind. It is a proud record, this story of medicine, for it is also the story of man at his best and highest, touching at times the majesty of total dedication to an ideal, the glory of a selflessness that can be matched by very few other professions. It is a heritage that demands the best in us, and it is a history that must awaken aspirations toward medicine in anyone who has the imagination to see and feel, as he reads, the cost in nerves, sinew, and sacrifice of the highly skilled medical service available today.

Magic, Myth and Medicine has the sound ring of truth. Much study has gone into it, and, we believe, much enjoyment also. Dr. Atkinson is to be congratulated on his success in marshaling the great procession so effectively in comparatively compact form. His book, we predict, will find a wide and appreciative audience outside the profession. And inside it—well, one may as well say, doctors love doctors too!

Dr. Max Thorek
Founder, International College of Surgeons,
International Surgeons Hall of Fame and
Museum of Surgical Science

Preface

Since early youth the author of these essays has read medical history for diversion and relaxation. During this time he formed the habit of making random notes of incidents which particularly interested him. It has since been his privilege to visit, on five continents, the sites of the labors of these heroes of medicine. As the years passed the notes gradually took form, without any idea, however, of their publication. Only in recent months have they assumed the shape in which they are now offered to the publisher.

Some space has been given in the text to what little is known of prehistoric medicine, as well as to Greek, Babylonian, and Hebrew medicine that has greatly influenced medical thought of later times. The lives of a group of very determined men of early historical periods have been more thoroughly reviewed. Their dogged perseverance was pitted against obstacles which for the time being were often insurmountable, but the unceasing exertions worked on future medical thought an influence that became so dominant as to revolutionize medieval and later medicine.

The written work, *A Cruising Voyage around the World,* by the pirate, Captain Woodes Rogers, has supplied me with little-known information relative to the trip to the South Seas of Dr. Thomas Dover, the first European physician to use ipecac as a specific in amoebic dysentery. His name still lingers with us in the famous "Dover's Powders" of our childhood. Much information came to me through other rare copies of the works of pirate surgeons which are now in my possession, chief of which is *A New Voyage and Description of the Isthmus of America* by Lionel Wafer. This British surgeon introduced so many new American drugs into England that the Royal Touch as a cure of disease, as well as the use of loathsome substances, such as animal ordure, in the treatment of the sick, were entirely done away with.

It may be interesting to note that, though the encouragement given to science during the lives of these pioneers was not great, the result of their labors manifests itself today in every country in the world where medicine is a science. To every thoughtful person the teachings and achievements of these men, many of them long denounced, will be regarded as the nucleus around which has grown practically every department of scientific medicine.

MAGIC, MYTH AND MEDICINE

1.

Magic, Germinator of Scientific Medicine

The waters of the Aegean Sea bathe the shores of Asia Minor and Greece, where it is believed that ancient medicine first sprang into existence. Let us embark in an imaginary craft and follow the meandering and tortuous coast line of these two cradles of early medicine. We may well compare the course taken on this journey to the ailments of primitive man, with his superstitions and taboos, gradually ambling onward during the dark ages of prehistory when magic held steadfastly to the minds of men. Then, after thousands of years, as history begins to dawn and taboos gradually fade away we still find magic in all its darker forms. For more thousands of years magic and the healing methods of primitive man lived on and held an overpowering influence over men's thoughts. One enemy sought magic workers to cast spells on some hated foe and, this result supposedly accomplished, soothsayers were employed to destroy the evil influence thus occasioned. Should the latter be thought to have succeeded, this assured life and health for his patient. Failing in this, the opposite result would ensue, and a worse fate awaited the magic healer, who, shorn of his laurels, was forthwith dispatched by his neighbors or fled for his life. More rational healers helped to influence their associates to improve the sanitation of their communities, but their work was frequently frowned upon. The forerunners of scientific medicine and sensible sanitation were often thought to be in league with evil spirits, the archenemies of mankind, and were the victims of persecution when they failed to stay the hand of epidemic diseases or to alleviate the sufferings of their neighbors, the more fortunate escaping the vengeance of the mobs only by flight and self-banishment from their homes and communities.

During the thousands of years that civilization has been shaping itself we have made great strides forward, but along the way we have shed few of the passions and destructive instincts of our primeval ancestors. Many of us carry loads of inherited characteristics which are an essential part of us. Hate, jealousy, revenge, and fear, which occupied the lives of our ancestors, still have possession of many of us. With our veneer of civilization, we in times of stress resort to inherited instincts given to the human family many thousands of years ago. These would control all our lives but for the development of our ability to think, which was generated by centuries of experience and by the further cultivation of the wholesome restraints of sympathy and conscience.

Our ancestors, shivering in fear in some unlit cave, had brains as large as, or perhaps even larger than those of later generations. A mighty warrior was primitive man and, so far as he could succeed, he destroyed those weaker than himself. His instincts thus served him well. But after long periods of devastation of others by brute force the weak were rooted out. Man perpetuated himself along with his great strength. His good points have resulted in civilization, but certain of his hereditary instincts remain fixed and, when not controlled, create our crime waves.

As we meander onward in this story we find the instincts of hate, revenge and jealousy gradually subdued by civilization. But fear remains, as one of the echoes from the lives of those before us, to play its role in the creation of disease.

There is, of course, much conjecture to be used in working out the medical history of primitive times. Magic in reference to healing occupied the minds of all early medical men. The doctor of that period was necessarily more or less of a sorcerer. One is reminded of a drawing on the walls of a cave in the Pyrenees, which depicts a witch doctor arrayed in the skins of animals, his legs heavily striped with colored earth, and wearing a pair of deer antlers as a headdress. It is believed that this oldest representative of the healing cult belonged to the Aurignacian race who lived here some fifteen thousand years before the Christian Era, at which time all European races were in the New Stone Age. As medicine is often the result of association, there can be no doubt that the superstitions of these early ages have been reflected through hundreds of years to those who followed the healing cult. Many of the specimens found in various parts of the world would indicate that the diseases which beset Stone Age people were essentially the same as today's. Evidence of rheumatoid arthritis is not uncommonly seen, the oldest example found being situated as a bony excrescence on the femur of the *Pithecanthropus erectus* discovered by Dubois in Java in 1891, its original possessor belonging to a race of ape men who became extinct thousands of years ago. Similar outgrowths have been found in the skeletons of lower animals that lived millions of years ago, such as the dinosaur tail vertebra recently discovered in a stratum of a Wyoming plateau.

While in London in May 1954, I learned of a rare find of human remains which had been unearthed from Stone Age barrows on an estate in southwestern England and which are now on display in the Tudor Museum of Southampton. I spent a few days in this institution and was well repaid by what I saw there. A skull particularly awakened my attention, not only because of its unusually massive proportions but also because of the advanced bony destruction owing to an abscess of the jaw, which showed evidence of having been operated upon. Much of the external wall had apparently been removed by a crude process of surgery. One could not help wondering what manner of treatment other than surgical this resident of Ice Age England might have been subjected to. That he died before recovering is evidenced by the fact that the margins of his bony wound were rough, with many overlapping scratches, showing that healing had not yet taken place at the time of his death.

That surgery was practiced by the ancient Briton is manifested in several instances, one case being that of a skull of a similar period found at Downs, Dorset. In this specimen is to be seen a trephine opening which seems to have healed before death. Nearly all of the other ancient Briton skulls which I have observed give evidence of abscesses at the roots of the teeth. This is due, no doubt, to the fact that their possessors lived in the cold and damp climate of a glacial period.

Examples of trephining of the skull which have turned up in Peru and in various places in Europe and Asia would seem to indicate that the purpose of these operations, at least at their beginning, was to liberate from the skull some malicious demons who either were thought to cause extreme pain, as in the case of migraine, or attacks of falling to the ground, as in epilepsy. Such operations were done at the hands of medicine men and were often resorted to. One specimen found had three distinct openings all well healed-over, as indicated by the smoothed-over appearance of the bones at their margins. That all such operations did not end so comfortably for the patient is indicated by the fact that in a large number of skulls thus treated several were seen in which the trephining had not been completed. This might have been due to the refusal of the patients to submit further to surgical procedures, or more likely it would indicate that the subjects had expired during the operation.

There can be little doubt that as time went on the operation of trephining was used in a rational manner in cases of depressed fracture. For instance, several specimens have been found in which smooth-edge trephine openings would indicate that they had recovered long enough for healing of the bone to have taken place. In some of these healed-over radiating fractures the results would suggest that the operation had saved the patient's life.

In numerous burial caves in France and Spain, bodies have been found covered with red ocher and other pigments. It is probable that these tinting substances had been put on the body before death, rather than as a post-mortem procedure. Red was a favorite color with our Stone Age ancestors as a means of restoring vigor to the body, as it still is in many parts of the world. A red light or red hangings in the sickroom of a patient with smallpox is still thought by many to prevent scarring. Inflamed joints are still wrapped in red flannel by the more primitive people in various parts of the United States; there are also some who believe that sore throats should be encased in red flannel or that red stockings should be tied around the neck. Observers call attention to the fact that a red thread strung around the neck and tied with nine knots is supposed by many in Scotland to prevent nosebleed. Perhaps it is because of this age-old superstition that chemists still are prone to color their pills and tablets red.

All of this is but an inkling of how ancient medicine got its start. A part of early medicine may, of course, be considered irrational, for it seems to be bound up entirely in magic. But many of the folk medicines cannot be viewed in such a light. They grew out of something innate in life which caused primitive man to seek help from the herbs and roots about him. That there is nothing irrational in this is indicated by the fact that our household pets instinctively eat grass when in physical distress, and are actually relieved.

2.

Geographical Relation in Early Medicine

In considering the early history of three advanced peoples, Egyptian, Babylonian, and Hebrew, we find that in the areas occupied by them, early civilization made more rapid progress than elsewhere. The reason for this was largely geographical. At first nomadic desert dwellers, these three peoples became agricultural when they learned to utilize their water supply. In Egypt, the Nile annually overflowed its banks, and it was discovered that with little labor crops of cereals, fruits, and vegetables could be raised in abundance. This gave the Egyptians leisure to engage in intellectual pursuits. They were the first, it is believed, to have perfected a method of making pictures on papyrus, which when put in certain sequences conveyed meaning. To the east in Babylonia, between the Tigris and Euphrates Rivers, another former desert people used a different form of characters, made with a stylus on wet clay. These are two of the earliest examples of the art of writing, which has aided so much in the growth of civilization.

Another desert people, the early Hebrews, moved between Babylonia and Egypt into what is now known as the Fertile Crescent. In this area the development of civilization was somewhat hindered by the fact that the region lay across the trade routes between Egypt in the west and Babylonia in the east. In this geographical situation, the Hebrews often met with great difficulties. In 586 B.C. Nebuchadnezzar the Great, of Babylonia, in retaliation for the favors he believed had been shown by the Hebrews to Egypt, carried most of the Jews into a prolonged captivity. This enforced sojourn was ended by Cyrus in 538 B.C., who allowed them to return and re-inhabit Jerusalem.

In the Egyptian writings taken from papyri found buried with mummies, we can read the story of the wailing women whose function it was to accompany the bodies of the deceased across the Nile to the burial places east of the river. Thanks to this custom, we have learned not only about Egyptian medicine but also, if to a lesser degree, about Hebrew and Babylonian medical practice. Because of the dry climate these papyri are to this day well preserved. Among the texts has been found a great collection of writings of the time of Imhotep, the world's first physician. In reading these we learn that the traditions of Egypt, Babylonia, and Jerusalem were much alike. Each had its doctrines relative to the creation of the world, of the fall of man, and of the flood, which are so similar as to seem to indicate a common source. During this early period Egypt and Babylonia are seen to have made much more progress in medicine than Jerusalem. Babylonia and Egypt had their physicians, but in Jerusalem the priests looked after the health of their people. They gave little medicine, depending for their success upon hygiene and sanitation. In these two arts they became so efficient that their laws governing health formed the basis of sanitation in the more advanced countries of the world for over two thousand years.

Egyptian Medicine

Egypt is, no doubt, the birthplace of medical science; yet until a century and a half ago it was a land clothed in mystery. Myth steadily gave way as newly found papyri were discovered. With each translation some mistaken tradition was cast aside and a fact put in its place. Now a voluminous Egyptian literature is at hand, carrying the history of Egypt back over seven thousand years and giving us more knowledge of the country, even of the earliest periods, than we have of England during the days of King Arthur's Round Table. In Egypt various gods, including Imhotep, who eventually acquired divine status, presided over the scene of medicine. Ra, one of the most popular, who is depicted with the head of a falcon, represents the sun god. Thoth, who had the head of an ibis, was the god of wisdom, and Sekhem protected the mother in childbirth. Horus, the god who had lost an eye in a battle with Set, the emblem of evil, finally regained his sight. A symbol for the eye of Horus became a popular charm to protect eyes and to promote health, and the sign which precedes our medical prescriptions is said to have been derived from it. It passed through many stages and eventually took on the appearance of our capital R, bearing an inclined dash, thus: ℞. Such a symbol was placed upon anything indicating danger; hence it found its way to the heading of the doctor's prescription, which, one would think, is somewhat of an obscure compliment.

From the first dynasty onward Egypt had a system of medicine more rational than the world was again to see for over three thousand years. Egyptian physicians, famous as teachers, visited and taught in Arabia, Persia, and Greece. Hippocrates, grandfather of the great physician by that name, was the pupil of an Egyptian. Medical knowledge in Greece, fused with Egyptian teaching, was handed down from father to son as a family heritage. In this way Egyptian medicine became the groundwork for Greek medicine as given to us by Hippocrates.

For centuries Hippocrates has been called the Father of Medicine. We know now that many physicians contributed to the science before he lived, that he was more a collector of the current knowledge of his day than an originator, and that the art which he practiced was to some extent an Egyptian product. From the Ebers Papyrus, discovered and deciphered some eighty years ago, we learn that the celebrated Hippocratic oath is but a résumé of the ethical admonitions formulated by the physicians of Thebes sixteen centuries before the Christian era. From a minute examination of this document, Egyptologists say that medical and surgical knowledge was as far advanced at the time of its writing as it was during Galen's time fifteen hundred years afterward.

In Egyptian tombs have been found a number of treatises devoted to the treatment of the eye, which indicate that the Egyptians were the earliest eye physicians. That their skill was recognized by the royalty of surrounding countries is borne out by a Persian tablet in the British Museum which states that Cyrus, the Persian king, imported an Egyptian oculist to treat the eyes of his mother.

The Egyptians were first to realize the importance of dividing the practice of medicine and surgery into specialties. The ancient historian Herodotus tells us that "each physician treats a single disorder and no more. Thus the whole country," he states, "abounds with medical practitioners, some undertaking to treat diseases of the eye, others the head, others again the teeth, others of the intestines, and some those complaints which are not local."

Discovery of the Ebers Papyrus

The Ebers Papyrus, discovered in a tomb in Thebes, Egypt, and still in a state of good preservation though it had lain for 3,400 years above a decomposing mummy, gives an extensive description of Egyptian science.

When this papyrus was written, Egypt was at the height of her medical achievement. The hieroglyphic name for Egypt which was adopted about this period was Kahmi. This name gave promise of the future of science, for from it came the term "alchemy." Alchemy, made up mostly of magic, was to travel a long and devious course and pass through many ramifications before it became identified with the science of chemistry. During this period the priests of Egypt appear to have had exclusive control of the treatment of the sick. One who became ill had but to send a description of his ailment to a temple of health, and a physician skilled in the treatment of the described disease would be sent to him. Much surgery was performed. The bladder was opened to facilitate the removal of stones. Amputations were done, and diseases of the eyes received special attention. Operations for cataract were performed by couching, that is, pushing the cataract back in the eye where it would not exclude light coming in through the pupil. There was a very sensible avoidance of pus or other discharge from open sores, and it is believed that patients afflicted by such discharges were isolated.

The Ebers Papyrus is of the greatest importance not only as an example of the medicine existing 3,400 years ago but as one of the oldest, most complete, and unspoiled books in existence. This remarkable find fell into the hands of Dr. Georg Ebers in 1872 in the following manner: An Egyptian went to Dr. Ebers and told him of an unusual mass of papyri which he had recently discovered and which he had managed to keep secret until he could find a suitable market for it. Returning the next day, he brought a roll of papyri which he exhibited with apparent pride. It did not take long for Dr. Ebers, thoroughly versed in Egyptology, to learn that this could not be the prized roll. Dr. Ebers told the cunning Egyptian that if he would produce the papyrus he had first described he would be paid handsomely for his trouble. The next day the Egyptian returned with a metallic case in which, wrapped in an old mummy cloth, was the precious document now known as the Ebers Papyrus, in a perfect state of preservation. The ink on it was as crisp and clear as if it had been written only yesterday. The price asked for the roll was more than Ebers could afford, but a wealthy friend provided the necessary funds. The famous document was soon taken and deposited in the University of Leipzig, where its translation was at once begun. Here Ebers determined that the age of the document was greater than he had suspected and he was soon able to fix the date on which it was written as 1553 B.C. This date has been verified by all the Egyptologists who have since examined it.

It was definitely established that this papyrus had belonged to Amenhotep, a pharaoh who controlled Egypt from 1557 to

1501 B.C., two hundred years before the more famed Tutankhamen came to the throne. The document has proved to be the most accurately written of any found in Egypt before or since. It is said that "not a line, nor a word, nor a letter is missing in the entire roll." While I have not had the privilege of examining the original, I have looked very carefully over an exact facsimile, which may be seen in the British Museum by anyone sufficiently interested to ask to look at it. The medical preparations described therein consist of a great number of pills, potions, poultices, suppositories, and plasters, suggestive of the shelves of the ordinary apothecaries of a few years back.

A large part of the document is given over to remedies for a condition with which the human family has been plagued for thousands of years, that of constipation. I have copied the translations of two of these, either one of which might be prescribed even today with some success. For an overtaxed colon the first prescription would be found superior in effectiveness to many of our modern remedies.

Take thou:

Fresh dates one part
Sea salt one part
Sebbet juice one part

Signa:

Mix in water, place in an earthen receptacle, and put therein: crushed gengent beans, cook together, cool, and let the patient drink warm. Thereafter let him drink sweet beer.

Take thou:

Honey one part
Sasa seeds one part
Wormwood one part
Elderberry one part
Berries of the una-tree one part

Kernel of the ut-'ait-fruit	one part
Caraway	one part
Aaam-seeds	one part
Sea salt	one part

Signa:

Form into a suppository and put into the patient's rectum.

Then as now indiscriminate eaters seemed to have been plagued by indigestion. The remedies prescribed for this ailment do not seem to be as well understood by moderns as those prescribed for constipation:

Take thou:

Onions

Signa:

Cook in sweet beer and drink the third part thereof for three days.

For gastronomic overindulgence the following might be found to be excellent:

Take thou:

One casserole, half filled with water, half with onions. Let it stand four days. After it has stood, beat to a froth one-fourth of the third part of the contents.

Signa:

Let him who is affected with vomiting drink it for four days and he will become well.

The surgery advised for minor ailments begins with the bite of the crocodile. To the surgeon confronted by this accident it is advised:

If thou meetest with a crocodile bite and thou findest the flesh equally fallen away, cover the site of his bite with raw meat.

Remedy to be used if bitten by a person:

Take thou:
One portion of raw flesh
Signa:
Put on wound, apply oil and honey. Then put on the bite oil in wax so he will become completely well.

To prevent burn wounds:

Take thou:
A portion of cale
The hair of a cat
Signa:
Crush together and apply thereto.

A remedy to cause delay in labor:

Take thou:

Sea salt	one part
The grains of wheat	one part
Female reed	one part

Signa:
Plaster the abdomen with this.

A remedy to hasten delivery of a woman in labor:

Take thou:
Peppermint
Signa:
Let the woman apply it to her posterior.

The Ebers Papyrus seems to be much freer from magic than that of the Edwin Smith Papyrus which was discovered at about the same time, though the former was probably written at a much earlier period.

Babylonian Medicine

In passing through the Louvre in 1951, I was surprised to come upon the pillar of stone, engraved nineteen hundred years before the Christian Era, giving Hammurabi's code of laws, many of them relating to the physician. I had long known of this early medical landmark but did not have any idea where it could be found. In perusing and making notes of its translation, I felt that I would not like to have been a Babylonian surgeon, for the inscriptions read: "If a doctor has treated a Freeman with a metal knife for a severe wound and has cured the Freeman or has opened a Freeman's tumor with a metal knife and cured a Freeman's eye then he shall receive ten shekels of silver. If the doctor has treated a man with a metal knife for a severe wound and has caused the man to die his hands shall be cut off." This is the first example I know of pertaining to bodily mutilation as punishment, though mayhem was at one time a part of England's legal code. Even in our own legal parlance, which we inherit from England, the term "at the risk of life or limb" is frequently encountered as a relic of the time of the Norman Conquest, when a poacher on His Majesty's properties, if so unfortunate as to be apprehended, had one of his hands cut off and for the second offense had his eyes burned out.

The Hammurabi laws seem to have discouraged the work of the surgeon in Babylonia, though some of them may have practiced their art in spite of fear of reprisals. It is noteworthy that the rules governing physicians consisted almost entirely of regulating magical methods of overcoming disease.

Herodotus, who visited Babylon in the fifth century B.C., states that many cures were brought about by laymen. It was then the custom to place the sick on pallets so that passers-by might give them advice regarding their ailments. No one, according to law, was allowed to pass a sick man without stopping to consult with him about his disease.

The large number of clay models of the liver found later in Babylon would indicate that the liver was considered to be the chief cause of physical ills. These models are thought to have been sold or given to the healed patient to be offered by him as a thanksgiving for his recovery.

Hebrew Medicine

For the principal sources of Hebrew medicine we have to refer to the Bible and to the Talmud. In both, disease was considered a result of the wrath of the Divine Being, and surcease from suffering was to be brought about only by prayers, fasting, and the observance of moral laws. For example, a passage in Exodus (15:26) reads: "I will put none of these diseases upon thee, which I have brought upon the Egyptians: for I am the Lord that healeth thee." But that there were physicians among the Jews is shown by the passage in Genesis 50:2 in which Joseph "commanded his servants the physicians to embalm his father." Such physicians were not always called upon, however, as evidenced in the case of the prophet Isaiah, who by Divine command ordered figs placed upon the diseased parts of Hezekiah, causing his prompt recovery (II Kings 20:1–7).

In the Bible greater stress was placed upon the prevention of disease than was given to the treatment of bodily ailments, and in this no race of people, before or since, has left us such a wealth of laws relative to hygiene and sanitation as the Hebrews. These important laws, coming down through the ages, are still in use to a marked degree in every country in the world sufficiently enlightened to observe them. One has but to read the book of Leviticus carefully and thoughtfully to conclude that the admonitions of Moses contained therein are, in fact, the groundwork of most of today's sanitary laws. As one closes the book, he must, regardless of his spiritual learnings, feel that the wisdom therein expressed regarding the rules to protect health are superior to any which then existed in the world and that to this day they have been little improved upon.

While Moses gave the world its first and possibly its most effective system of sanitary science, the basic attitude in the Scriptures seems to have been a dependence upon Divine help rather than medical treatment. It may have been held that dependence upon mere medical help evidenced a lack of faith in Jehovah; a passage in Exodus 15:26 reads, "for I am the Lord that healeth thee," and in II Chronicles 16:12, Asa is the subject of censure, because "in his disease he sought not to the Lord but to the physicians." In the Epistle of James (5:14–15) this passage appears: "Is any sick among you? Let him call for the elders of the church; and let them pray over him, anointing him with oil in the name of the Lord: And the prayer of faith shall save the sick . . ." There are some valuable therapeutic measures, however, mentioned in the Bible, for instance, bathing in the River Jordan. And something in Gilead seems to have been recognized as curative; the balm of Gilead must have had certain remedial properties. The psychological effect of music is shown by David's playing of the harp to soothe the mental depression of Saul.

The story of Saul is of interest to every psychiatrist, for Saul was an unfortunate victim of melancholia. In desperation Saul says to his armor-bearer, "Draw thy sword, and thrust me through therewith"; on his servant's refusal, Saul resorts to self-destruction: he "took a sword, and fell upon it." (I Samuel, 31:4).

The build-up to this unfortunate condition of Saul can be seen throughout the story of his life, and in his severance he is but following a suicidal urge relating to his disease. When he came to Naioth in Ramah he denuded himself of his clothes and "lay down naked all that day and all that night." Just before this time came his depression, for "an evil spirit from the Lord troubled him," and though his depression was soothed by the soft strains of David's harp, the "evil spirit" was still with him and "he prophesied in the midst of the house" (I Samuel 18:10). Many other examples of mental derangement are recorded in the Book of Books; for instance, the insane boy who was, as his father says, "sore vexed for oft times he falleth into the fire and oft into the water," which points distinctly to the sacred disease of the Greeks or to our epilepsy. In Matthew 9:32 and 12:22 are seen two cases of those possessed with evil spirits: one with dumbness and the other with total blindness and dumbness. Most of these cases may easily be interpreted in the light of modern medicine, and the cause of the disease as well as the correct diagnosis can be ascertained.

Daniel 4:33 points to the lack of mental health which existed in that period in the account of the affliction of King Nebuchadnezzar, who in distress of mind "was driven from men and did eat grass as oxen, and his body was wet with the dew of heaven, till his hairs were grown like eagles' feathers, and his nails like birds' claws."

It is most singular that a description of leprosy, as found in the thirteenth chapter of Leviticus, could have been written so long before our time. It is to be noticed that such an accurate description of this dread malady as it appears in the Biblical narrative is not to be found in the literature of any nation for the next seventeen hundred years. Leprosy occurs in three forms: the nodular, or skin type; the maculoanesthetic type; and the mixed type. The first variety is now spoken of as tuberculated and the second as nontuberculated; these terms, however, cannot be applied arbitrarily. In medical literature there is still more confusion in the symptomatology regarding the various types of leprosy than is to be found in the Biblical narrative.

Many diseases described in the Bible are unrecognizable to the modern physician. But it seems clear that the disease mentioned in 1 Samuel 6:5 was that of bubonic plague, because the mice died and marred the land. It is possible that these rodents were in reality rats, for this disease is spread to human beings by fleas from the rat, an animal which itself readily succumbs to the plague.

It is noticeable that the Jews in Palestine gave very little thought to surgery, though no people in the world are more meticulous in having their male children undergo surgical operation than are the Jews. This operation, as everyone knows, consists of circumcision. But it is quite evident from Genesis 17:24–27 that the Jews many years before the Christian era practiced circumcision. Abraham himself submitted to the operation and the same day Ishmael, his son, was also circumcised "and all the men of his house, born in the house, and bought with money of the stranger, were circumcised with him."

But according to the world-famous Egyptologist, Professor Elliott Smith, the rite of circumcision was in general use in the Nile Valley in predynastic days, which represents a time long before the covenant made between Jehovah and Abraham. A bas relief of the operation of circumcision has been found in an Egyptian temple, and Professor Smith has mentioned other representations of the rite of circumcision, carved two thousand years before Rameses II.

It is singular that, while the Old Testament contains many commands that males submit to the rite of circumcision, there is only one passage in the Bible which gives in detail the method of performing this surgical rite. The operation was done by Zipporah, the wife of Moses (Exodus 4:25), who "took a sharp stone and cut off the foreskin of her son." The passage is said to be the only description of an operation occurring in the Bible, which indicates the primitive stage of surgery among the Hebrews of the period.

Wounds, however, were dressed with oil, broken bones were set, and the roller bandage was in use to assist in their union, as suggested by a verse in Ezekiel 30:21: "Son of man, I have broken the arm of Pharaoh king of Egypt; and, lo, it shall not be bound up to be healed, to put a roller to bind it, to make it strong to hold the sword."

The belief in maternal impressions, or the marking of offspring, was generally accepted. In support of this, there is a passage in the Bible which has been the subject of much discussion since the law of heredity was discovered by Mendel, himself a priest of God. It occurs in the book of Genesis and states that Jacob wreaks his vengeance upon Laban for the chicanery which had been practiced upon him regarding Leah and Rachel, by introducing a method of raising among his herds spotted and speckled calves. As this incident is in contradiction to the conclusions of the scientific world, I shall pass it over without comment.

It is interesting to note here that in obstetrical cases the stool upon which the prospective mother was placed during labor, a contrivance still in use in all Oriental countries, was employed by the midwives of the Hebrews. In the first chapter of Exodus, Pharaoh commanded the midwife to do away with all male children "when ye do the office of a midwife to the Hebrew women and see them upon the stools."

3.

Early Medicine in Greece

The belief that there was no surgery in early Greece and that surgical diseases were taken care of in Greece solely by the healers in the temples was disproved by the archeological findings of Dr. Heinrich Schliemann. His excavations in the mound of Hissarlik led to the discovery of the site of ancient Troy and did much to prove that Homer's *Iliad* had a basis in historical reality. Many incidents in the *Iliad* are of especial interest to us, and Schliemann made us alert to the fact that much of the myth lay in our own belief that there was no surgery in Greece at that time. Reading the *Iliad,* we get accounts of spear wounds and arrow wounds among the advancing soldiery and of leeches (surgeons) "skilled in medicine and busy healing their wounds." The army also had its attendant nurses, for a gravely wounded soldier is told to "sit where thou art," a prevention against shock, until the fair Hakameda "shall heat warm water . . . to wash away the clotted blood." When an archer was pierced by an arrow, Machaon, son of Aesculapius, breaks the cruel barb, "sucks out the blood and spreads thereon soothing drugs." None of these incidents took place in the temples; all give the impression of the battlefield.

The earliest Greek practitioners of medicine of whom we have any direct knowledge were the Aesculapians or priest-physicians who endeavored to heal the sick by a fusion of superstitious rites and practical means suggested by a patient study of disease, which they believed to be the work of demons. This, no doubt, was what was most practiced on the island of Cos, where the great Father of Medicine, Hippocrates, was born. It has not been decided whether or not any of the original healing temples of Aesculapius are still in existence. There were so many later Greek physicians practicing their art in Egyptian temples and teaching medicine that it is difficult to say which belong to Aesculapius and which to later physicians. It is clear, however, that all physicians of the time had the same ideas in common, that physical conditions to a marked degree would respond to mental states. The function of the priest-healer then was to direct the patient's mind into wholesome channels. Next to this came the art of dietetics in treating the sick. All Greek schools of medicine taught the sick to select their food well, to eat less and thus to live longer. Third in the list as a help to the sick was that of drugs. There were few of these, chief among them being purgatives, and these were only seldom administered. But the patient was urged to eat deliberately, to chew his food well, and to seek repose after meals.

These three rules are still sheet anchors in the care of one's health. While now incorporated into modern medicine, they came first from what may be called the early Greek school, and they are destined to remain a part of modern thought for which due credit should always be given to the Greeks.

Just how much the treatment of the priest-physicians consisted of magic and how much of logical medicine is not known, but at any rate Hippocrates in his writing makes little reference to their teachings, though he was born at Cos where a temple of healing dedicated to Aesculapius was then at its height of popularity. How Hippocrates was able to free his mind entirely of magic is unknown; neither is it known how he managed to gain such a vast knowledge of diagnosis and treatment. It may have been, as some suppose, that the priests turned over to him all cases in which the diagnosis had not been made, and that he also assisted them in the treatment of cases not responding to the magic of Aesculapius. Others believe that though he was born on the island of Cos, the home of most of the Aesculapians, he, in fact, did not teach there, for it is possibly more than tradition that Hippocrates gave clinics and taught on the island of Rhodes.

Just as Hippocrates disassociated himself from all Greek magic of healing, it appears that he gave no recognition to the early emblem of the Greek healing art, the caduceus. At any rate, I have not been able to find in any authoritative writings of Hippocrates reference to this emblem. This healing wand with the entwined serpents, no doubt, had its origin long before the birth of Hippocrates, and he must have been familiar with its tradition. Probably it originated in or about Athens but later was taken to Cos and there stood as an example of healing, except that in Cos two wands with two serpents attached were representative of the art of healing by magic. From Cos it returned to Athens, and after the fall of Greece the slave physicians taken from Greece to Rome carried their beloved caduceus with them. But the Romans, while tolerating both, would have nothing to do with the caduceus as a medical emblem and little with the Greek physicians. The word *caduceator* was adopted in Rome, however, to apply to the function of any type of Roman peace commissioner.

The Hippocratic writings give us a clear outline of Greek medicine of his period. Even though some of this may be spurious, through it all runs a thread of what might be called original therapeutic facts. This could not have been imagined. His aphorisms or concrete sayings, still as apt as they were when he wrote them, could not have grown up in the minds of his contemporaries, who were ignorant of healing except by incantation, amulets, and the casting of "spells." Such a state of mind existed for nearly two thousand years before men were prepared to see the therapeutic value of the teaching of Hippocrates.

The aphorisms of Hippocrates, some extracts of which follow, are such that anyone who reads them carefully may see the reasons for them:

"When sleep puts an end to delirium it is a hopeful sign."

"When on a starvation diet the patient should not be allowed to become fatigued."

"Old men usually have less illness than young ones, but such as they have last, as a rule, till death."

"Some diseases are more prone to occur and to grow worse at certain seasons."

"Pleurisy, pneumonia, colds, sore throat, and headache are more likely to occur during winter seasons."

"Consumption usually attacks those between the ages of thirteen and thirty-five."

"When one oversleeps, or fails to sleep, the condition suggests disease." It is not to be expected that Hippocrates had correct views relative to anatomy and physiology. These sciences were to come much later. His great fame grew out of the fact that he investigated every description of disease at the bedside. There was no magic in his conclusions, and he manifests often a distaste for the belief that disease was the result of a visitation from one of the then many gods. This is well set forth in his book *The Sacred Disease*. Here he used the term only to identify it, and he states that the falling sickness, which we now know as epilepsy, was not, in fact, any more sacred than other diseases visited upon mankind, but that it had a natural cause which was not understood.

In his book on prognostics Hippocrates writes that the attention of the physician should be called to the position of the patient in bed, to the nature of his expectoration, and to the character of his breathing. This was more important to him than the mere name of the disease, which he seldom mentions, and he writes, "Do not regret the omission of the name of any disease. For it is from the same symptoms of all cases that come to a climax at the times I have stated." In his prognostics Hippocrates describes many symptoms which indicate unmistakably what disease he is dealing with. He tells his students that they may be guided greatly by the appearance of the patient's face, which will indicate whether or not death is near. This suggestion has come down through the ages and is used by the modern doctor to apply to the Hippocratic facies which often precedes death. In this a sharpening of all the features of the patient, particularly of the nose, is seen, along with deeply inserted eyes, thinned-out temples, and a turning outward of the lobes of the ears, which are cold to the touch. Before death the face is parched and the facial skin dry and yellow and "very dusky." Shakespeare, who appears to have known more than any man of his time of life and death, gives a Hippocratic description when he says of Falstaff on his deathbed that "his nose was sharp as a pen" and that he "babbled of green fields."

While Hippocrates did not deign to name the diseases he treated, we of later experience may supply the names for him in almost every case, as here:

"Phillipus lived by the wall. He took his bed with an acute fever and sweating on the first day. His nights were uncomfortable. On the third day he was seen to have lost the fever but toward night acute fever came again with more sweating, great thirst, and a dry tongue. The fifth night was distressing, leading to irrational talk with black urine and cold sweat. At midday of the sixth day he died. Breathing through the course of the disease was as if he were recollecting to do it." This sentence will be recognized by all physicians as what is now known as Cheyne-Stokes respiration, and, according to modern clinicians of experience, Hippocrates was describing accurately blackwater fever.

Another case gives its own diagnosis: "The daughter of Nevios, a beautiful maiden of twenty years, was playing with a girl friend who struck her with the open hand on the top of the head. . . . On getting home this girl was taken with a fever and redness of the face. On the seventh day there was discharged from the right ear much reddish pus which seemed to bring her some relief. But soon the fever returned and she became comatose with the right side of the face drawn. Her tongue and eyes became paralyzed, and she died on the ninth day." It is probable that this girl had been struck not on the top of the head but near the right ear with the cupped hand, which caused a rupture of the drum membrane. The pus of red color was the result of an infection of the middle ear. This was followed by mastoiditis and later with a rupture upward of the mastoid antrum, ending in a subdural abscess and later in meningitis and death. While Hippocrates often did surgical operations, the fact that the girl's life might have been saved by an early mastoid operation did not occur to him, and it was many centuries after this that such operations were ever attempted, but he dreaded pus as a modern surgeon does. He set fractures as well as reduced dislocations, and it is likely that he trephined the skull, for an operation describing this procedure seems to be suggested in his book *On Wounds of the Head.*

As a suggestion for the care of the surgeon's hands, he states that "the nails should either be cut short or be allowed to extend to the fingertips. The thumb should be well opposed to the fingers. With practice both hands should be made equally efficient, and the surgeon should be ready to work at all times with ability, speed, precision, and readiness."

I have been over the ground of the supposed sites of Hippocratic teaching in Rhodes, and I left convinced of the authenticity of claims that Hippocrates taught there. The remains of a temple of health are plainly visible. This is a more probable site for the center of his activities than Cos. It is on an elevated site overlooking the Aegean Sea, where salubrious breezes constantly blow. The view is enchanting. These two factors must have had much to do with the cures of Hippocrates, by acting as incentives to cheerfulness.

It is thought that there were two reasons why Hippocrates might have selected the island of Rhodes for the principal site for his teachings. He had long known that states of mind are influenced by one's surroundings. The island of Rhodes (the island of Roses) was a place more attractively situated than were the surroundings of any other of the places where Hippocrates supposedly taught. Though its famous Colossus fell as the result of an earthquake before Hippocrates ever saw the island, this celebrated wonder of the ancient world was, no doubt, placed there because of the extreme natural beauty of the site, which attracted thousands to the island in the same manner as its loveliness does today.

The natural charm of the island of Rhodes was enhanced by its warm and sunny climate. Roses of a great variety grew in profusion and hung over its walls in a veritable tangle of beauty. Also in abundance were the same native blossoming plants of varied and entrancing colors which are to be seen there today. Here also are myriads of butterflies, which end their larval stage on the island and on sunny days make vivid panoramas of exquisite coloring seen nowhere else in the world. All this, it is thought, must have attracted the great physician and caused him to select Rhodes as the chief site for his teaching and healing activities.

Though Hippocrates grew up in the shadow of the supposed healing virtue of serpents and the wonder workings of the Greek priests, he seems not to have been influenced in any way by these traditions. It is evident, however, that though not impressed by priestly philosophy, he at least lived in harmony with the temple healers and had the opportunity of studying the symptoms of their patients who came there for relief. It is also apparent that he had the opportunity of taking advantage of some practical therapeutic measures which had been instituted by older physicians. It was probably here that he began the career of teaching which was to occupy him throughout his life, and that here he at least amended a document much older than his period, which his students were encouraged to subscribe to. This was what the world now knows as the Hippocratic Oath. Until recently, every American medical student had to subscribe to it before he was given his diploma of graduation:

Oath of Hippocrates

I swear by Apollo the Physician, by Aesculapius, and by all the gods and goddesses, making them my witnesses, that I will carry out, according to my ability and judgment this oath.

To hold my teacher in this art equal to my own parents; when he is in need of money to share mine with him;

to consider his family as my own brothers and to teach them this art, without fee or indenture; to impart precept, oral instruction, and all other instruction to my own sons, the sons of my teacher, and to indentured pupils.

I will use treatment to help the sick according to my ability and judgment, but never with a view to injury and wrongdoing.

I will not administer a poison to anybody when asked to do so, nor will I give a woman a pessary to cause abortion. But I will keep pure and holy both my life and my art.

I will not use the knife on sufferers from stone, but I will give place to such as are craftsmen in this art.

Into whatsoever houses I enter I will endeavor to help the sick and I will abstain from all intentional wrongdoing and harm, especially from abusing the bodies of man or woman whether bond or free.

And whatsoever I shall see or hear in the course of my profession, or in my intercourse with men, if it be what should not be published abroad I will never divulge it, holding such things to be secrets which are holy.

If I carry out this oath and break it not, may I gain forever a good reputation among all men for my life and my art; but if I transgress it, may the opposite be my portion.

While we know little of the life of Hippocrates, his name stands out before us as one of the first definitely historical personages to give himself wholly to the study and the practice of medicine. Many anecdotes have arisen which seem to throw some light on his life, but they seem to be more or less fabulous. They leave us where we were at the beginning, with little knowledge of the life of this greatest of all ancient physicians.

Some historians believe that the ideas of Hippocrates may have grown out of the various schools of Greek philosophy. This is improbable, for the Greeks of his time, while masters of philosophy, knew little of medicine. They appealed to their gods for help in time of sickness. With them therapeutics was a matter of secondary importance until long after the time of Hippocrates. Aside from the priestly functions of the temple, Hippocrates and his colleagues depended much on the curative effect of rest and relaxation. The claim that he practiced venesection is not very well founded. But the use of thermic baths as therapeutic measures may, it is thought, be traced to him. When occasion arose he prescribed purgation and emesis for his patients. In emergency he set and splintered fractures and reduced dislocations. The use of squills, opium, rosemary, saffron, honey, and a number of other remedies has also been ascribed to him. But above all he was a keen observer and in his writings describes with great clarity symptoms by which physicians even today can arrive at the nature of the maladies, regardless of the fact that the present names of the diseases often have no relation whatever to the terms used by Hippocrates.

Hippocrates died in 377 B.C., but the wonder workings of the Aesculapians were destined to live several hundred years longer, occasionally cropping up, until the beginning of the Christian Era, in various parts of Africa, Europe, and Asia. In Europe such traditions did not become extinct until some time after the rise of Christianity, for, at the site of the buried city of Pompeii, I have seen two good examples of what remained in Italy of Aesculapian medicine in 79 A.D.: One is a plaque from the house of Vettii that represents a serpent reposing on a table on which is spread what appear to be sacrificial offerings; the other, a shrine along the Via della Bondanza, recently excavated, which represents five figures holding offerings that they apparently are about to place on an altar under which two huge serpents are entwined. But, however influential the cult of Aesculapius, it was short-lived in comparison with the ideas promulgated by Hippocrates, which are now and have been for centuries the foundation of both medicine and surgery.

Pythagoras, c. 550 B.C., besides being a philosopher, is thought to have been one of the first regular medical practitioners of Greece. What he knew and practiced appears to have been a direct transference of Egyptian medicine to Greece. He is known to have founded a Greek school at Crotona, and from here students of medicine flocking in from other parts of Greece and from Rome carried Egyptian medicine over a broad area. It is probable that Hippocrates had been a student of the writings of Pythagoras, since there is great similarity between the treatments used by these two great first physicians.

There were many Aesculapian temples scattered over Greece and the islands of the Aegean Sea. I have visited the most important of these sites, at Athens, Cos, and Rhodes, names which are inseparably linked with early Greek medicine.

Pythagoras, it was believed during his life, was a direct descendant of the god Aesculapius, yet historians have noted that in no writing attributed to him does such a claim appear. From the evidence extant we believe that he was brought up in the worship of Aesculapius as it was then practiced on the island of Cos. He, no doubt, was familiar with all the treatments of the priest-physicians sojourning there. These consisted largely in measures to turn the anxious patient's mind away from his ailments. The supplicant was encouraged to rest by the playing of soft music. Large openings in the temple walls permitted the passage of soothing breezes to promote sleep. Most remarkable of all was that the Greeks were indoctrinated with the Aesculapian idea that great healing virtues rested in the touch of the sacred snakes of the temple. These were bulky but harmless creatures taught to nestle closely to the sufferers, their cool bodies, it was thought, bringing relief to the inflamed areas. The knowledge of the use of serpents as healing agents has come down to us through a great number of scultpured reliefs from the various temples of health in Greece, though a number of Egyptian steles still may be seen representing a single serpent, or two serpents, clinging to an upright staff. In the present day, as any discharged soldier knows, military medical authority in both Great Britain and America is represented by two serpents entwined about a central staff known as the caduceus.

In the Museo Capitolino in Rome may be seen a relief representing a Greek priest of about the fifth century B.C., clothed in the characteristic garb of the period. Among his priestly accouterments is a serpent entwined about his neck. Here also is a plaque, of about the same age, showing Aesculapius standing in a commanding attitude before his altar, which is laden with material for sacrifice. Beside him is a statuette representing Hygeia. While the text accompanying the figures bears no legible inscriptions, it is evident that sacrifice and votive offerings were considered essential to healing in the particular temple from which these figures were derived. It is evident also that the serpent played an important role and, though location of the temple is not now known, the work is typically Grecian and suggests a period of from three to five centuries before the Christian Era.

Another group in the Capitolino collections is that of a girl offering a sacrifice to Hygeia, whose image stands upon the altar before her. A votive relief of the same period portrays Aesculapius accepting sacrificial offerings. It is interesting to note that these reliefs are among the oldest of their kind in existence and that they have a direct relation to the science of hygiene as the world knows it today.

Some have believed that it is anachronistic to speak of the periods we are discussing in relation to the temple of healing at Cos, but a number of stone steles said to have been excavated in Epidaurus in 1881 indicate that the temple at Cos dates back to the fourth century B.C., and it is further claimed that this temple was built upon the site of a former one, the date of which there is no accurate way of determining.

Alexander the Great conquered Egypt about 332 B.C. but did not disturb Egyptian science. Soon after this the school of Alexandria became the leading medical center of the ancient world. Every modern student of anatomy is reminded of this when in his study of the brain his attention is called to the *torcular Herophili,* named for Herophilius, the Greek anatomist.

In about 3000 B.C. Imhotep, the first of the world's great physicians that we have any knowledge of, lived in Egypt. In Greece his name has been associated with Aesculapius, the god of healing.

It is probable that Alexandrian medicine was for a long time governed by the school of thought engendered by Imhotep.

The Greeks in Alexandria knew much of the Hippocratic teachings and eventually, following in the footsteps of Hippocrates, made many discoveries which they put into practice in Alexandria and gave less thought, therefore, to the magic formulas of Egypt.

Alexandria must be looked upon as, at least, a connecting link between Egyptian magic and the more rational treatment which eventually found its way into Europe. It is known that the earlier Egyptians did no scientific dissecting. It is probable that the removal of the contents of the abdomen and of the brain preparatory to embalming was done by the slaves. So to this day we have learned almost nothing regarding anatomy from early Egyptian sources, but the studies of the Greek anatomists in Alexandria, Herophilius and Erasistratus, are to be regarded as among the chief guides which were accessible to Vesalius, whose life is reviewed later in this book, and the work of these two great scientists is accepted as classically correct by all modern anatomists.

4.

Medicine in Early Rome

Little was heard of Roman medicine during the period in which the practice of Greek medicine was in vogue in Rome. Greek physicians seemed to regard Roman medicine as being of no consequence scientifically. In addition to this, the Roman physicians were antagonistic to the medicine of the Greeks and made perpetual jibes at their physicians, claiming that it was their secret purpose maliciously to destroy the Roman world by the use of their medicines. The Greeks, as a retaliatory measure, resolved not to make reference to any Roman writings, thus relegating them to scientific oblivion until the fifteenth century when Pope Nicholas V found in the Vatican a number of manuscripts which indicated that the periods from Celsus to Galen were entitled to more recognition by the scientific world than they had received. These manuscripts were at once recognized as a key to early Roman science. Celsus, it was seen, had written extensively on agriculture, a subject in which he was vitally interested, and he wrote in one of his prefaces that "As agriculture provides food to the healthy, so also does medicine pave the way to health for the sick." His first two books are taken up by a consideration of the effect of proper food upon health. His mention of many varieties of food proves that the Roman of this time was supplied with an extensive larder. Celsus' attention to the therapeutic value of bleeding is believed to have been responsible for the subsequent use of this treatment for over nineteen centuries. Celsus also turns his attention to fevers and disorders of the heart, as well as dropsy and consumption, and discusses the four cardinal signs of inflammation: redness, heat, swelling, and pain, still as important to the student of medicine as it was in his day. He goes into the question of surgery, giving a rational and concise description of the wounds most often inflicted at that period. He gives complete descriptions for the methods of removal of arrowheads, of the operations required for removing stones from the bladder, and for operations for hernia. He also discusses blindness owing to cataracts "within the eye." For this he advises "pushing a needle through the two [*sic*] coats of the eye, and as soon as it creates in the surgeon a feeling of resistance this will indicate that the needle has entered into the cataract." The hand of the operator is now elevated and by this act the cataract will be carried down "so that the light will again enter and the patient will be relieved of his blindness."

Celsus gives the attributes of the surgeon who undertakes delicate surgery: "He should not be beyond middle life in age, and he should have a steady hand and be able to use both hands with equal ease." He also should see well what he is attempting to do, should work calmly and continuously and should be unmindful of the patient's cries, so as not to attempt to work too rapidly or to neglect doing what should be well done. He describes a number of surgical instruments of the time, some of which were later unearthed from the ruins of Pompeii.

Galen and Roman Medicine

Galen was the next great writer on medical and surgical subjects of the Roman world, and nearly everything he advocated was in vogue throughout Europe from the time of his death until Paracelsus thundered against his theories and practices and thus did much to open up the way for the medical renaissance.

Galen looked upon the human body only as a receptacle for the soul, and this view was respected by Mohammedan and Christian alike for several centuries. This led to extreme disapproval of anything which would throw disfavor on the conclusions of Galen. This adamant view was so fixed upon both Moslem and Christian that it led often to the persecution of dissenters. It was because of this, as will be noticed later, that Vesalius was obliged to make a tour of repentance to the Holy Land.

Galen was born about 130 A.D. in Pergamum, Asia Minor, of a very intellectual father and, it is said, a psychopathic mother. Galen writes that she used to scold continuously at her husband and in fits of anger bit her serving maids. Galen was a man of mild temper, blessed with the genius of his father. In early youth he was sent to Alexandria for his education. He studied surgery and seems to have developed a gift in this art, for on his return to his home in Pergamum, though still very young, he was appointed surgeon to a group of gladiators. This experience provided him with much material for putting into actual practice what he had learned. His success became so great in Pergamum that he soon felt impelled to go to Rome, where greater opportunities for success might await him. He spent several years of noticeable accomplishment in Rome, but when the plague broke out he returned to his native city. His Roman opponents claimed that he did this through cowardice and that he had run away to protect himself when he was needed. So far as I can learn, this view is still held by most medical historians.

While Galen was in Rome the Emperor, Marcus Aurelius, had taken note of his ability and had remarked that in reality the world had but one physician and that was Galen. This encouraged Galen to return to Rome, where he worked and wrote until his death.

Galen in his work in Rome followed the methods of medicine and surgery laid down by Hippocrates and thus did much to help perpetuate the fame of the great Greek master. He is said to have been the first to call attention to the merit of the Father of Medicine. Following Hippocrates' precepts, Galen used diet, massage, and gentle exercise in his management of the sick, and, while he prescribed the drugs which Hippocrates had used, he mentioned but a few of these in his writings, and these have come down to us under the term "galenicals."

In perusing the writings of Galen and comparing them with those of Hippocrates, one sees the difference between the characters of the men; whereas Hippocrates was a mild and modest writer, Galen on the contrary was often arrogant and boastful. This characteristic appears to have been the chief reason for the loss of approval he suffered from a later scientific world.

Galen's fame rests upon his experimental work rather than upon his clinical writings. He was far advanced for his time in knowledge of anatomy, though he never dissected a human body. His anatomical investigations were carried out by dissections upon pigs and Barbary apes, now extinct except in Gibraltar, where a few specimens still exist under careful protection. Using the apes' anatomy as a guide, he worked out a rather good outline of the muscles of the human being and made a careful study of the brain. Besides describing the optic and the auditory nerves, he gives the first glimpse we have of the sympathetic nervous system. He also anticipated the work of the anatomists to follow by claiming that the "pneuma," or inspired, air entered the lungs during the act of breathing and was then mixed with the blood. But he believed that all the blood was formed in the liver and was brought from the intestines by the portal vein. At the time this blood or "natural spirits" passed to the right ventricle and was carried through "imperceptible openings" between the walls of the ventricles and became intermingled with the blood arriving from the lungs by the "arterial vein," as he termed what we now know as the pulmonary artery. Much of the blood in the body was thought to reach the brain, where it became the "pneuma of the soul" and where it was carried by way of the nerves, which were thought of as hollow tubes throughout the body, resulting in direction and motion.

Galen's work was the highest peak of Greco-Roman medicine and continued to be revered for several centuries, during which time to dispute him was to earn the reprobation of society, as in the case of Paracelsus, who was so imprudent as to burn

Galen's writings in the lecture hall and as a result had to flee for his life.

It may be true that when Rome invaded Greece she did very little to advance the cause of medicine, though she instituted a system of sanitation and water supply which is a marvel to all those who view its remains today. But regardless of this, disease, including plague and malaria, continued to take a frightful toll of the inhabitants. The latter disease is thought by some modern historians to have been responsible, more than other cause, for the downfall of Rome and the recall of the Roman legions from Britain, thus making way for the Anglo-Saxon invaders to whom many of us trace our lineage.

5.

Nestor and Arabian Medicine

Taking any part in religious controversies has never been the function of the medical profession. Regardless of this, most medical men the world over are grateful for the foresight of Bishop Nestor of Constantinople in saving from oblivion many of the scientific works of Egypt, Greece, and Rome, which were later to influence the medical thought of the Renaissance.

Very little is known of the early life of Nestor. It is supposed that he was born in Syria in about 380 A.D., but the exact date is not known. He died a natural death, however, in the land of his birth in about 450 A.D.

Many historians believe that Nestor had been trained as a physician, for when he fled to his native country after an accusation of heresy and excommunication by the Church of Rome, he had in his possession practically all of the Greek, Roman, and Egyptian medical classics in existence.

The Nestorian sect, the first unitarians among the Christians, had at that time made great progress in medicine and had accumulated copies of a vast amount of Greek and Roman manuscripts, notable among which were the writings of Hippocrates, Galen, and Celsus. Fleeing before the anti-heretics, the Nestorians made their way gradually eastward by foot, mule, and camel, carrying their meager belongings with them and taking care to preserve their precious documents. Some of these Nestorian Christians continued their journey until they reached China, where a number of their descendants still have retained their identity. Some of them stopped in Palestine, where I have met and talked to their descendants, but the majority of them made their way into Arabia and gave origin to a renaissance among the natives, who eagerly studied and helped translate into Arabic all these ancient manuscripts. While the Arabians did not dissect human bodies, as this was forbidden by the Koran, they by virtue of these documents became the most enlightened people of the world of that time from the standpoint of former Greek, Egyptian, and Roman medicine.

While I was in Damascus in 1934 a monk of the Nestorian Christians explained to me the great geographical extent of this religion, which he declared covered much of Asia, as far east as China. After returning home, I was sufficiently interested to investigate what the monk had told me. I had the good fortune to find an account of the partial Christianization of Cathay (China) by the Nestorian Christians by means of convents similar to the one I visited in Syria. This is fully set forth by the British author, Colonel Henry Yule, in a preface to *The Travels of Marco Polo*. By this new evidence the story told by Marco Polo about the Christian, Prester John, formerly thought to be spurious, may now be accepted as a historical fact.*

The monk reminded us that in coming from Beirut to Damascus we had crossed the route taken by the Nestorian Christians on their historic flight from Constantinople over one thousand years ago. A remnant of this long-persecuted sect has remained in eastern Syria and Lebanon since Nestor's time. During World War I, the monk stated to me, they existed in sufficient numbers to cause the British nation to take steps for their protection.

I learned that at the beginning of its persecution this indomitable group came to eastern Syria because Nestor had been born there. From Syria many of his followers moved southward into Arabia. Having formerly met persecution on every hand, the

* *Memoirs of Sir Henry Yule,* by Amy Frances Yule, L. A. Society, Aut. Scot, 1926.

Nestorians received a warm welcome from the Arabs and their manuscripts were eagerly seized upon and translated into Arabic.

After the death of Mohammed, Arabian medicine developed rapidly, and the Arabian armies which invaded Spain carried along the most complete array of classical medical literature then to be found in the world.

Two of the greatest physicians of the Arabian Renaissance (c. 625 to c. 925 A.D.) were Rhazes and Avicenna, who translated all the then known Greek and Roman medical manuscripts and soon established themselves as teachers of medicine in both Asia and Africa. Those of us who have read the *Arabian Nights* and came across the name of Harun-al-Rashid may not have recognized in this quaint character an Arabian ruler in Spain who patronized all the sciences, particularly that of medicine, and one who should be given much of the credit for the dissemination of the knowledge of Arabian culture throughout the civilized world.

In 639 A.D. the Arabians forced their way into Egypt and later traversed North Africa and conquered Spain. Their Arabian scientists were now steeped in all the ancient lore of Greece and Rome, both philosophic and medical, and at Cordova, Spain, established what was one of the most enlightened medical schools of the time. To this center came many Europeans, who familiarized themselves with the ancient culture.

In Damascus in 1160 was founded one of the first great hospitals erected by the Arabs. I was shown its ancient site during my visit there. This had been built later than other noted Arabian hospitals in Bagdad and Cairo. A system of state medicine had been put in effect in all these institutions, and the poor were treated free, medicines also being dispensed to them without charge. The hospital at Damascus had attached to it a laboratory where decoctions and tinctures were prepared and shipped by caravans to the more affluent in various other parts of Arabia. Alcohol was distilled here for the whole nation. About this time a Jewish traveler and writer visited the Damascus hospital and wrote that the fires in its laboratories had never gone out since they were lighted.

During this period there crept into the *Tales of the Arabian Nights* a story unearthed and translated by E. W. Lane, known to the world as "The Story Told by the Jewish Physician," in which a description of an amputation of the hand is given in detail. This would indicate that at the time this was written something was known regarding Greek surgery. "As soon as I had said this," relates this patient, a son-in-law of the governor of the province, "they cut off my hand and scalded the stump with boiling oil, and I swooned away. They then gave me to drink some wine, by swallowing which I recovered my senses, and I took my amputated hand and departed." This method of amputation was in vogue in Europe until the days of Ambrose Paré, who first used ligatures to control bleeding. It is believed that the *Tales of the Arabian Nights* depict quite accurately the life of the people among whom these stories grew up and were passed along by word of mouth for centuries before they were written down. Other stories from the *Arabian Nights* give evidence of an infiltration into Arabic of the anecdotes of Greek and Roman medicine, which they first learned from the Nestorians.

One story, translated from the Arabic by Sir Richard Burton, is of an Arabian girl who was the slave of an improvident young heir to a fortune. He had squandered all his substance except this slave girl. Her former master had evidently been a physician. She seems to have given way to her love and sympathy for this young spendthrift by suggesting to him that he sell her and with the proceeds free himself of debt. He realized her unusual talents, knowledge, and value and decided to do this. He therefore offered her for sale to the caliph. The caliph, hoping that he had found a very useful addition to his harem, decided first to have her examined by the learned men of his court. Soon the girl astounded her interrogators with her knowledge of law, philosophy, and astronomy. On the subject of medicine she was familiar with such anatomy as the Arabs knew. She was also acquainted with the humoral theory of Hippocrates, which had found its way to Arabia through the writings of Galen that were among those carried away from Constantinople by the Nestorians. This slave girl proved to be familiar with all the superstitious ideas of the age in reference to the "natural spirits" in the liver, the "vital spirits" in the heart, and the "animal spirits" in the brain. While these three contentions constituted the greatest fallacies of ancient medicine, this story is mentioned simply as an indication that the vellum scrolls of the Nestorians, with all their facts and fancies, got into the hands of the Arabians, probably in the neighborhood of Damascus.

In 641 Alexandria was captured by the Arabians. Here a great mass of classical medical manuscripts had been gathered together which, contrary to the general belief, were rescued from their famous library before it was burned. The Mohammedans, having a passion for old classics, had already translated these works into Arabic, and they were among the treasures which were carried into Spain. During the period in which the Arabians were being driven out of Spain, in the eighth century, they managed to take with them nearly all their precious scrolls. By the Spanish conquerors these were contemptuously passed over as a mass of waste paper, and their transportation was not interfered with. How the Arabians with these documents finally made their way back to Arabia and Palestine, where during the Crusades they came in contact with European physicians; how they fraternized with these physicians, who soon grasped the importance of this medical wealth; and how in returning to Europe the crusading physicians carried copies of these manuscripts to Italy, thus ushering in the renaissance of medicine in Europe, is one of the most engrossing stories in medical history. The knowledge of Arabian medical science also flowed into England from Rhodes and Malta, where the Hospitalers for long periods maintained hospitals for returning pilgrims from the Holy Land.

Before the expulsion of the Arabians from Spain, Cordova had become the principal center of medical learning in the world. One of the greatest teachers in Cordova at this time was Abulcasis. Cordova was then a populous city which contained fifty hospitals and a medical library of over 100,000 volumes. Abulcasis had personally collected over five hundred works on surgery alone, and his courses were attended by surgeons from every part of Europe. He did much to bring surgery back from the crude work of the itinerant charlatan to the best that the sciences could offer anywhere in that day, and in his book, *al-Tasrif,* which gave a complete account of surgery as practiced by the cultivated Arabians, he did much to pave the way for surgery as it was later practiced after the expulsion of the Moors. Abulcasis' work was later translated by Guy de Chauliac, one of the great surgeons of medieval times, and thus it found its way to all parts of Europe. Abulcasis was somewhat of a fatalist, for he writes that surgical operations are of two kinds: that which cures the patient and that which kills him. Among the greatest physicians of Cordova, Avenzoar, who lived in the twelfth century, stands foremost, and his book, *al-Tëisir,* or "Assistance," was widely translated and had much to do with bringing about the later medical renaissance.

Another great Arabian physician was Moses ben Maimon, often referred to as Maimonides, of the late twelfth century. He was also renowned as a teacher of medicine. Born in Cordova when Arabian medicine was at its highest peak, he was later expelled from that city for clinging to Jewish traditions in religion, and migrated to Cairo, where, in spite of his faith, he was later appointed as personal physician to Saladin, then the acknowledged leader of the Moslem world. It is believed that this great personality of medicine was to give origin to the Jewish physician El Hakim in Sir Walter Scott's *Talisman.*

Maimonides spent most of his life in taking care of the sick and needy, both Moslem and Jewish, and in his book, *True Counsel,* he emphasizes the worthlessness of worldly lucre and stresses the great importance of building character. Aside from being a renowned physician, Maimonides was a great philosopher. In his book, *The Guide of the Perplexed,* he showed the close relationship which should exist between medicine and religion. He died in 1204 and was buried in Tiberias, in Israel, a place of pilgrimage for medical men, where the writer of these lines reverently stood as one of a group of appreciative physicians in 1934. With Maimonides passed much of the glory of Arabian medicine. For centuries the Arabians have been represented as a beacon light in both medicine and surgery, and it is only because of them that many of the priceless manuscripts of Greek and Roman medicine have been preserved for us.

Geoffrey Chaucer, the great English poet, knew much about the great Arabian doctors, so much, in fact, that for many years after his death those who wished to get information on the subject went directly to Chaucer for it. The answer to this apparent mystery has been cleared up since then. Chaucer, who was one of the most learned citizens of England, had a passion for investigation. Naturally, he attracted to himself the most erudite members of the realm, and as medicine was even then a great and learned profession he must have known some of the physicians who returned from the Crusades with stories of the culture of Arabia and especially of Arabian medicine. The English physicians had been greatly disillusioned by their ancestors who had been in the Holy Land and who had developed considerable respect for the achievements of the Arabs. They must have been an iconoclastic lot, for Chaucer states that the study of the physician "was but little of the Bible." There seems to be little doubt that in this way Chaucer became acquainted with the names of these Arabian celebrities of medicine and was regarded as the greatest authority in England on the subject.

In the British Museum I came across an account of the journey Chaucer made to Italy in 1373. He was appointed by the crown to confer with the city of Genoa on the establishment of a port where trade facilities might be open to both countries. For a period not established by the accounts he later turned into the royal household, he also made his residence in Florence, and while there undoubtedly had the opportunity of conferring with returning pilgrims who had visited the hospitals of Rhodes or Malta. Thus he amplified his knowledge of medical science in general, and got particular information on Arabian medicine. An excerpt from his *Canterbury Tales* displays some of this knowledge:

> There was here also a Doctor of Phisik,
> In al this wide worlde was ther non him like
> To discuss phisik and surgerye;
> For he well knew astronomye.
> He kepte his pacient wondrously well
> In all houres by provn magik natural.
> He could guess well the ascending of the star.
> Wherein his pacients fortunes were.
> He knew the cause of each maladye,
> Were it cold, or hot or moist or drye,
> and where engendered, and of what humour;
> He was a perfect practisoin.
> The cause knowen and of its right misiere.
> Then he gaf the syke man a cure.
> Always rede hadde he his apothecaries,
> To make him drugges, and electuaries,
> For each of them made the other for to wynne;
> Their friendsheipe was not newe to him
> He knew well the old Esculapeus,
> and Descorides and Rufus too;
> Add Hippocrates and Haly and Galien;
> Serapyon, Razis, and Auycen;
> Averrois, Damascen, and Constantyn;
> Bernard, and Gatisden, and Gilbertus.
> Of his diete mesurable was he,
> For it had in it no superfluitee,
> But of norishing gret and digestible.

6.

Gilbertus Anglicus

The most unusual character of English surgical literature may be found in the person of Gilbertus Anglicus, who roamed over Europe until his name became so associated with the Continent and the surgery of the time that after his death his English friends, seeking to claim England as his birthplace, referred to him as the English Gilbert, or Gilbertus Anglicus. Chaucer, summing up the world's authorities in surgery in his famous poem, makes mention of him.

Little is known of the life of Gilbert. Joseph Payne (*British Medical Journal,* November 12, 1904), who made a careful study of his life, believed that he was born about 1170 and died about 1230. It is probable, then, that his *Compendium,* the only writing which can certainly be attributed to him, was produced during the most constructive period of his life, that is from 1200 to 1230. Whether he died in his native England or succumbed somewhere on the Continent is not known. But that he traveled far is attested to by Payne, who states that some of the work attributed to him was written in Syria while he was a very young man. It seems likely that his jaunt into that country was more or less of a youthful adventure and that he was turned back because of his lack of knowledge of the Arabian language, and that certain notes written there later found their way into the *Compendium.* This much is certain about the writings of Gilbert: While the *Compendium* was written mainly to give an account of the condition of medicine on the continent of Europe, as others have observed, several chapters are devoted to the surgery which came under Gilbert's direct notice during his wanderings. On the Continent surgery was then a despised profession, engaged in only by a lowly type of barber, and it continued to bear this unsavory reputation until the sixteenth century when Ambrose Paré, by his work as a barber surgeon in the French Army and by his voluminous writings, elevated it to respectability. But this was some three hundred years after the time of Gilbert.

It was not until 1540 that barber surgeons in England were recognized by an act of King Henry VIII dealing with a quarrel between the apothecaries and the barbers, though a former grant of arms to the London Company speaks of the barbers as "Masters of barbery and surgery within the Craft of Barbery." Members of this Guild were usually avoided by the people in general, who referred to them as "evil coxcombs who flourished razors." In Queen Elizabeth's time the barbers seem to have lost the prestige granted them by Henry VIII, and the people, now fearing them, became convinced that "a medicine is provided for every ill." About this time Bullien, in his *Bulwarke of Defense against all sickness, sores and wounds that do daily assault Mankind,* thunders against the barbers, and Bordes, in *The Brevaris of Health wherein doth follow remedies of all manner of sickness and diseases that which may be in Man or Woman,* condemns the work of the barbers.

Considering the condition of surgery and its almost total relegation to the itinerant at this period, it seems most remarkable that Gilbert almost three centuries earlier managed to bring together so many facts regarding the new science of "barbery," that are so devoid of the superstition of his age as to make them seem almost modern. As an example of this, let us first notice his "alder button" for end-to-end anastomosis, or repair of severed intestines. A quite similar device only a half a century ago was popularized by John B. Murphy in his " Murphy's Button" and for a time was generally used for end-to-end anastomosis throughout the entire surgical world. This is in no sense a suggestion that Murphy ever heard of Gilbert's method. He probably never had. But it does suggest that many great discoveries have in fact been born, lived, died, and been forgotten by all the world, as Gilbert's alder button was forgotten.

The following is Gilbert's description of the alder button and its use:

"If some part of the intestine has gotten through the wound in the abdomen and is either cut crosswise or lengthwise while the remainder remains uninjured, it should be noted if the intestine is warm or cold. If it is cold some small animal like a puppy should be killed, split open and placed over the intestine until the intestine is vivified by the natural heat of the applied animal. Then a tube of alder is to be prepared, its peth hollowed out and its bark removed. . . . It is now to be introduced into the gut and be stitched into position with a small square pointed needle carrying fine silk. The opening in the alder tube should be of such a size as to carry through it the contents of the intestines. When this is finished a sponge and warm water should be employed to cleanse the intestines from all foreign matters. When the intestine is thus cleansed it is to be returned to the abdominal cavity through the wound of the abdominal wall. The patient is then laid upon his back and gently shaken so that the gut will fall back of its own weight. The primary wound may have to be enlarged for this purpose. The wound in the abdomen is to be kept open until the wound in the intestine is thoroughly healed. So soon as the wound in the intestine is healed the abdominal wall, if still open, may be sewed up."

Such wounds of the intestines were of course caused by serious accidents or as the result of arrow, sword, or spear cuts in hand-to-hand warfare. The description of this procedure as outlined by Gilbert, contrary to the general belief, gives precedence to him and to the surgeons of his time for a method of end-to-end anastomosis which sprang into being in America only a few years ago.

But Gilbert in his chapter on fractures includes in his description of wounds of the head a suggestion which must have been the cause of death in many of his patients: namely, that all such wounds should be explored with a probe or with the finger. We should, however, be lenient with him in this, for exploration of wounds by the probe continued to cause death in the lowly as well as the great for more than six centuries after Gilbert's time. We must remember that the wounds of two of our martyred presidents, Garfield and McKinley, were thus explored, one of such operations being performed in an unsanitary railroad station by anxious surgeons attempting to find the bullet.

Many of the head wounds described by Gilbert were the result of penetration by arrows. He notes that when the arrow wound passed directly through the head the results were not necessarily fatal. This has long since been proven by the famous crowbar case of New England, in which a workman in attempting to remove a charge of unexploded dynamite from a tamped-out receptacle in a quarry caused it to ignite. The detonation, set off by sparks from steel striking against granite, drove the large tamping iron through his skull. No permanent harm resulted in this case, although the workman, who later drove a stagecoach, developed a violent temper and was given to frequent outbursts of profanity.

For such penetrating wounds of the cranium, Gilbert fortunately reverses himself and, instead of advising the use of the finger to explore the opening, suggests that nothing be done beyond dressing the wound as in a case of fracture.

In cases of wounds in which the arrow is lodged in the thorax, Gilbert recommends that the surgeon first trephine the thorax wall and extract the shaft and then withdraw the arrowhead through this opening. In the event that the head of the arrow is lodged just within the ribs, its removal, he states, will be much more difficult. The ribs may then be spread apart by a wedge, after which the removal of the arrowhead will be greatly facilitated. The wound is then to be covered in a regular manner, well soaked in goose grease, and with a protruding portion left outside so that the dressing will not slip inside the chest wall and be lost in the chest cavity.

Gilbert, with little knowledge of the physiology of the nervous system, observes that wounds of the spinal cord which are in line with the normal contours of the spinal column, thus splitting the cord, are much more favorable than transverse wounds of the cord, which he considered to be incurable.

Wounds of the nerves, Gilbert suggests, are to be dressed with a mixture of earthworms and oil beaten together. He makes the shocking suggestion that before the wounded nerve is treated it should be cut across to relieve pain and to prevent lockjaw. But before passing judgment upon this early surgeon for this astounding suggestion, we should consider the age in which this advice was given and its almost total ignorance of the anatomy and physiology of the human body.

The renowned Antonio Scarpa some two hundred years later, as mentioned in my book, *External Diseases of the Eye,* states that he was called to consult with some military surgeons on the case of a young woman thought to be dying of smallpox, and that he made the recommendation at once that he be allowed to burst her eyes. Shortly after this was refused, the patient, he states, expired. During the ensuing grief, Scarpa states with a noticeable degree of self-assurance, the parents of the young woman, when it was too late, regretted that they had not given way to the general opinion, that is, that they had not permitted him to burst their daughter's eyes. This was about two centuries before Gilbert was born, and we may remember also that Italy, the home of this ancient author, was at that time considered to be one of the European leaders in surgery, and that Scarpa was then a man whose fame was almost world-wide.

Gilbert was the first writer, so far as I can learn, who recommended splinting and bandaging a fracture of the extremities and encasing such fractures in plaster. This suggestion is made in an outline of the treatment of fractures of the humerus, or what he terms the upper arm bone. The cast, he states, is to remain in place until the union of the fracture ensues, but he suggests that the arm should be carefully watched for signs of swelling and inflammation. Should this appear, he advises that the plaster be taken off and the arm well bathed with a warm solution of soda, after which the plaster is to be reapplied. In cases where spicules of bone have penetrated the skin, they are to be carefully drawn out, the wound dressed, splinted, and bandaged and small openings left in the cast over such openings as exist in the skin, to provide for the liberation of discharges that are likely to follow such perforations of the skin by bony fragments.

For cases of fracture of the forearm Gilbert recommends careful comparison of both arms placed side by side before the arm is bandaged, then hot fomentations are to be applied and, with some degree of extension, the arm should be splinted and bandaged.

But possibly one of the most practicable suggestions of Gilbert is made for cases of "broken neck," or dislocation of the atlas-axis articulation. His method of reduction is the first I have been able to find in ancient surgical literature, and, while I have never seen it put into use, the feasibility of this method, I believe, will appeal to the modern surgeon. First the patient is placed upon his back on the floor. As a preliminary to reduction the mouth is to be held open by a wedge. A slip of gauze is then placed under the patient's chin, and the surgeon, sitting behind him, places his feet upon the patient's shoulders and makes traction upward upon the bandage, reducing the dislocation. The head is then to be supported with large splints, after which bandages are to be carried across the forehead and around the chest to keep the reduced dislocation in place.

Gilbert took note of the fact that when the lower jaw is dislocated a complete malocclusion of the teeth occurs, and the condyles of the jaw protrude beneath the eyes. To overcome this malposition of the lower jaw, he advises the jaw should be grasped by the hand and forcibly dragged down until the teeth of the lower jaw fit those of the upper jaw. When correct apposition of the teeth is accomplished, a gauze band should be placed under the lower jaw, carried over the top of the head, and tied. It is interesting to note here, in support of the adage that there is nothing new under the sun, that the Egyptologist

Edwin Smith found an account of the reduction of a dislocated jaw in a papyrus only slightly later than that of the Ebers Papyrus, which contains the following:

"If you examine a man having a dislocation of the lower jaw, should you find his mouth open and his mouth cannot close for him, you should put your two thumbs upon the ends of the two rami of the mandible, inside his mouth, with your fingers under his chin, and you should cause them to fall back so that they may rest in their places."

In cases of dislocation of the shoulder Gilbert advises that the patient be put upon the floor, after which a small stone encased in wrapped yarn is to be placed in the armpit. The surgeon presses upon the padded stone with his foot and, by making traction downward forces the head of the humerus into place. This procedure will certainly not be new to the American country doctor; one will rarely be found who has not practiced the same method of reducing dislocations of the shoulder, except that the stone wrapped with yarn has been supplanted by the doctor's heel in the armpit. In young patients Gilbert advises that nothing more is needed to reduce such dislocations than a closed fist in the armpit, by means of which the humerus goes back into place as the young patient is lifted upward.

For dislocations of the elbow Gilbert advises passing a strip of cloth into the bend of the elbow; by placing his foot into a loop in this cloth, the surgeon makes a counter extension and guides the dislocated articulation into place with his hands. Then a bandage should be carried around the upper arm so that the patient himself can flex his lower arm and prevent stiffness of the elbow. This method of reducing dislocations was old even in Gilbert's day, for I have found in the British Museum a book entitled *Chirurgri,* written by Roger of Palermo in 1080, which recommends this method of reduction.

All that is necessary in dislocations of the wrist and fingers, Gilbert writes, is that the fingers be pulled gently downward, as the forearm is pulled upward.

Gilbert devotes several pages of his *Compendium* to the

treatment of hernia, and he seems to apply this term to hydrocele and orchitis as well as to protrusions of the viscera through anatomical openings. He advises that when the testicles seem swollen and otherwise distended the patient should be placed upon his back and kept entirely quiet. Should there be a large mass in the scrotum, the hips are to be elevated, after which the mass works its way upward as the result of gravity. A bandage made of silk is now to be snugly fitted to keep the protrusion from redescending. Apparently he is describing what we know as a truss, and if so, this, I believe, is the first time such an appliance is mentioned in medical literature. If this simple procedure is not followed by relief, he advises pushing the intestines upward and then with a red-hot iron searing over the opening, the object of this being to produce sufficient adhesions that will, with the scar tissue formed, provide a support to prevent a redescent of the intestines into the scrotum. The patient is then to be kept on his back with hips elevated for a period of forty days.

Considerable space is given by Gilbert to what seems to have been the plague of Middle Ages, gravel in the bladder. This, he notes, frequently obstructs the male urethra and prevents micturition, owing to striction of the urethra. In the female this occurs more rarely, because of the shortness of the urethra. He advocates the use of soundings to push the offending stone back into the bladder. At some later time, he suggests, when inflammations and swellings have subsided in the urethra, soundings may be discontinued. If this fortunate finale to a trying condition is not accomplished, he suggests the services of a lithotomist, who will remove the stone through an artificial opening in the bladder.

Much of the surgery which Gilbert describes was needed as a result of the terrible hand-to-hand conflicts in the warfare of the period. The pike was then a much-dreaded weapon in the hands of an enemy, as numerous ancient paintings in various art galleries will indicate, the artists not glossing over the horrors of warfare but, on the contrary, often depicting the pike passing into the body of a fallen soldier who, with the spearhead held in his hand, attempts to force it back toward his adversary. In one such picture the despair in the face of the victim undergoing penetration and the sadistic gleam depicted in the eye of the one about to conquer are calculated to awaken in the beholder a disgust for all warfare, ancient or modern.

Before the days of the more humane bullet wound, the arrow, next to the pike, was the greatest destroyer of life in warfare. It is said of the English soldier that with the long bow he was the most dreaded opponent in the world. This was the result of long practice. Besides working for his lord of the manor every weekday, he was expected to practice archery on Sundays. This greatly developed not only his skill in sending his arrow straight and far but developed the muscles he used in drawing the bow. If his practice shaft went astray and killed a bystander, he had the protection of the law. The skilled archer was thus trained to be a terrible opponent. His arrow could penetrate a one-inch oak plank at fifty yards, and he could place it as near to the mark as the average recruit of later years could put his bullet. This arrow was of chisel-shaped steel, sharply ground. With it he could penetrate the armor and body of his opponent at a distance of fifty yards, pinning him to an iron encasement from which he could not extricate himself.

Next to the English soldier in accuracy and strength was the French archer. But when the French and English armies met at Agincourt the French proved no match for the English, many of whom were so sick with dysentery that they were ordered to leave their pants on the field before the battle began. With no heavy shields to contend with, the English archer literally nailed the French to their own armor. It is not a wonder, then, that early authors such as Gilbert gave so much space in their writings to wounds made by arrows.

As with all writers on the subject of medicine, from Hippocrates until a hundred years ago, Gilbert believed in drawing blood for the relief of pain. He relates, to prove the efficacy of this treatment, that he once saw a woman with so much pain in her right wrist that it caused her to scream out. She was a full-blooded person who had not controlled her appetite for food.

He accordingly bled her from the right hand and the left foot to the amount of one pint. This procedure he repeated in an hour, drawing off another pint of blood from the right hand and the right foot. The pain, he states, then entirely disappeared, but the woman attempted to have him bleed her again from the hand. The following is another interesting case which Gilbert describes:

"Once in a case of gout accompanied by great pain in an aged man I asked the patient if he had pain in the feet or in the other hand. He replied that he had had pain in the right hand but not in the feet. I accordingly bled him from the right foot. A physician who had treated him before had bled him from the right hand, thus quieting the pain in this right but directing it to the left hand." "When I questioned him about this," he adds in self-approval, "he at once understood that I knew more about medicine than the other doctors did."

Just how to unravel the reason for the treatment set forth in these two cases I find not easy, nor will it be for the modern reader. Yet I feel that Gilbertus Anglicus, hedged in as a result of centuries of superstition and an age of unreasoning tradition, has upon the whole given us a glimpse into the surgery of his period which should cause admiration for the insight and prowess of this first of English surgeons.

7.

Balavignus and the Rebirth of Sanitation

The most cursory study of history will find the footprints of the Jewish scientist everywhere along the paths of progress. In all departments of human endeavor he has cut deep his niche, and often he has accomplished this in the face of oppression and ostracism. Though he has been despoiled and spurned, he has usually preserved an inimitable optimism.

In medieval times the Jewish doctor of Europe was confined within the limits of a ghetto. This was an expedient to block his progress, instituted by gentile physicians who realized that they could not compete with him. Ghetto life was accepted by the Jew uncomplainingly. In many ways he believed that it was to his advantage. It preserved for him his racial ancestry, which he regarded as a priceless heritage.

In the early part of the fourteenth century at Thenon, near Strassburg, lived the Jewish physician Balavignus. Though he was distinguished among his people, his life was confined to narrow limits, and his services were not in demand except by his own race. In medieval Europe the Jew, unless he bore a concession, went beyond the limits of the ghetto at his peril. Occasionally the monotony of ghetto life was broken for the commercial Jew, whose financial aid and advice in matters of commerce were often sought. To the commercial Jew, however, was extended a prerogative which never fell to the Jewish physician. Gentiles were forbidden to employ a Jew as a medical practitioner, and severe penalties were imposed upon the Jewish physician who was found a party to the infringement of this law.

For the part he was to play in saving his people from the devastations of a great epidemic, fate early made of Balavignus a student of Arabian sanitation, a science unfamiliar to the gentile physicians of his time. Sanitary science, almost modern in principle, was brought into Moslem Europe by the Mohammedan conquerors. In some of the cities of Spain may still be seen the street paving and other evidences of sanitation put there by the Moors at a time when London was reeking with filth and Paris threw her refuse into the gutters. Many of the greatest physicians under Moslem rule were Jews. Among these was the renowned Maimonides of Cordova, whose work, *Tractatus de Regimine Sanitatus,* written over seven hundred years ago, is still a classic.

Balavignus was also a master of Jewish tradition and was in a position to apply literally the principles of Pentateuchal sanitation. These writings of Moses contain most practical instructions relating to disinfection and the incineration of refuse. The laws of health laid down in Leviticus are the basis of modern sanitary science. Moses ordered that cases of leprosy should be segregated, that dwellings from which infected Jews had gone should be inspected before again being occupied, and that persons recovering from contagious disease were not to be allowed to go abroad until examined. The modern quarantine harks back to these sanitary regulations of the Old Testament.

Besides being familiar with the Pentateuch, Balavignus was also a student of the Talmud, and Talmudic writings contain a great mass of medical information, setting forth scientific facts antedating many supposed modern discoveries by centuries. The Talmud shows the Jews to have been far in advance of their time in anatomy. Dissections of the human body had been performed and the results carefully noted. They had a passing familiarity with surgery, for they operated for stones in the bladder, inserted artificial teeth, and even performed the Caesarean section. Their thoughtful and progressive medical spirit is indicated by Talmudic writings which describe rabies and pleurisy and mention jaundice, giving its pathology as bile in the blood. These studies so shaped the career of Balavignus that the ghettos under his supervision were entirely free from the filthiness so general throughout Europe.

In 1346 the plague broke out in various places in Europe. In a year's time it had reached Strassburg, where it swept away the inhabitants by thousands. Many were struck as if by lightning and died in the streets. Others took flight and expired in the roads outside the city. Many walled themselves up in their homes and either died of the disease or starved to death. Grass grew everywhere in the streets. Great vats were dug, and to these corpses were hauled at night and thrown in. An ominous silence reigning everywhere was broken only by an occasional wail of distress or the rumbling of carts laden with corpses.

Boccaccio says that "amid this general lamentation and woe, the influence and authority of every law, human and divine, vanished. Most of those who were in office had been carried off by the plague, or lay sick, or had lost so many members of their families that they were unable to attend to their duties; so that henceforth everyone acted as they thought proper. Others, in their mode of living, chose a middle course. They ate and drank what they pleased, and walked abroad carrying odoriferous flowers, herbs, or spices, which they smelt at from time to time in order to invigorate the brain, and to avert the baneful influence of the air infected by the sick and by the innumerable corpses of those who had died of the plague. Others carried their precaution still further and thought the surest way to escape death was by flight. They therefore left the city; women as well as men abandoning their dwellings and their relations, and retiring into the country. But of those also many were carried off, most of them alone and deserted by all the world, themselves having previously set the example. Thus it was, that one citizen fled from another, a neighbor from his neighbors, a relation from his relations; and in the end, so completely had terror extinguished every kindlier feeling that the brother forsook the brother, the wife, her husband; and at last, even the parent deserted his own offspring and abandoned them, unvisited and unsoothed, to their fate."

By the Christians the plague was considered a visitation of Providence and was allowed to run its deadly course unchecked by sanitary measures. Sewerage at this time was a thing unknown among the gentiles. The people were crowded together, and refuse was thrown in the streets. The example of a great number of consecrated men, living in sackcloth and ashes, was emulated by the poorer classes whose dwellings were unspeakably filthy. Erasmus tells us that at this time the floors of gentile homes were made of rushes and were strewn with an ancient collection of "beer, grease, fragments, and everything nasty." The plague being carried by rats, no condition could have been more conducive to its spread than was afforded by this general uncleanliness.

Balavignus insisted that no better setting for an epidemic could be staged than this general lack of sanitation which was to be found in the homes and premises of his neighbors, both Jewish and Christian. Immediately following the advent of the epidemic, he instituted a cleanup movement among his people. In his campaign to promote general cleanliness it cannot be presumed that Balavignus had the modern conception of the cause of disease, but it is an undisputed fact that he sensed in some way the relation between dirt and disease and attributed the plague to filth. How much more advanced were his ideas than those of the European gentile physicians is indicated by the following extracts from a report of the College of Physicians of Paris, an institution which excluded the Jew and whose members frowned upon the idea that he could be anything but a charlatan.

"We, the Members of the College of Physicians of Paris, have, after mature consideration and consultation on the present mortality, collected the advice of our old masters in the art, and intend to make known the cause of this pestilence more clearly than could be done according to the rules and principles of astrology and natural science. We therefore declare as follows:

"It is known that in India, and the vicinity of the Great Sea, the constellations which combated the rays of the sun, and the warmth of the heavenly fire, exerted their power especially against that sea, and struggled violently with its waters.

"We are of the opinion that the constellations, with the aid of nature, strive, by virtue of their divine might, to protect and heal the human race: and to this end, in union with the rays of the sun acting through the power of fire, endeavor to break through the mist. Accordingly, within the next ten days, and until the 17th of the ensuing month of July, this mist will be converted into a stinking deleterious rain, whereby the air will be much purified. Now, as soon as this rain shall announce itself, by thunder or hail, every one of you should protect himself from the air; and, as well before as after the rain, kindle a large fire of vines, green laurel, or other green wood; wormwood and chamoile should also be burnt in great quantity in the market places, in other densely inhabited localities, and in the houses. Until the earth is again completely dry, and for three days afterward, no one ought to go abroad in the fields. During this time the diet should be simple, and people should be cautious in avoiding exposure in the cool of the morning. Rain water must not be employed in cooking, and everyone should guard against exposure to wet weather. If it rain, a little fine treacle should be taken after dinner. Fat people should not sit in the sunshine."

Compare these conclusions with the ideas of Balavignus:

Following the sanitary laws as set down in Leviticus, Balavignus had all refuse burned. Naturally the rats left the ghettos and gravitated to gentile quarters in search of food. The Jews consequently suffered less from the disease than did their Christian neighbors, the mortality in the ghettos being five per cent of what it was among the Christians. This was so noticeable that the Jews at once fell under suspicion. It was observed that they covered their wells and took away their buckets. This led to the belief that they were not only escaping the plague themselves but were in a conspiracy to destroy the Christians by the disease. One day it was said that someone had seen a Jew deposit a bag containing poison in a well. This report so infuriated the people that a general massacre of the Jews was begun. Hecker tells us: "In this terrible year an unbridled spirit of fanaticism and thirst for blood caused the death of nearly all the Jewish population in Strassburg. Torture was always inflicted upon the victims before they were thrown into the flames. At Eslengen the whole Jewish community in despair burned themselves in the synagogue. Mothers were seen to throw their children on the pyre and then precipitate themselves into the flames." A visitor to Strassburg today may see there a monument erected to commemorate the death of over two thousand Jews who fell victims at the hands of fanaticism during this terrible year.

Balavignus early fell under suspicion of being the one man of his race capable of producing the poison which was thought to be responsible for the disease. Dazed and driven insane by excruciating tortures, he made a confession implicating other Jews and a number of Christians. Thousands upon thousands during these dark ages made similar confessions, accusing themselves of the most absurd and impossible acts, simply as a means of bringing their torture to an end. The spirit which made confession inevitable also brought about conviction, and Balavignus was condemned. The same night, in the courtyard of his prison, a sentence was read, the faggots crackled, the mob chanted, "Justice shall prevail," and soon in the smoking embers lay the mortal remains of this great man who, had his advice been heeded, would have proved to be one of the world's greatest benefactors.

In examining the following quotations from documents written by the Scribe of the Court to the Mayor of Strassburg, it is difficult for us, today, to understand the psychology of the sort of justice exemplified by the following:

Answer from the Castellan of Chillon to the City of Strassburg, together with a copy of the inquisition and confession of several Jews confined in the Castle of Chillon on suspicion of poisoning. Anno 1348.

To the Honorable Mayor, Senate, and Citizens of the City of Strassburg, the Castellan of Chillon, Deputy of the Bailiff of Chablais, sendeth greeting with all due submission and respect.

Understanding that you desire to be made acquainted with the confession of the Jews, and the proofs brought forward against them, I certify, by these presents, to you, and each of you that desire to be informed, that they of Berne have had a copy of the inquisition of the Jews who lately resided in the places specified, and who were accused of putting poison into the wells and several other places; as also the most conclusive evidence of the truth of the charge preferred against them. Many Jews were put to the question, others being excused from it, because they confessed, and were brought to trial and burnt. Several Christians, also, who had poison given them by the Jews for the purpose of destroying the Christians, were put on the wheel and tortured. This burning of the Jews and torturing of the said Christians took place in many parts of the country of Savoy. Fare you well.

It remained for a Bavarian Jew, John Peter Frank, to open wide the trail toward sanitation blazed by Balavignus. His great work on public hygiene, *A Complete System of Medical Polity,* which gave plans for correct sewerage and water supply, and a life spent in arduous study and teaching were means of greatly minimizing the epidemics of Europe.

Sanitation has now practically abolished the plagues from the world. In extending our gratitude to those who have made these results possible, let us not forget a great man of science, the just and humble Balavignus.

8.

Simon de Covina Establishes the First Quarantine

In the middle of the night the mother of a first child has become alarmed about the condition of her offspring. He complains of headaches. She feels his forehead and it appears hot. She then looks at his tongue. While its surface is not much coated, she observes there a number of bright red spots which make it appear like the surface of a ripe strawberry. And when she peers at the tongue she sees redness in the back of the throat, which alarms her. With increasing apprehension she bares his body and feels for tender points which might help her in determining his trouble. Immediately her fears increase, for much of his skin is covered with a rash. Now thoroughly alarmed, she decides to call her physician, the family doctor who had ushered her into the world twenty-five years earlier. He tells her that he will be right over, and soon his step is heard at the front door. The doctor enters the room, carefully examines the little patient, and turning to the mother says, "Johnnie has scarlet fever. Don't be alarmed. He is not very sick and it is probable that this is no more than a mild attack." He opens his satchel, leaves some powders with explicit directions for their administration, and says to the mother: "The board of health will quarantine you for a short time. You and Johnnie will be required to remain indoors and no one may come in. After the card 'Scarlet Fever' is tacked to the door no one will wish to enter anyway. This may be something of an inconvenience, but it is the law and a very good one for all concerned." The patient soon makes an uneventful recovery, no one contracts scarlet fever from him, and what might have been an epidemic is stopped in its tracks by quarantine.

The question is often asked: How did quarantine come about? Most of the answer to this is lost in the mist of past ages, but this much is recorded as history. In the early part of the fourteenth century there lived in Venice a physician by the name of Simon de Covina. He was a man of deep insight, and he had sufficient influence to cause the Venetian Republic to appoint a council for the protection of the city's health.

During the days of Covina, Venice was the most powerful metropolis in the world, having been made rich by the traffic between it and Palestine brought on by the Crusades. But it was beginning to suffer the fear of extinction because of the great plagues which appeared continually and seemed to come in from Asia and Africa by a circuitous route through Florence and Perugia.

First Covina had the Strait of Messina closed to all shipping. He then selected Ragusa, in 1377, as the first quarantine station of the world. Knowing that all ships passed this point, he believed that if these ships were held there for a period of thirty days, the plagues coming by water from the East might be held in check. This was first called a *trinatina,* from thirty-days isolation. After a trial it was found that ships leaving there and secretly carrying persons afflicted with plague passed the sickness on to the next port. It then occurred to the council of the city that thirty days was not a long enough time to isolate the passengers of ships, and that a longer period would prove more effective. Forty days was then decided upon. It was soon found that this practice was much more effectual in controlling the plagues; hence, *quarantina,* which means forty days of isolation, was first put in force at Ragusa, and a like measure has later been practiced in all civilized countries of the world. Though the quarantine is now somewhat relaxed, because of our better understanding of the diseases which brought it into being, it exists in modified forms in all countries and is of immeasurable value to us as a barrier to the spread of communicable diseases.

The establishment of the quarantine was the world's first great example of international medicine. From Ragusa physicians the French got the idea of establishing quarantine stations in all the ports of Southern France. In 1533 Paris established an isolation post outside the city where goods were checked and, if they came from plague-ridden territories, barred. Plague victims were also to be quarantined, and their quarters, marked with crosses, were to be cleaned; the streets before these houses were to be flushed and the cesspools walled up. As an example of international medicine, during the great plague in London nearly all the then known measures of the quarantine were put into use, though they were, of course, ignorant of the fact that the plague was caused by the rat flea. But the cleanliness instituted by the health authorities no doubt had much to do with driving the rats out, for London began to burn the refuse which previously had been thrown into the streets to feed and keep alive the actual cause of the plague.

At about this time a great step forward was taken; people turned to the belief that natural causes, rather than Divine wrath, were responsible for disease. Many advanced thinkers, among whom was Daniel Defoe, believed that the plague might be caused by organisms existing in filthy matter, and accordingly harangued the populace, urging them to clean up the city. This did much to bring the plague in London under control.

The famous surgeon, Sydenham of London, wrote extensively on the plagues at this time, and his works, widely read in America and elsewhere, did much to do away with epidemic diseases and to establish in the minds of the people a need for understanding among the physicians of all nations. The quarantine, in the modified form of segregation, has been of immeasurable benefit in lessening the spread of leprosy. This method relentlessly applied has been responsible for freeing England from the great prevalence of leprosy which it experienced in the fifteenth and sixteenth centuries. This step was not taken, however, until Sweden, Iceland, and Norway, because of national intercommunication, showed an alarming gain in the frequency of leprosy cases. An example of the benefit of segregation in the fight against leprosy is given us by Norway, where a rigid national quarantine was introduced in 1856. Ninety years later the health authorities were able to report that Norway had only five per cent of the number of lepers that were there before segregation. Similarly favorable reports come to us from Finland and Sweden, where enforced segregation of lepers had also been instituted. With the continuation of segregation and with improved methods of treatment for leprosy, the outlook for vanquishing this loathsome disease, which has plagued the world for over three thousand years, seems favorable.

The quarantine failed ingloriously, however, in controlling a new disease possibly from America, the so-called *mal français* or syphilis. A severe epidemic broke out in Europe in 1494, a year after Columbus returned from his discovery of the New World. Charles VIII of France in that year invaded Italy. The fighting in this campaign was desultory, but circumstances which made it necessary for Charles to employ adventurers and mercenaries from several countries were unfortunate, inasmuch as these soldiers served to disseminate the new disease throughout Europe after the army was disbanded. On the way South, Charles stopped for three months in Florence. Here the Spanish mercenaries infected many Italian women. The same situation occurred in Rome and Naples. To such an extent was this true that the *mal français* in France was long called the Neapolitan disease. After the war was over the Swiss, German, and Slav mercenaries of Charles' army, returning home, carried the disease to their respective countries. Infected French soldiers transplanted it to their homelands. It was only a step across the English Channel to England, where the *mal français* soon spread.

At the time Columbus returned to Spain there was a Dr.

Roderick Diaz de Isla of Barcelona, who, according to his book *Against the Reptilian Disease,* had a rich experience in treating those afflicted with the new disease, commonly called in Spain the "bubas." In 1521 this book was rewritten and dedicated to John III, King of Portugal.

Diaz claimed that the so-called *mal français* was an entirely new malady and that the sailors of Columbus, disregarding moral laws, had cohabited with the women of Hispaniola and Haiti and thus contracted it. Later, he said, many infected Spaniards joined the army of Charles, which accounted for the great prevalence of the new disease in the French Army. While the Indians in the island of Hispaniola called the disease *guaynares,* this author believed his name of reptilian disease should be considered more appropriate than any other, because of the horrible reptilian appearance of the victim's skin during the period in which skin eruptions occurred.

Diaz believed that the reptilian disease had been on the island of Hispaniola for so long that the natives had become partly immune to it and that they had originated a treatment for its control. This treatment consisted of the administration of guaiacum. Diaz stated that he depended more, however, upon inoculations of mercury than he did upon guaiacum therapy, and he was one of the first to believe that mercury was more adapted to the treatment of the condition in Europe than it was in America.

There is a refutation of the claim of Diaz in that, although he treated the *mal français* among the returned sailors of Columbus, he did not mention the word "syphilis," using instead the term "bubas." But the term "syphilis" did not come into existence until 1530, when a certain Dr. Fracastoro of Verona published a poem in Latin entitled "Syphilis sive Morbus Gallicus." Because so many names had been given this condition, Fracastoro's poem caught on at once and syphilis became the universally recognized term for the so-called "new disease."

Further Spanish corroboration of the theory that syphilis was an American disease comes from Las Casas, the so-called Apostle of the Indies. Las Casas' father was with Columbus during his first visit to America, and as a young man Las Casas was himself present when Columbus returned to Spain bringing a number of Indians from the island of Hispaniola. It was the opinion of this well-informed observer that syphilis, appearing among the Italians as the *mal français,* was in reality the same disease as that of *guaynares,* long a plague to the Indians of the Carib Islands.

For the control of this new disease sprung up so suddenly in Europe, quarantines were set up in France to protect the French from the Italians; in England to help keep the inhabitants of the tight little isle free from the disease, and in Spain to shield the Spanish from the infected French. But none of these steps had the slightest effect in controlling the spread of syphilis. Humanity was then just beginning to learn the severe lesson that this disease is no respecter of persons, that the rich and the poor, those in high stations and those of low origin, were alike subject to its ravages. As represented by a European artist of the period in "The Dance of Death," a grim reaper, tripping lightly over the fallen corpses, mows down all alike. Here the quarantine failed and will always fail until human nature changes and man becomes a more exalted and self-controlled creature than he now is.

During my visit to Venice in 1953, a physician of the city pointed out to me the house where de Covina is supposed to have lived. While his quarantine did nothing to control the black plague of from two to five hundred years ago, his method for the control of epidemics in general cannot be said to have failed. The quarantine, linked with sanitation and science, has practically driven the epidemic plagues from the world. Cholera has become almost a thing of the past, typhus is no longer a deadly menace, yellow fever has been entirely routed out, and smallpox is under absolute control for those who do not avoid vaccination. In extending our gratitude to those who have made these results possible, let us not forget this great man of science, Simon de Covina, who first established the quarantine.

9.

Agrippa and the Beginning of Psychiatry

Only in recent years has man been able to banish a fear of the unseen which for thousands of years had kept him in perpetual torment. Everywhere about him in the long ago were disembodied spirits, evil, malicious, and cunning. Invisible forms, lurking in every shadow, were thought to be ready to hurl at him some great and terrible misfortune. From the storm reached the outstretched hands of the denizens of the unseen world, and malignant spirits, bent upon his undoing, leered at him from the lightning's flash. Witches with burning eyes cast malevolent glances from the darkness as they swung through the air on unholy errands bent, and salamanders, wreathing and hissing in the flames, set the sparks flying vehemently across his hearth.

Every calamity that had befallen friend or neighbor was believed to have been the culmination of the malicious design of some abominable demon. It was thought that life itself would soon have suffered a frightful termination but for the guardianship of the friendly spirits who waged a perpetual warfare against the innumerable monsters of the air.

Such beliefs were as real to the medieval mind as are the phantoms conjured up today by the imagination of the child. When we recall the visions which sometimes accompanied our childish nocturnal adventures, when every lurking shadow held a possible enemy, we can realize something of the paralyzing terror of these mental children of the past whose paths were so beset with the creatures of their imaginations. The existence of these apparitions was rarely doubted. A great fabric of evidence was at hand to prove the prevalence of such enemies of the human race. Hundreds of persons believed that they had met these demons face to face, and thousands more were thought to have gone down to untimely deaths at their hands.

During certain phases of the moon these enemies of mankind were thought to be particularly hostile, and at such times their frenzy could be allayed only by seizing upon a victim. The bodies of the seized then became the habitats of these dreaded personalities, and the resulting symptoms, which we now know to have been insanity, were but the reflected conduct of the Evil One himself. We have an illustration of this tradition in the word "epilepsy," which we get from the Greek and which literally means "seizing."

It was argued by medical men of the time that moonlight was a factor in producing disturbed mentality, because it gave the demon sufficient light to pursue his nefarious work. An echo of this delusion comes down to us in our English word "lunatic," from *luna,* the moon, a term used by the old masters of medicine to designate any mental departure from the normal. It was thought the moon also had the power to create physical ills and its debilitating rays were often the cause of death. It was known that the moon influenced the tides, and it was thought that at the turning of the tide death often hovered over the sickbed. We have a reminder of this weird superstition in the case of Shakespeare's Falstaff.

During this period of human history physical disorders were nearly always attributed to spirits who had evaded the protecting sylphs and forced an entrance into the body. Failing in life to accomplish their ends, it was believed, they often succeeded in getting control of the disembodied soul after death. To frighten away these unwelcome neighbors, bells were rung at nightfall. This was the origin of the curfew. As Professor Henry Draper suggests, the bells today given to children as toys had a medieval significance very different from the modern. At that time they were put into the child's hands not to afford him amusement but to act as a safeguard to his life. If these childish beliefs had not been accompanied by acts of supposed retribution, the history of this time would be of interest to us today only as an amusing study in psychology. Instead of this it gives us the most appalling examples of cruelty known to the world.

As already noted, a common belief during the Middle Ages was that of demoniacal possession of the living. Many persons, it was thought, were in league with the devil, the archenemy of mankind. Possessed persons were accused of making storms at sea, of being responsible for periods of drought, of causing hailstorms, of stunting the growth of children, and of a thousand other impossible crimes. Because of this superstition thousands upon thousands of men, women, and children suffered the most excruciating tortures. They were suspended to ceilings by their thumbs, famished in dungeons, stretched on the rack, and broken on the wheel. Only in death which left them beyond the reach of their tormentors were they to find deliverance. So fearful was the torture which usually preceded the executions of these victims that a great many confessed themselves guilty of the most impossible deeds. Accused persons were known to have admitted that they had caused children to vomit crooked pins, that they had inhabited the bodies of wild animals at night and were enabled thereby to commit the most diabolical acts. Thousands confessed themselves guilty of witchcraft, knowing that such a confession meant death.

The psychology of these confessions has long been a subject of mystery. It is probable that they were made in the hope of a few minutes surcease from pain or as a means of ending an unbearable existence. Some, no doubt, confessed because the terror occasioned by their accusation drove them insane. It is estimated by Samuel Laing that during the eighth century in

Germany alone, over one hundred thousand persons suffered excruciating deaths for the crime of maintaining an alliance with the devil.

This popular delusion had a long life. Even as late as the seventeenth century we find Sir Matthew Hale of England condemning two women to be burned for witchcraft, and every American school child recalls the fate of a large number of innocent persons who were executed as witches on this side of the Atlantic. It is remarkable that humanity clung so long to these superstitions. The only explanation for this lies in the fact that for centuries the world was governed by fear. With fear humanity stands still; it is courage alone which is responsible for human progress.

In the treatment of the mentally deranged, as in all other things, we find the hand of evolution. By this process the execution of the insane gradually gave way to punishment without death. For centuries these unfortunates were starved, exorcised, and seared with hot irons, under the belief that the demons would find their bodies such an uncomfortable abode that they would vacate the premises for a more agreeable residence. Gradually several of these methods of punishment were supplanted by a therapeutic method with which medical history abounds for centuries. This remedial agent was the whip. So great was the belief in its merit that, until a century and a half ago, it was dispensed to the great as well as the lowly. George III, during his attacks of dementia, it is said, was flogged on more than one occasion, and as late as 1810 we find Sir Thomas Moore of England advocating the public flogging of lunatics, and yet Moore was considered a humanitarian and even today is spoken of as one of the greatest philanthropists of his time. Even Shakespeare countenanced the treatment, as is indicated by one of his characters, who speaks of the lunatic as meriting a dark house and a whip. Gordonius, an authority on various means of outwitting witches, declared whipping a specific in cases of nervous irritability, and he suggests, "If the patient be young and disobedient flog him soundly and often." Reverend S.

Baringould tells us of a German physician of the seventeenth century who suggested whipping, on the theory that "it cleared the brain, stirred up the stagnating juices, circulated the blood, and braced the nerves." Whipping the insane was really meant for compassion and intended rather as a chastisement of the demon who dwelt within than as a punishment of the patient. Only through such harsh measures, it was thought, could the evil spirit be induced to vacate the bodies of the possessed.

Another method of dealing with victims diabolically possessed was "torture insomnia," the subjects of mental disorder being kept continuously awake. No form of treatment could so successfully have defeated its own end. Sleep is as necessary to the human body as food is. It is only while we sleep that brain repair goes on. During our waking hours something which may be called brain waste is stored up within us and if not eliminated by sleep will, of itself, destroy our reason. Is it a wonder that none recovered? Even if mildly insane, the victim was chained to a stake in an upright position and all the devices of perverted ingenuity were used to keep him awake. The inevitable was the result. What would have been a temporary disorder under rational treatment became a hopeless disease.

In 1486, a time when the infamy and horror so long directed toward the insane was at its peak, a child was born at Cologne who was to cross swords with the swarming myriads of ghouls and infesting spirits, and whose influence, sweeping down through the centuries, was to be the means of banishing them forever from the world. This child was Henry Cornelius Agrippa.

Agrippa was a favored son of Cologne. He lived at a time when the ninety and nine were born into feudalism, were ill-nourished, half-clothed, and poorly housed serfs whose ceaseless toil went to maintain an aristocracy and to support a brutal military employed to keep them in bondage. Agrippa, of the one per cent which history is pleased to call noble ancestry, was destined to throw away his birthright in the hope of bringing to a close the orgies of superstition and inhumanity toward the insane which so long had cursed his country. He was further destined to grope his way alone through a maze of intolerance and ignorance, maligned, opposed, and suspected. And, as a friend of the oppressed, he was to meet with a persecution that was to end only with his death.

Agrippa's accident of birth gave him the opportunity of a liberal education, which, by the way, in medieval times consisted largely in storing the mind with mistakes and studying in detail various and sundry events which had never happened. The universities turned out an insipid product taught to conform, whose thoughts followed the beaten path of convention. This, however, seems not to have affected Agrippa.

By some Agrippa is believed to have graduated from the University of Cologne. Others say that he was expelled. At any rate he carried away from his university a salutary ambition to hew out a name for himself. What appeared to be a channel to this end was soon open. The court of Emperor Maximilian I was in need of a secretary. He could fill the requirements from the standpoint of both blood and education, so he applied and was duly installed; but his new post brought him only disillusionment, and soon he left, disgusted with the jealousy and frippery of court life. In 1509 he studied divinity at the University of Dôle, in Burgundy, and later became its professor of Hebrew. Here his utterances against the popular belief in witchcraft made him enemies, but he worked on, patiently and aggressively, ever ready to strike with his caustic pen at wrongs which for centuries had been blighting humanity. Later he took up the study of medicine. He received his degree in 1515, after which he traveled in France and England.

In 1518 Agrippa became the syndic at Metz. Here he was appalled at the treatment of the insane, who were either confined in dismal and repulsive quarters or languished in the most wretched dungeons. Incurable cases wore an iron belt about their bodies with a ring attached, through which ran an upright bar. They could sit and stand, but this unhappy contrivance prevented their lying down. In this way they were doomed to spend their miserable lives. The prisons for the insane had no drainage and no proper ventilation. Disinfection was unknown. Shut away from the sunlight, eating improper food, and drinking contaminated water, they soon sickened and died. Two or three years was the average life of an inmate.

Agrippa began to advocate the treatment of the insane with humane methods and sought to prove that the padded cell was more efficacious than the iron collar and chain then used on nearly all cases. Contending that the prevalent superstition as applied to the insane was fatal to even a moderately disturbed intellect, and impatient at the credulity of his contemporaries and the cruelties which their ignorance encouraged, he resolved at any cost to hew a path through this jungle of popular superstition.

One day a demented old woman was dragged through the streets, having been accused of witchcraft. Agrippa made an impassioned plea in her defense, upholding the view that the supposed witches were really victims of disease of the brain and that they should be treated with mercy instead of abuse. The result of this innovation was inevitable; he was openly denounced by the medical profession, his friends forsook him, and soon the mob was at his heels. Savan, the Inquisitor of Metz, was preparing to bring him before the Inquisition for disturbing a popular belief, when he fled the city. To remain would have meant death at the stake, the inevitable fate of those of the time whose personalities were not lost in conformity, or whose characters were not dominated by submission to authority.

Agrippa was still essentially an aristocrat, and in 1523 at Lyons he was made court physician to Louis of Savoy. But he was not long to enjoy peace. His enemies began their intrigues anew, and he was repaid for his services by being banished. His compensation was withheld and he again found himself a penniless wanderer. In 1528 he was once more a court physician, this time to Margaret of Austria, regent of the Netherlands, at Antwerp. Here he wrote his book, *On the Vanity of the Sciences.* This work was a general condemnation of the medical science of the time, in which the part played by the medical profession in promoting the witchcraft delusion and its resulting cruelty to the insane was set forth in scathing language. His ideas on insanity, embodied in this book, may be considered the nucleus around which has grown the science of psychiatry.

Soon after the publication of Agrippa's work he was imprisoned in Brussels. After a year he was released and returned to Lyons, where he was again thrown into prison. In the year 1535 at Grenoble, France, the great humanitarian, with a broken heart and a body wasted with disease, succumbed to an acute illness. Much prison life had done for him that from which he had given so much of his life to save others.

In 1816 Philippe Pinel at the risk of his liberty instituted the reforms which Agrippa sought to bring about nearly three hundred years earlier. Pinel succeeded in striking off the chains of insane prisoners, liberating them from close and musty cells and placing them in humane surroundings. Thus was the dream of Agrippa to become a reality.

The subject of this sketch was the first man in history to strike a blow in favor of the persecuted insane. Since that time all advocates for reform in the treatment of the mentally diseased have but followed the footsteps of this great physician, humanitarian, and searcher after truth.

10.

The Part of the Pirates in Early Medicine

A halo of respectability had hung over the profession of piracy for two centuries. Many of the great had joined the ranks of the pirates for the purpose of preying on Spanish shipping and Spanish colonies in America. "Singeing the king's beard" was the term applied to these sea rovers. Both Francis Drake and Henry Morgan had been knighted by the British Crown because of their success in bringing back booty, much of which went into royal coffers. The Earl of Cumberland, an M.A. of Trinity College, made twelve piratical trips to the Spanish Main and returned each time loaded with plunder. The Earl was held in high esteem by Queen Elizabeth I and until his death carried upon his person a glove Elizabeth had given him. Thomas Lodge, another English pirate, and the son of Sir Thomas Lodge, Lord Mayor of London, engaged in several piratical expeditions to the Spanish Main, and in one of his works he speaks of "my book, rough as hatched in the storms of the ocean and feathered in the perilous seas." His novel, *A Margarite of America,* was written during one of his piratical expeditions.

Much of our knowledge of buccaneer medicine came from the pen of Alexander Esquemeling, surgeon to the notorious pirate, Henry Morgan. Esquemeling wrote in the Dutch language, and for that reason he is thought to have been a native of Holland. He sailed to the West Indies in 1665 and, not being fitted for a life there because of his lack of knowledge of the English language, he joined the buccaneers. These buccaneers had grown out of a band of former uncouth French sea rovers who made their living on the island of Santo Domingo by capturing and killing the wild cattle found there. The beef thus obtained was smoked and roasted on iron grills and then sold to various wolves of the sea who were preying on the shipping of the Spanish Main. Since the grills were known as *boucans*, these beef merchants became known as *boucaniers,* or the roasters of beef on boucans. Everything was peaceful enough for these beef smokers until Spain decided to rid Santo Domingo of their dangerous neighbors, so she landed a force on the island and after weeks of search succeeded in freeing the area from the wild cattle. Deprived of their means of livelihood, the buccaneers now kept the island as a base from which to prey on Spanish shipping. Increasing in numbers and courage, they at length began to attack the least protected of the Spanish settlements and the reign of terror on the Spanish Main was soon in full blast. This was the type of seaman that Esquemeling fell in with, and he seems to have been present in all the great exploits of the buccaneers. Of these he writes in a startling and forceful manner. His account of the sacking of Panama states that Henry Morgan sailed away to Jamaica, leaving him and his buccaneer friends with no ships, no money, and with little of the spoils from Panama. His book, *The Buccaneers of America,* setting forth the almost inconceivable hardships of himself and his companions as they wandered over Central America, was later sent to Holland and published. In 1684 this book was translated into English and published in London. From it is derived almost our total knowledge of the life of these wandering buccaneers, all of whom Esquemeling claimed he at one time or another came in contact with. The book is said by historians to be authoritative, and it gives us a complete account of all the atrocities committed by these various bands of outlaws.

Esquemeling all the while was observing the plants which were used by the Indians as remedies for the cure of their ailments. In these modern days of polypharmacy the discoveries of Esquemeling may not be taken at face value, but as compared with the therapeutics of his time and with English medical preparations of the period, which we now know to have had little or no medicinal value whatever, they stand out quite prominently.

Matico, an American product brought over by pirate surgeons, was for many years prescribed to control hemorrhage and as an astringent in cases of quinsy. Sarsaparilla came next into vogue with pirate surgeons in the treatment of syphilis, where it was used as a vehicle for mercury in controlling this disease. If it did nothing else, its use modified the disastrous effects mercury had when not compounded with sarsaparilla. Guaiacum, or *lignum sancta,* was also used by pirate surgeons for the same malady, and it brought to exporters considerable wealth, being sold at a very high price. A knowledge of coca, from which we get the local anesthetic, cocaine, first came to America on pirate ships; it had been used by the Incas from time immemorial. Even stramonium, the famous jimson weed of the early colonies, reached England from the British colonies on board pirate ships.

Lionel Wafer

The man who had most to do in causing the relegation of English pharmacology, and putting in its place the names of many useful drugs, was the pirate surgeon, Dr. Lionel Wafer. Wafer, because of an explosion of gunpowder which occurred when he was deep in the country of the Darien Indians, in Central America, was compelled to remain behind his party. He was soon adopted by the Indians, and when he was rescued over a year later was painted just as all of the Darien savages were. These Indians were at that time and still are the most uncivilized of all the known tribes of Central and South America.

Wafer's adoption by the Indians after the other pirates had

abandoned him came about in this way: He succeeded in explaining to the Indians that he was English and an enemy of the Spanish. This fact undoubtedly saved his life, as the Indians had suffered at the hands of the Spanish so often as to become their avowed enemies. So they gladly took Wafer into their tribe. "Being now forced to stay among them," he writes, "and having no way to alleviate the anguish of my wound the Indians undertook to care for me." Here, he relates, he found an Indian who had been a slave to the Spanish and who had learned from them the Spanish language. "This," says Wafer, "was of much use to me, for having a smattering of Spanish and a little of the Indian taught by the aid of the escaped slave who acted as an interpreter, I was able to learn much about the country and its people and more particularly the Indian's method of treating the sick with native drugs than could have been procured so completely without a much longer residence in the country." By long and tedious treatment with native plants, which Wafer mentions but does not describe, the wound on his knee was at length healed, and he was free to wander about with the interpreter and to make inquiries regarding the various medicinal plants which grew in the neighborhood, with the use of which the Indians had long been familiar.

The Darien Indians' mode of living and their present treatment of the sick is much as it was when the pirate surgeon lived among them in 1701-02. They had spent many generations in study and observation of native plants. Dr. Leon S. De Smidt, author of *Among the San Blas Indians of Panama,* the modern name of the Darien Indians, has managed through friendly contact, fair dealing, and fidelity to learn much of these American Indians least friendly to the white man. Having spent much time among them, he has developed a respect for their honesty and for their mode of living. A similar spirit of fair dealing was responsible for Wafer's success in learning about their drugs. Wafer succeeded in bringing back to England a knowledge of 352 American plants. His original book, containing a complete description of these plants, published in 1704, is one of the most prized possessions in my collection of pirate lore.

Wafer managed the following year with the aid of some former companions to escape from the Indians and sailed before the mast on a small pirate ship from the Gulf of Mexico bound for Philadelphia. Here he took advantage of the general pardon which James, his king, made to pirates who would promise forever to forego the life of piracy.

Wafer's famous book gives us first-hand knowledge of his studies of the method of treatment employed by the Indians. To the medical historian it would seem clear that this residence of Wafer among the Indians had much to do with what may be termed the second medical renaissance in England, resulting from the infusion into England of the knowledge of American drugs, the most valuable of which had been brought to them from the surgeons on pirate ships.

Much that formerly had crept into medical literature relative to such drugs as cinchona, of which quinine is the active principle, and ipecac, is now seriously questioned. The story of the Empress Cinchona's being cured of malaria by the Brazilian Indians is thought by many to be pure fiction. The English writer A. W. Hagis, investigating this old legend, studied the diary of the Countess of Cinchona and has proven therefrom that the Countess of Peru died in Spain before her husband, the Viceroy of Peru, went to South America and that he was accompanied to the New World by another wife. This second wife was not ill in Peru until her death, and, as she never returned to Spain, she could not have been the means of popularizing the remedy, as claimed in the early accounts which most physicians will remember having studied in their various schools of medicine. McKenzie, in his *Infancy of Medicine,* states, "Although I think the general impression is that European medicine obtained cinchona from the folk medicine of Peru it is necessary for us to note that although it was probably a folk remedy for malaria in South America strict investigation has, so far, failed to give us definite proof that this impression is correct. . . . It is reported that the natives of that country were unaware of its virtues. . . . Moreover, Markheim notices the curious fact that the wallets of the native itinerant doctors, who from father to son have plied their art since the days of the Incas, never contain the bark."

McKenzie, quoting Binz, says that the remedy, though unknown to the Peruvians, was familiar to the inhabitants of the more northern countries. That would include Central America, and it is more probable that it came from the Darien country and was included in the 352 plants described by Wafer in his book, but under some name originated by Wafer himself, as is the case with all the drugs which Wafer describes. As an example of the confusion in the names of drugs from the New World at this period, the Indian *hiwowrake* became "quaicum." Lionel Wafer describes a drug which he called "dysentery vomit," and there can be little doubt that he was alluding to ipecac, a drug which the natives had used from time immemorial for the cure of amoebic dysentery, a condition which is still prevalent in the Darien country. This drug was reportedly sold to Louis XIV by Helvetius, a charlatan, for four thousand dollars as part of a secret cure to be administered to the King's son. However, it soon died out in France, and the drug first came into general use as an ingredient of Dover's Powders.

The English remedies before the days of the pirate surgeons were almost wholly superstitious and failed to compete with the drugs of the buccaneer doctors. These seamen had returned from America with drugs of proven therapeutic value, and their work caused the doctrine of signatures and magical treatments in general to disappear in England.

The pirate surgeons were among the first to discard the belief in the royal touch for the cure of disease. This mode of cure had made its advent in England during the days of Edward the Confessor and grew in popularity during the next two hundred years. From England it crossed the channel to Paris and at the hands of Louis XIV became the chief method of treatment for all manner of diseases. Louis XIV is reported to have touched over sixteen hundred persons during one Easter Sunday. In England on one occasion Charles II was so beset with scrofulous patients that in a stampede to get to His Majesty's side six patients were crushed to death. From the time of King Henry VIII rings were given by His Majesty to epileptics for the purpose of preventing the recurrence of this disease, as well as for warding off cramps. They were known as cramp rings. When Anne Boleyn was young, beautiful, and in good favor with the king these rings were put in her care for distribution; an extant letter from Anne Boleyn to a certain Mr. Stephens states that she is forwarding a number of cramp rings and prays him to distribute them "as you think best." The future Queen Elizabeth was provided with one of these marvelous rings, which, it is recorded, she wore between her breasts.

It was thought at that time in England that nature had provided mankind with an infallible rule, in that any type or shade of flower or plant which resembled the characteristics of a certain disease could be used to great advantage in the treatment of that disease; thus the red blooms of poppies would indicate at once the use of these flowers in cases of anemia, when the blood lacked a normally red color. It became the theory of the physicians that nettles would cure nettle rash and that yellow dandelions would cure jaundice. Absurd as this theory may appear, it was destined to be of long life. Many of the supposed remedies of that time became so fixed by conventional habits of thinking, that they disappeared, it might be said, only yesterday. As an example, much of the medical literature until sometime in the last century advocated the use of euphrasia as a medicament to be used in the treatment of eye disease, because the spot in the corolla of the flower was black in color, resembling the pupil of the eye.

The surgeons on pirate ships who had been to America and had learned about the therapeutics of the Indian were the first to rebel against the irrational but conventional theories and treatments of their colleagues in England.

Thomas Dover and Robinson Crusoe

Almost every member of the English-speaking world has been thrilled by the story of Robinson Crusoe's long life as a castaway on the island of Juan Fernández in the Pacific. And this Robinson Crusoe is now known to have been a pirate whose real name was Alexander Selkirk, which causes the label of Dover's Powders to take on renewed interests and adventure. There are few persons of middle age who during their childhood have not had prescribed for them a preparation known as Dover's Powders as a remedy in attacks of common intestinal derangement. Dover's Powders until recently was such a popular corrective for such complaints in children as to have become almost a household word.

In 1708 Thomas Dover, then practicing medicine at Bristol, England, joined the pirates with a joint command by Woodes Rogers and himself. They then sailed in the *Duke* and *Duchess,* two ships fitted out by the merchants of Bristol, with the avowed purpose of making a piratical attack on Guayaquil, South America, then believed to be the least protected of any of the Spanish colonies in America. After having rounded Cape Horn, they stopped for water at Juan Fernández, a lonely island in the Pacific Ocean off the coast of Chile. Approaching the shore, they saw a light and, fearing it might be a Spanish fleet, drew off, passed to the other side of the island and there anchored for the night. Early the next morning, not seeing any trace of ships, Dr. Dover and his boat crew went ashore. Before landing, they noticed a strange human being clothed in goatskins "more savage in Appearance," Woodes Rogers, Captain of the *Duke,* later wrote, than "the original possessors of them." This striking character ran toward them and then retreated, acting in this strange manner for several minutes. This was done, he declared later, to make sure they were English and not Spanish. Satisfying himself in this respect, he came boldly forward with outstretched hand and told Dr. Dover and his crew that his name was Alexander Selkirk and that he had been left on the island three years previously by the pirate, Stradling. Selkirk was taken back to the *Duchess,* where he recognized another pirate, William Dampier, now famous in English maritime history. After hearing Dr. Dover's good promises, Selkirk agreed to again take up his old profession and join the ranks of the pirates. He was later put in command of the *Bachelor,* a ship that had been taken from the Spanish. Rogers and Thomas Dover then sacked Guayaquil, but the entire crew was soon taken down with a plague of flux. Many of them died, and it was here that Dover got the idea from the Indians that ipecac was a specific treatment for this most distressing complaint. Two hundred years of its use has proven that in this he was correct. Taking advantage of what he had learned about this drug, the remainder of his crew soon recovered and were on their way to England. Returning homeward, they attacked and took an Acapulco ship, famous for carrying Spanish treasure to Spain, and then proceeded around the world and arrived home with total booty of a million pounds sterling.

Dr. Dover then gave up piracy, went to London, and put out his celebrated remedy, Dover's Powders, with the active ingredients of ipecac and opium, which soon proved to be a favorite remedy with doctors on both sides of the Atlantic.

Alexander Selkirk also gave up piracy about this time and was soon appointed mate to H.M.S. *Weymouth,* which office he held until his death in 1721.

Dr. Dover was celebrated for two hundred years as an originator of a sedative powder, which is a rare distinction for a pirate. But Alexander Selkirk's reward was greater; he was immortalized in literature not only in *Robinson Crusoe* but also by Cowper in his famous lines, "I am monarch of all I survey. My right there is none to dispute."

11.

Medicine of the Middle Ages

In wandering through the various art galleries of Europe, one can find many paintings which give excellent examples of what medical and surgical methods were practiced during medieval times. But a greater variety of illustrations may be seen in such storehouses of historic manuscripts as the British Museum and the Museum of The Royal College of Surgeons in London. Much data and several illustrations reposing in these great storehouses of medical and surgical lore had been taken advantage of by this writer before the bombing of the latter institution took place during the recent war. In many other museums throughout Europe may still be seen illustrations which indicate the trend of surgical thought during the fourteenth and later centuries. Of these the most understandable is that of the "Wound Man," which represents the many injuries to be treated by the medieval surgeon during the terrible hand-to-hand conflicts of the period. There are also numerous illustrations depicting the methods then in vogue for reducing dislocations, producing extensions in fracture, and draining and dressing wounds. Human dissection was a favorite subject for the artist during the early period that followed the lifting of the ecclesiastic ban on human dissection, which was formerly thought of as the desecration of the human body. The urologist is also depicted in many paintings in almost every quarter of Europe, the great number of which reveal the physician peering into a glass of urine, while the anxious members of the family eagerly study the examiner's face and await his decision. This was the period when frequent bleedings were thought to be necessary measures in all cases of serious sickness, and a number of extant charts show the then supposed courses of the veins, indicating the approved locations where these were to be opened in order best to serve the patient's welfare. Belief in astrology, or that the various positions of the stars in one's horoscope either promised health and long life or pointed the way to calamitous happenings ending in disease and death, was generally accepted, and ancient figures representing the signs of the zodiac turn up in nearly all European museums. Here are depicted life at its best and death at its worst, which epochs were supposed to be governed solely by the position of the stars.

Somewhat later than the time we are considering, a belief became general that for every human ill there had been provided a remedy. This was the golden age of the herbalist. The medical man of this period was so imbued with the thought that all diseases were to be cured by the barks and seeds of herbs that he spent his time in the fields and had little leisure left for his patients. That this was a step forward, inasmuch as it reduced the great numbers of useless and repugnant remedies formerly in use in medicine, seems self-evident. For it was destined that the studies of the herbalist were to pave the way to the new science of botany in medicine, which was to continue until very recently when synthetic drugs largely replaced the use of vegetable remedies. The use of simples, or simple herbal remedies, still has its place in many a family household, as have several of the older superstitions in medicine, such as the reading of horoscopes by some member of the community. In the more primitive communities in both the United States and Great Britain stress is still placed on the various phases of the moon which are said to indicate the most favorable periods in which farm animals may be castrated with the least risk, and which give promise of the hardiest progeny of breeding animals.

The Christian Church and the Spirit of Medicine

During the Middle Ages the Christian church had a marked influence over what at least might be termed the spirit of medicine. Contrary to the conclusions of writers often put forth in the last century, while monastic medicine may have been somewhat intolerant of lay physicians, the examples of pity and charity which were everywhere extended to the sick might today be incorporated in modern medicine more than it seems to be. No one was turned away from these monasteries who was ill or suffering. The hospital at Rhodes, which I have had the privilege of visiting and examining thoroughly, strongly suggests the work of the monks of the time who devoted their lives to the care of the sick. Here, for a period of more than two centuries, pilgrims going to and returning from the Holy Land were cared for, and these patients, worn, diseased, and discouraged by the hardships of travel, no doubt in the majority of instances finally succeeded as a result of this care in reaching their homes much improved in health. The ideals of this ancient healing institution are still in abundant evidence in thousands of hospitals throughout the world conducted by various orders of Christian nuns.

May we not say here in answer to the charges that the early church discouraged the practice of medicine that one Peter Hispanus, born in Lisbon in the middle of the thirteenth century and for years following the profession of medicine and surgery, later became pope. When Hispanus practiced medicine, Pope Gregory X appointed him as his personal physician. Soon after this Hispanus himself was elected to the papal chair as Pope John XXI. Among his writings *Thesaurus Pauperum,* "Treasury of the Poor," is best known. In it is embodied much of the charity which he believed the church would at all times perform for the ailing sick throughout the world, a prediction which nearly all doctors, especially the surgeons who have operated in the Catholic hospitals, have seen many times exemplified.

The Anglo-Saxon in Early Medicine

The Anglo-Saxons, after having overrun England, were in possession of a number of manuscripts written in the eleventh and twelfth Centuries which give us a clear-cut idea of the mixed herbal and magical practices of the times. Several examples of these old and tattered documents are now to be seen in the British Museum. One of them, of the date of 1050, contains a large number of drawings of "simples" and other plants which are well executed and which identify perfectly the types of the various plants to the modern botanist. Another manuscript of a slightly earlier period contains a number of recipes for charming away, by a mixture of magic and herbal remedies, the ills which they recognized in their midst. One condition which they strove to overcome by combined magic and herbals was "mental vacancy and folly." The remedy contains "fennel, agrimony, cockle and marche," and it is directed that the one so afflicted shall drink thereof.

Certain other Anglo-Saxon remedies were wholly magical, as is the following for the relief of warts: "Take seven little wafers and write upon each these names: Maximianus, Malchus, Marche, Johannes, Martianius, Dionysius, Constaninius. As a charm sing their names into the right ear, then into the left ear; then let one who is a maiden go to him and hang the charm upon his neck. He will be well in three days." As another example: "For a woman bewitched: Take at night, while fasting, a root of radish. After this the unseen cannot harm her." "In case of a woman suddenly become dumb: Take pennyroyal and rub to dust. Then wind it up in wool and place it under the woman. Soon she will be well."

The Anglo-Saxon believed that disease was either the result of an elf shot or of demons, or was due to the destruction of the body by worms; these worms are pictured in their manuscripts as monstrous creatures and they, as well as the demons and elf shots, were to be dealt with by charms or by the administration to the patient of nauseating and repulsive remedies which were meant to disgust the elfish enemies and thus drive them away. From one manuscript may be gleaned these two remedies: "For devil sickness feed to the possessed wolf's flesh. Recovery will be immediate. For loss of sleep lay a wolf's head under the pillow —the unhealthy shall then sleep."

The Anglo-Saxon superstition regarding disease and its management persisted for centuries, and many of their disgusting remedies were carried in English pharmacopoeias until the influx of pirate drugs from America caused them to be done away with. But they still persist to a degree in the American states which grew out of the early British colonies, principally in the New England states. They also occasionally crop up in the more primitive parts of eastern Canada. It would be hard to convince some of the natives of these areas that a mixture of beef gall and honey does not have especial curative values for a myriad of ailments, this being a direct transplant of the views of their Anglo-Saxon ancestry. Dan McKenzie, F.S.A., M.D., mentions the famous and supposedly efficacious Album Graecum of a century ago, which was supposed to have a specific influence upon sore throats. This is an echo from the Anglo-Saxon remedies which invaded England in the tenth century. Album Graecum was composed chiefly of the droppings of a dog. In parts of New England and in Canada, where I was born, the droppings of cattle are still a favorite remedy for painful inflammations. This remedy reached the British colonies in America over three hundred years ago. In northern England and in Scotland it is still in use, having been planted there by the early Anglo-Saxons.

The Stocks and Pillory

In England in the early part of the thirteenth century crime was on the increase, but it was noticed by King Henry III that, while this appeared to be so, capital offenses had in reality become less. But a wave of petty law violations had increased the total number of court hours necessary for their disposal. Until this time decapitation, hanging, or long terms in prison had been the approved procedures for almost all criminal offenses, but it occurred to King Henry that if all the lesser offenses were dealt with by the old sentences of death or imprisonment the jails would be so overcrowded that they would thwart their own purpose, and if an increased number of criminals were executed this would soon deplete the Royal Army of able-bodied fighting men. Among the many lawbreakers of this period were apothecaries without licenses, who sold all manner of nauseous concoctions. Other offenders were barbers unlicensed to practice their art as barber surgeons. These the king decided must be dealt with in an effective manner but not by any type of punishment which would unfit them for future military service. Accordingly, in 1266 Henry passed his Statute of the Pillory. By this law all small offenders were to be punished by being placed in the pillory. A somewhat similar device was known as the stocks. The pillory was a strong wooden post with two crosspieces in which were three openings through which the culprit's head and hands were inserted and held fast by wedging the crosspieces together.

Before being placed in the pillory, the guilty one's head was often shaved, but the king's statute particularly ordered that no material harm should be done to the prisoners. This, no doubt, was because he anticipated further military service from the more fit among those to be punished. But there was no clause in the act which forbade tormenting the prisoner to add to his discomfort and increase his punishment. How many apothecaries and would-be surgeons suffered this type of degradation is not known, but, as England was replete with this kind of quackery, the number could not have been small.

In 1637 the use of the pillory was prescribed for all who published printed matter without authority. Thousands have been thrilled by Daniel Defoe's story of *Robinson Crusoe,* but not all of these may know that its author was once compelled to stand in the pillory and to receive the abuse of those who passed, and, though it is not recorded, the possibility exists that Defoe was pelted with overripe eggs and stale vegetables. This was also the fate of many unlicensed barber surgeons and apothecaries. The stocks came to the New World with the early colonists and the provisions for their use are to be found in the United States statute books until 1839. And further, this antiquated form of punishment was not abolished in the state of Delaware until 1905.

The quarrel between the barber surgeons and the apothecaries of England, despite the stocks, continued with unabated bitterness until 1540. In this year the barbers, by a degree of influence which had not been accorded the apothecaries, managed to be heard at court, and their spokesman succeeded in favorably interesting King Henry VIII. A charter was proposed, setting forth their rights and decreeing that henceforth they were to be honored as barber surgeons and were to be accorded the title of "Mister." The followers of this group, now the acknowledged surgeons of the British Empire, evidence a pride in this ancient charter, especially in the title of Mister, which still almost always appears on their doorplates and their professional stationery instead of the conventional M.D.

Theriac Resurrected to Become a Medieval Cure-All

About two and a half centuries after the death of Hippocrates there lived in Pontus a ruler by the name of Mithridates, who studied the use of poisons on the persons of criminals and who claimed to have discovered a cure for all manner of poisons, including the bites of venomous serpents, which continued in vogue for eighteen hundred years. This was the first attempt at immunization known. Mithridates arrived at his conclusions after long periods of experimentation in which small doses of a poison were first administered, the amount being increased until enormous quantities, it was said, could be taken without harm. To prove the efficacy of his remedy, Mithridates became his own guinea pig, so to speak, and demonstrated upon himself his poison cure. Its use became so well known that it spread over the then civilized world. I have noticed that *The Pharmacopoeia of the Royal College of Physicians,* as late as 1724, gives the recipe for this ancient preparation. Throughout the ages in which this popular remedy lived many voices were raised condemning its use. During the period of the "sweating sickness" in England this remedy, then known as theriac, was widely used, and Caius at Shrewsbury, England, in 1552 severely condemned it and wrote that one of the chief reasons for the tremendous mortality of the disease lay in the indiscriminate use of this outmoded prescription. But the use of theriac was destined to live for almost two centuries after this, until it received its deathblow at the hands of William Withering, who wrote in 1770 an essay on "Mithridatium and Theriac," which in England added still another controversy to the many that had preceded it, and caused this fanatical preparation to be removed from the English pharmacopoeia. It has been suggested with some reason that the English adage "to kill or cure" had its origin in the use of this grotesque remedy.

The Medieval Hospital at Salerno

The hospital and medical school at Salerno, Italy, during the Middle Ages provided a type of education not found anywhere else in the world. Its fame spread far, so that pilgrims from great distances flocked to it. Among the many famous patients who visited the hospital for treatment was Robert, son of William the Conqueror. Robert had gone to Jerusalem with a Christian crusade and had received while there an arrow wound which for many months refused to heal and which had terminated in a fistulous opening that daily discharged a large amount of pus. It is said that at Salerno, by the advice of his physicians, the poison was sucked from the wound by Robert's wife, and because of this he made a slow but perfect recovery.

Before he left for England the faculty of the medical school of Salerno dedicated to Robert a poem which has brought this institution more fame than have its cures. The poem was written in Medieval Latin, then understood by all who could read, and was meant as a guide to health, not only for this royal patient but anyone who would be wise enough to read and profit by it. The novelty of the fact that it was the first medical work set to rhyme caused many to read and remember it; whereas it is probable that had it been written in prose it would soon have been forgotten. For a familiar example of how the mind clings to illustrations which have reached it in rhyme, we have only to remember the verses of Mother Goose, whose doggerel has indelibly fixed itself upon a large percentage of the English-speaking world for more than two hundred years.

This poem, *Regimen Sanitatis Salernitanum,* was widely published through the next four centuries and translated into nearly all the languages of Europe.

Sir John Harington during Queen Elizabeth I's reign made an English translation of this work and attempted to transpose it in rhyme from Latin to English. Notwithstanding the fact that Harington succeeded in giving us the substance of the poem in English, his strained efforts to reproduce the rhymes caused him to lose, to a great degree, its original meaning. Since then many authors have tried to remedy this defect by putting all or a part of the poem in blank verse.

During the Middle Ages the *Regimen Sanitatis Salernitanum* evidently served the purpose for which it was intended, for it not only has kept alive a knowledge of the work done at Salerno, which otherwise would likely have been forgotten, but it served as a code of health to the more intelligent laymen and gave valuable lessons on diet, rest, exercise, and general hygiene, lessons that even when disseminated among many who could not read left their fruits which may be remembered today in many parts of Europe. The following are examples of essential parts of the poem, freed from some of the effects of Sir John Harington's efforts at rhyme:

Advice to the Laymen

If thou would have health and vigor
Shun cares and avoid anger.
Be temperate in eating
And in the use of wine.
After a heavy meal
Rise and take the air
Sleep not with an overloaded stomach
And above all thou must
Respond to Nature when she calls.

Regarding Wine and Women

Our use of Greek and Candia wine
Dulls our wits and stores up fat
Red wine causes one to talk loud
And taken as a habit grows.
Tis said canary wine will make one lean
This advice causes one to laugh
It means they lean upon a staff.
Thus to wine, women, and baths
By Nature we are inclined
But if abused they do us harm.
Some love to drink new wine
If you care for health you will abstain.
For new wine causes fluxes
And if drunk much of will create stones.
Others foolishly drink only water.
But for me they may drink alone
For water and small beer
Are enemies to good digestion
And Horace proclaims the fact
That water drinkers make poor verses.

The Wine Bibber

Bold he is and fit for all company
Inclined to be fat
Given to loud laughter
Loves music and mirth
And he little cares
Of what may come after.

Dietetics

Be wise in selecting food.
Choose peas and nuts and rue
But chief neglect not garlic
That oft has proved to save from death
Bear with the unsavory breath which follows
And do not scorn it though some think
It makes men more to drink
And makes their breath to stink.

That this part of the poem was written by a doctor for other doctors as well as for the public is well set forth in the following advice to the physician:

Let doctors array themselves well.
Sparkling jewels are not amiss.
When you have them show them.
Ride in a well-attired vehicle
For when you are well dressed
You may charge a higher fee.
Patients always pay a doctor best
If he appears to be well dressed.
While those who go in shabby clothes
Must put up with small fees.
There always will be poor doctors
Who get a pittance for their work.

On Bleeding

To bleed often cheers
The pensive mind
And it is well known
That this alone will serve
To cool the fires of burning love.

On Virtue and Vice

You cannot read from the face
One's worth or virtue or vice
The street roué is nothing nice
He loves wine, women, and song
Likes stirring tales and cards and dice.

So far as adding anything of importance to the knowledge of medicine and surgery, the school at Salerno was a failure and became decadent. In anatomy there was no dissection, and the studies of the then almost unknown science were carried on by opening and viewing the viscera of a pig once annually. Nothing worthy of note was taught on the subject of physiology. In the late thirteenth century the course of medicine in Salerno was increased to five years; at the University of Paris it was still three years. This discouraged prospective students, and the institution declined rapidly. It is said to have been closed permanently by Napoleon Bonaparte in 1796. I visited the site of the University of Salerno in 1933 and found nothing to indicate its former glory. A few of the original buildings are said to remain, but of this I was not convinced. The huts which now occupy the original site give evidence of being hastily constructed and are occupied by the poorest of Italian peasants, whose goats wander at will from one dooryard to another. Unless one's expectations are low indeed, a visit to the site of old Salerno must be accompanied by disillusionment. The school at Salerno occupied a unique position in medieval medicine, but the amusing, though instructive, poem we have been considering indicates the low social status of the physician of the time, who in his dealing with his patients was often unscrupulous.

12.

Paracelsus, the Father of Therapeutics

We have seen that until a comparatively recent date medical science was an outcast. During the Middle Ages and even much of the Renaissance, the rational therapeutics of Greece and Rome gave way to charms, amulets, talismans, and various and sundry substances devoid of therapeutic properties. The following prescription from *A Short Manual of Physic,* published in the seventeenth century by Dr. William Solomon of London, is a good example of the therapy of its period:

"Recipe. Gold, one half ounce, Powder of a lion's heart, four ounces. Filings of a unicorn's horn, one half ounce, ashes of the whole chameleon, one and a half ounces. Bark of witchhazel, two handfuls. Earthworms a score. Dried man's brain, five ounces. Bruisewort and Egyptian onions of each one half pound. Mix the ingredients together and digest in my spirits Universalis, with a warm digestion, from the change of the moon to the full, and pass through a fine strain."

Another prescription by Dr. William Pullyem, one of the most eminent English authors during the reign of Edward VI, suggests the prevailing trend of therapeutic thought. This preparation, which he styles "Electuarium de Jemini," is prepared as follows:

"Take two drachms of white perles; two little pieces of saphyre; jacinth, corneline, emerauldes, garnettes, of each an ounce; setwal, the sweate roote doronike, the rind of pomecitron, mace, basel seeds, of each two drachms; roots both of white and red behen ginger, long pepper, spicknard, folium indicu, saffron, cardamon of each drachm; cinnamon galinze, zurubeth, which is a kind of setwal, of each one drachm and a half; thin pieces of gold and silver, of each half a scruple; of musk, half a drachm. Make your electuary with honey emblici, which is the fourth kind of mirobolans with roses, strained in equall partes, as much as will suffice. This healeth cold, diseases of ye brain, harte and stomache. It is a medicine proved against the tremblynge of the harte, faynting and souning, the weaknes of the stomacke, pensivenes and solitarines. Kings and noble men have used this for their comfort. It causeth them to be bold spirited, the body to smell wel, and ingendreth to the face a good coloure."

As seen from the foregoing, precious stones were supposed to have a particular virtue in healing disease. These were often taken internally. By those not able to afford such costly medication they were rented for a monthly stipend and carried about on the person. We find an echo of this superstition in the modern watch charm. Literature abounds with reference to charms of many kinds which were worn for their supposed therapeutic value. Scott in his *Talisman* mentions the healing effect of heliotrope, or bloodstone, which "stancheth blood, driveth away poison, preserveth health; Yea, and some maintain that it provoketh rain and darkeneth the sun, suffering not him that beareth it to be abused." We read further that "the topaz healeth a lunatic person of his passion of lunacy and the garnet assisteth sorrow and recreates the heart." From the same author's *Lay of the Last Minstrel* we find mention of the charm being used as a hemostatic in these lines: "She drew the splinter from the wound and with a charm she stanched the blood." Charms were used for the cure of malaria and smallpox and to assist in the union of broken bones. The color of the charm was believed to have a direct bearing upon the disease. It was thought that flannel dipped nine times in blue dye was a cure for scrofula. Spiders hung around the neck were said to be a specific for malaria, and we have it on the authority of an English physician of the seventeenth century that this method of treatment when applied to ague fits "will drive them away God be thanked."

"How the fever was cured by a spider shut up in a nutshell," lines from Longfellow's *Evangeline* have reference to this superstition regarding the cure of disease. In the National Museum at Washington may be seen an interesting exhibit of charms which have been used in the past and are still used by some to ward off diseases. Among this incongruous array several specimens are seen which remind one that folk medicine still exists among us. Here are the rabbit's foot, the horse chestnut, the patella of the sheep, and rings made from a coffin nail. Many primitive people in this country still cling to the idea that curative virtues are in some way bound up in these amulets. Everyone, perhaps, is familiar with the madstone for the cure of hydrophobia. This stone was originally used as an amulet. Some charms were made of herbs and roots. We find the remains of this superstition in the Irish potato carried in the pocket to cure rheumatism, in the asafetida worn about the child's neck to prevent contagion, and in the string of roots which, even today, primitive-minded mothers place about their babies' necks to facilitate the process of dentition.

The belief that scrofula could be cured by the touch of royalty was common, as indicated by the following words put by Shakespeare into the mouth of Malcolm in *Macbeth*: "Tis called the Evil, a most miraculous work in this good King: Which often since my here-remain in England, I have seen him do. How he solicits heaven, himself best knows; But strangely-visited people, all swollen and ulcerous, pitiful to the eye, the mere despair of surgery, he cures—Hanging a golden lamp about their necks, put on with holy prayers; And 'tis spoken, to the succeeding Royalty he leaves the healing benediction."

The credulity of the times caused even medical men to accept prevailing delusions with implicit confidence. Climbing out of a mental rut is a painful process.

Two great events occurred in the last decade of the fifteenth century: America was discovered, and at Marie Einsiedeln, in Switzerland, a child was born. This child was to go through the world burdened with the name Aureolus Theophrastus Bombastus von Hohenheim, or Paracelsus. It was also decreed that he was to live a life of turmoil, was to go down in defeat, and that many years afterward his works were to be revived and used as a means of sounding the death knell to the medical stagnation that had hung over Europe since the time of Galen.

The father of Paracelsus was a physician and his mother a hospital superintendent. This explains his reason for saying "from my swaddlings I have understood disease." It is well that he had this early training. Children's minds are impressionable. They catch the ideas of others, and after a time these ideas become fixed upon the sensitive plates of their minds, and, without any effort upon their part, are stored away for future reference.

At a very early age Paracelsus was recognized as a precocious child, and before his fifteenth year he had picked up an unusual amount of medical knowledge mixed with prevailing ideas of alchemy, astrology, and the occult. At nineteen years of age he was studying chemistry with Abbot Tritheim, a Benedictine monk. A little later he is in the laboratory of Sigismund Fugger in the Tyrol, where he studied the relation of chemistry to metallurgy. During the next few years he wandered about in France, Italy, and Germany, visiting one university after another but not remaining long enough in any to obtain a degree. Next we find him leading the life of a vagabond or wandering physician. In this capacity he traveled over Southern Europe and visited India and Egypt. He collected information as he went, associating with the physicians with whom he came in contact and, it is said, with bath keepers, fortune tellers, barbers, hangmen, and gypsies.

When accused of keeping low company he remarked that a gem was a gem whether found in a jewel case or in a garbage heap. For a time he held a commission as surgeon to the Imperial Army of Italy. Returning to Basel in 1527 he was appointed city physician and occupied the chair of medicine in the university.

Early in his career Paracelsus acquired the animosity of the profession by writing his prescriptions in German. This was an innovation which caused his contemporaries to charge him with ignorance and with the heresy of making medical mysteries known to the laity. The medical man of the sixteenth century wore a wig and a scarlet coat and carried a staff. This conventional dress, with the exception of the staff, Paracelsus discarded and in doing so fell under the charge of vulgarizing the profession. At the university Paracelsus taught his students in their own language, instead of in Latin, and again he was accused of cheapening medical knowledge. As teacher, Paracelsus strove to throw off the ossified wisdom of his time and to supplant tradition with facts. As opposed to the conformists, he was ever ready to strike a blow at harmful traditions which had been handed down from antiquity. Such a man could not go long unnoticed at a time in which it was a crime to differ from current opinion. The desire to conform has ever been a weak point in human nature. Even today, let us remember, we shrink from having our conventional habits of thinking disturbed. In the past this human failing evidenced itself by an arrogant intolerance, an intolerance which presumed that all was known that could be known. The history of science is largely made up of innovations on the one hand and, on the other hand, attempts to crush every semblance of original thought. As an illustration of this, we find in England, during the reign of Henry VIII, a law with the object of compelling all persons to think alike. It may still be seen in musty legal archives and is entitled "An Act for Abolishing Diversity of Opinion." This spirit of intolerance unmodified by centuries would have prevented Koch, Metchnikoff, Pasteur, Ehrlich, and Wassermann from being blessings to humanity. Fortunately, the world has moved on a little since the days of Paracelsus.

Conventional intolerance caused Paracelsus to be denounced as an impostor. Invective hurled at him might have crushed him early in his career had not a sturdy common sense caused him to overlook the disdain with which he was received. He had a happy vein of humor, and this is an asset which always leads toward success. Instead of growing sour, he ridiculed the pedantry of his opponents. His good-natured jibes elicited the sympathy of the people, and when the people are with a cause they carry it a long way forward; when they are against it, alas for that cause; its epitaph is written.

For his audacity in condemning the medical practice of his time, Paracelsus reaped the reward which has been the lot of the great majority of innovators. Soon his colleagues at the university were up in arms against him. Perhaps the worst would not have come had he not found his students, despite his teaching, clinging to the moss-grown ideas of Galen. One day in a fit of disgust and anger he collected all the works of the great author and burned them in the lecture hall. This indiscreet act intensified the animosity with which he was held by his opponents, and, in addition to this, it awakened in the public mind a bitter antagonism toward him. The Canon of Lichtenfels, who seemed to have a particular hostility against him, taking advantage of the popular clamor, now accused him of sorcery. The City Council of Basel eagerly accepted this indictment and Paracelsus was compelled to flee the city. Had he remained the results may well be imagined.

From Basel he went to Nuremberg, but the malignancy of his enemies preceded him. Here he met with difficulty everywhere and was abused as a charlatan. We find him during the next fifteen years at Munich, Regensburg, Augsburg, Mindelheim, and finally in 1541 in the Tyrol, where death put an end to his wandering.

Paracelsus lived at a time when originality led often to the rack, the scaffold, or to violent death. Whether he met the latter end or not is still a question of dispute. It was said by his enemies that he died from the result of carousing and dissipation, but many years afterwards his remains were exhumed for reburial and a fracture was found in his skull. To this fracture his death has been attributed by many historians, for it points strongly to the probability of a murder at the hands of his enemies. If this be true, his is but another name added to the long list of medical martyrs.

No manipulator of the pestle and mortar has ever created such a revolution in medical thought as did Paracelsus. He was the first man in centuries to relegate precedents to the past and to stand firmly on deductions drawn from reason and experience. Through his teachings he accomplished more for humanity than did any other physician of his period. Besides caring for a practice of such magnitude that he became famed throughout the world, he wrote five books on medicine, gathering data for these works wholly from his own records. By introducing the use of chemicals in medicine, by opposing the polypharmacy of his time, and by demonstrating the restorative power of nature when it is not handicapped by promiscuous drugging, Paracelsus may be considered the father of rational therapeutics.

With the exception of Agrippa, Paracelsus was the first physician to condemn witchcraft. He was the first to describe cretinism and to give a true clinical picture of ophthalmic goiter and the first to describe phthisis (consumption), then known as miner's disease. He introduced iron, arsenic, lead, and copper into European pharmacopoeia and was the first to demonstrate conclusively that mercury was beneficial in syphilis. Despising the parrotlike repetitions of the old masters, he awakened progress by holding up to derision absurdities which for centuries had posed as science. "Mother Nature," he said, "is the internal physician who, if left alone, will attend unassisted to most of the body's ills." Nature failed when the patient had the "seed of disease," and then only was medicine indicated.

By taking a positive stand against the wound treatment of his contemporaries, Paracelsus was a reformer in surgical practice. At that time it was thought necessary to infect a wound in order to promote its healing, hence the old term "laudable pus," and we may remember that "laudable pus" did not cease to be laudable until a little over a half century ago. Fresh wounds were to be let alone; only old and sluggish wounds were to be disturbed and that solely with the curette for the purpose of removing debris.

Paracelsus washed his wounds with wine. This treatment was rational, for wine at that time was about twenty per cent alcohol, and alcohol is a disinfectant. It evaporates and leaves the wound dry with free adhesive surfaces. Especially true to nature and minute in every detail is the clinical picture of hospital gangrene in his book *Chirurgia Magna,* a manual containing many important discoveries in surgery not to be renewed until the days of Lister.

Turbulent as was the life of Paracelsus, he caught vivid glimpses of a profession idealized. "One of the most necessary requirements for a physician," he said, "is perfect purity and singleness of purpose. He should be free from ambition, vanity, envy, unchastity, pomposity, and self-conceit, because these vices are the outcome of ignorance and are incompatible with the light of divine wisdom which should illuminate the mind of a physician."

Paracelsus is known in medical history as its greatest iconoclast, and it must be said of the iconoclasts that they have stood erect in the face of all circumstances, have fearlessly stated what they have thought to be true and have been willing to abide by the consequences, preferring any end rather than the soul sickness of mental coercion. This characteristic has made them enemies to hurtful tradition, but through it they have blessed the world.

Paracelsus was the first medical apostle of the school of observation and experience. "If you wish to be a true physician," he wrote, "you must be willing to do your own thinking and not merely employ the thoughts of others. What others teach you may be good enough to help you in your search for knowledge, but you should be able to think for yourself and not cling to the coattail of any authority, no matter how high-sounding the letter of the latter may be. The best of popular physicians are the ones who do the patient the least harm. Unfortunately, some physicians poison their patients with mercury, and others purge or bleed them to death. Then there are some whose learning has driven out all their common sense, and there are others who care a great deal more for their own profit than they do for the health of their patients. . . . A physician must be the servant of Nature, not her enemy; he must be able to guide and direct Nature in her struggle for life, and not throw fresh obstacles in the way of recovery.

"To be a good alchemist is to understand the chemistry of life. Medicine is more than a science. It is an art and does not consist in compounding pills and drugs of all kinds; instead it deals with the processes of life, which must be understood before they can be used as a guide. A powerful will may seem to cure, where doubt will end in failure. Thus it will be seen that the character of the physician acts more powerfully upon the patient than all the drugs he may employ."

Sir William Osler and Professor Sudhoff have done much to lift from the name of Paracelsus the stigma of being a wandering charlatan. Sudhoff calls him "one of the founders of the medieval period of medicine," and Osler speaks of him as medicine's greatest reformer of the period. The world still needs men of this type to clear up the debris of stagnant thought; to those of the past we owe a lasting debt of gratitude.

13.

Basil Valentine and the Development of Early Medicine

As mentioned in a former chapter, alchemy, transformed, has come down to us as the science of chemistry. As stated, it had its origin in Egypt, the use of the term itself having been taken from the word *Kahmi,* the ancient name given by the Egyptians to their country. Rome, by her early contacts with the Egyptians, had become imbued with the belief that the alchemists among these intellectual people had once found, and then lost, an elixir made from the philosophers' stone, which if it could be re-discovered would one day cause the lives of many of those among them to continue forever. The two substances, the philosophers' stone and the elixir of life, were thought to be allied, and the belief arose that when the one was discovered the other would be an essential part of it and with it they could transmute any or all of the baser metals into gold.

Before the fall of the Roman Empire the armies of Rome had invaded nearly all the territory which is now Europe. In mingling with these conquered peoples, Rome carried this and other myths and legends with them. Aside from the science of government, the Romans had little passion for facts. The conquered barbarians came to believe that by a strange magic they also could learn to brew a substance which would cause life everlasting, and so superstitious were these simple people and so anxious were they to find this unknown mixture, called by the Romans *elixir vitae,* that their imagination gave way to a belief that the formula for this unfamiliar substance had been found by some of their neighboring barbarians and had again been lost. Such legends grew with the years, and long before the advent of Christianity in Europe men were working over glowing fires in close cellars and caves, brewing mixtures of all manner of weird substances, even various animal excrements, in a frenzied search for this elusive mixture which would cause their lives on earth to be unending. Then one day, by mere chance, into one of their retorts was thrown the antlers of a hart, or male deer, and a lesser amount of the hide of the same animal, which had been found in a dunghill. Experiments on the resulting brew were carried further and furnished them with the observation that chips from different metals would be changed in color when placed in this mixture. Believing that in this they had found the key to the transmutation of metals, they named their new preparation "spirits of hartshorn," a synonym for ammonia which is still used in chemistry. Then they excitedly continued their experiments, which to a marked degree have culminated in our commercial productions, ammonium chloride, ammonium carbonate, ammonium iodide, and other ammonium salts.

Centuries passed in which the belief in the philosophers' stone and the elixir of life throve. Then in 1604 appeared a very remarkable book, written by a most extraordinary man, or by several individuals, as a number of medical historians soon after the beginning of this century suggested. At any rate, this work is still in existence and comes down to us in its original state. It is entitled *The Triumphant Chariot of Antimony* and was written by Basil Valentine. It gives us a clear insight into the great amount of myth believed in by the doctors of that period, and their dependence upon forms of medical treatment which reach the ultimate of improbability. The writer's description of how he discovered antimony indicates that he was an alchemist as well as a monk and physician. The peculiar circumstances which led up to the fact of his having obtained knowledge of the properties of this metal, and of how it occurred to him that it had great remedial qualities, have been remarked upon by many of his commentators. Valentine, it is said, while at work in his alchemist laboratory at the completion of a long series of experiments on a then unknown metal, threw the chemical residue from his tests into a trough at which a number of pigs were being fed. Its appeal to the pigs' appetite was evident at once; they disposed of the refuse containing the experimental salt in a surprisingly brief period, so he noted down that this metal was good to the taste. He later noticed that the swine thus fed soon developed intense intestinal irritation, following which their appetite for all kinds of food was enormously increased. They soon became much fatter than other pigs in an adjoining pen. Then it occurred to him that some of his brother monks were in a poor state of health and very thin in flesh, and he thought it would be an excellent idea to restore them to health. Fortunately, he had kept exact notes of how the salt had been obtained. But how was he to give them the advantage of the administration of this wonder-working remedy? Without a doubt, he reasoned, they would refuse to be a party to the experiment. Then he decided to give them the salts of this new metal clandestinely, which forthwith he proceeded to do. From the beginning he noticed that these unconscious partners to his experiment failed to improve. On the contrary, they had intense intestinal derangements, perspired profusely, had attacks of fainting, and coughed violently. Then, to Valentine's great distress, some of them died. Other versions of this story leave out the demise of the subjects of his experiment, but all relate that the monks became ill and so continued throughout long periods.

Now, Basil Valentine, in jotting down the disappointing results of this experiment, noted that although the salt of this metal was good for pigs, it had the opposite result when applied to members of his order. In casting about for a name for the new metal, he decided that the name given it must not lead to error, so he created from two Greek words—*anti,* opposite to, and *monachos,* solitary—the word "antimony"—a remedy not good for solitary monks—and to this day the name remains.

The appearance of *The Triumphant Chariot of Antimony* attracted wide notice in all European countries and did much to popularize the administration of mineral salts in the treatment of disease. Mercury soon came into general use as a treatment for syphilis, but it was noticed that after its indiscriminate administration loosening of the teeth and often necrosis of the jawbones followed. These complications did much to discourage the use of metallic substances in the treatment of disease.

It is said that Paracelsus used antimony under the name of stibium. This seems quite likely, for this keen investigator dabbled in alchemy as well as in astrology and other mystic methods of relieving the sick, and unquestionably ran across methods of obtaining various salts from stibium and other metals. Following Paracelsus, numerous illicit and floating practitioners of medicine greatly abused the use of antimony and other mineral salts, thereby adding greatly to the ills of suffering humanity. This, no doubt, was why the use of these mineral preparations was legislated out of France. Later investigations reveal why this prohibition was made. Antimony in moderate doses is a powerful heart depressant, slows the process of breathing, is an excitant of the mucous membrane, and causes vomiting and purging. In excessive doses the symptoms induced by its administration are all intensified, and often end in death, with symptoms similar to those of arsenic poisoning. But just as the rich and influential of several countries engaged Jewish doctors as personal practitioners after the Jews had been banned from practicing their art upon gentiles, so did those of influence in France employ medical itinerants who were known to be using the forbidden metallic drugs.

In 1687, when Louis XIV was so ill with what is now believed to be typhoid fever that his subjects despaired of his life, there appeared at court a traveling charlatan who sought the privilege of curing the king. After long consultation, he admitted that he wished to use the barred antimony. Promising to put his own life in forfeit should the king not recover, he was permitted to display his skill. He at once administered to the king a salt of antimony, and forthwith the king made a speedy recovery. As a result, preparations of antimony soon became more popular in France than they had ever been before, and mineral remedies were again in the medicine trays of French doctors and remained there until by their use a historic personage proved to his own satisfaction and to that of his physician that they were poisonous: When Napoleon, as a prisoner on the island of St. Helena, began to complain of violent pain in his stomach, a doctor, Antimarchi, administered tartar emetic, the tartrate of antimony and potassium. This gave the former emperor a violent attack of nausea and vomiting. A few days later Napoleon again complained of great stomach distress, and his physician then brought him another dose of tartar emetic disguised in lemonade.

After the physician withdrew, Napoleon's attendant, Montholan, appeared and asked, "What did the doctor bring you?"

"Lemonade, only lemonade," Napoleon answered. "What can lemonade do for a pain in the stomach?"

Then, handing the glass to the attendant, he said, "You drink it."

Realizing the harmlessness of lemon and perhaps tempted by the daintiness with which it had been prepared, Montholan put the glass to his lips and drained its contents. In a few minutes he was retching, vomiting, and writhing in pain. When Doctor Antimarchi reappeared Napoleon, in a tirade of abuse, claimed that he was being purposely poisoned and summarily dismissed him. Ever after Napoleon refused to take his medicine, and it is known that Antimarchi never ventured again to use the drug.

It is probable that Basil Valentine's studies in alchemy began with a search for a method which would transmute baser metals into gold, as this fact is evident from a study of his work. It is evident that by the many experiments he made in this baffling search he was able to store up a great deal of knowledge regarding the properties of metals, and these he kept fresh in his memory by his practice of making numerous notes. That he was a physician as well as a monk is indicated by the way he treasured each of his discoveries that might in any way be useful in medicine. Many of his laboratory experiments may be viewed as first steps in the science of chemistry which was soon to follow.

That the monk physician who later became Pope John XXI was in his early years an ardent alchemist has been noted by James J. Walsh. Others have noted that not only did he spend much of his life in quest of a method of turning baser metals into gold but, with visions of personal success, he sought to discourage his followers from going further with their experiments.

It is recorded that Bernard Treveson, one of the most noted and respected alchemists of Europe of the fifteenth century, had as an associate a Franciscan monk who labored with him until, overcome by work and privation, he succumbed, leaving Treveson to work alone. Treveson, greatly discouraged, then went to Vienna and established another laboratory with a monk by the name of Henry. These two men followed the elusive dream of creating gold by means of the philosophers' stone which they felt they were certain to discover, but after months of weary hours in their stuffy laboratory both were compelled to cease their efforts. Treveson's death occurred in 1490 as a result of inhalation of poisonous fumes. It is believed his monk associate died at about the same time of a like cause, for his return to his monastery is not recorded.

That alchemy occupied the attention not only of the learned but also those of royal power is indicated by many incidents of history. During the Middle Ages the governments of the several European countries had their own alchemists who were engaged in the search of methods of transmuting metals, and there are extant records to the effect that various nations gave honors to alchemists in order to obtain their services. Some of these reached exalted ranks, even becoming members of the nobility. Rudolph of Prague was a confirmed alchemist and for long periods attempted to create gold from baser metals. The results of his labors, which are still to be seen in Vienna, consist of bars of lead that Rudolph had spent years in attempting to change into gold.

Aside from the celebrities of the church, intellectuals among the laymen delved deep into alchemy. Sir Isaac Newton was not above accepting the alchemist's quest, and at Trinity College, Cambridge, he set up a laboratory where he attempted to create gold out of baser metals. For many months this quest seems to have occupied all of his time as well as his thoughts. Who knows but what in his reverie in the orchard he was seeing visions of gold when kind fate permitted the apple to fall upon his head, thus enabling him to give us the law of gravitation? But great achievements did not dissuade him from seeking the philosophers' stone, for he was still meditating on the subject when later he wrote to his friend, Francis Astor, who was about to start on a journey throughout Europe "to observe the products of Nature in several places, especially in mines and if you meet with any transmutation those will be worth your noting. . . . As for particulars these that are to follow are all that I can think of. In Hungary, they change iron into copper by dissolving the iron in vitrolate water." Newton was so greatly interested in the proposed work of an Indian company who claimed that they had an effectual method of transmuting other metals into gold, that he is said to have later sought to influence the president of the Royal Society with a view to repealing the act then on its statutes against those who would multiply gold.

While the trend of the last few years has been toward the discrediting of Basil Valentine and his work, I do not think the grounds for believing that he did not live and write the book accredited to him are well founded. While it may be true that no authenticated record of his life and work has been turned up in any monastery of the order to which he was supposed to belong, the book shows every evidence of having been written under such communal surroundings as the old monasteries afforded. The work speaks for itself as the product of the long life of a secluded though intellectual individual with a passion for investigating the properties of unknown substances, at a period when alchemy was giving way to the birth of the new science.

Other monks before Valentine's time had studied physical science, the most outstanding of them the English Franciscan monk, Roger Bacon. Secreted in a cloister while still an alchemist, untrammeled by the world's cares, Bacon was free to turn his mind to subjects scientific, and as a result he wrote a number of brilliant essays on chemistry and other subjects. He studied the action of explosives, and it was as a result of his many experiments that saltpeter was made to explode, thus leading the way to the discovery of gunpowder. He believed that the principle of explosive energy would one day carry ships across the seas without sails and that carriages powered by explosive energy would be made to drive through the streets. It was largely by the ridicule which attended these predictions that Roger Bacon's name has come down to us, who now drive through the streets and cross the oceans by the principle of explosive energy as a driving force. Roger Bacon in his cell became so famous that his name was on everyone's lips in England. The experiences of this humble monk clearly demonstrate that monastic life did not destroy the spirit of investigation.

As alchemy passed, a new science was born, and may I remark, in honor to the church, that with an ecclesiastical background it gradually forged its way forward into chemistry. To give but a single example of this trend in the church; Saint Thomas Aquinas, while devoting most of his energies to theological subjects, found time to give to chemical experiments, and his writings had much to do in breaking down the early prejudice toward chemistry, which had been thought of as an offshoot of alchemy and, therefore, was in many parts considered as a pseudo science. Much of the work of the modern chemist had its origin in the patient labors of the alchemist. Even most of the utensils used in his laboratories were invented by these early workers in the unknown, and the names given to them at that time are still unchanged. Among the many of these is the pipette, a tube with an expanded center, now glass though first of metal, employed by the alchemists in transferring boiling liquids from one vessel to another. Also the crucibles, cauldrons, and retorts were first made by the alchemist, all of which are now requirements of the modern chemical laboratory, to say nothing of the mortar and pestle, names with which everyone is familiar, which were first used by the alchemists in reducing resistant materials first to fragments and then to powder.

The thought that life could be made to exist forever occupied the minds of many men of intellect who, becoming enmeshed in the toils of alchemy, spent their lives over fires and stewing vats. Modern investigation finds that this strange delusion existed in every European country, causing men, often those of genius, to endure privation and seclusion which ended only in death in the search for the elixir of life that would promote an existence which, if not eternal, would continue much beyond the span of ordinary life. This delusion influenced the thoughts of many men otherwise wary. Every school child is familiar with a famous character of history, Ponce de León, who was the embodiment of a desire for never-ending life. Ponce de León was a man of sufficient importance to have been appointed tutor to the royal household of Castile and later to have been made governor of Puerto Rico. But he firmly believed that his youth would be everlasting if he could discover the famous fountain which the Indians told him about. In 1521 he lost his life in this odd adventure.

The idea of eternal life died hard, for we find it cropping up many times in a search for a panacea for all ills, which was believed to renew youth and prolong life indefinitely. But it must be admitted that during the persistent search for this goal alchemy was kept alive until the light of reason at last fell over this pseudo science.

In the writings of Basil Valentine there is sufficient evidence for us to conclude that, besides being a churchman, he practiced medicine. At that remote time there was no way of determining that any one man was a physician except by the fact that he appeared to have a knowledge of drugs and that he was a practitioner of the art of medicine. There can be no doubt that Valentine prescribed for those associated with his monastery and probably for others in the community, because he opposed the practice of other physicians who gave drugs the properties of which they knew little or nothing. Paracelsus, also an alchemist and a physician, made a similar complaint that the practitioners of his day did more harm than good by following in the footsteps of leaders who had no understanding of the remedies they were prescribing. Valentine insisted that each physician should personally prepare the remedies he prescribed. James J. Walsh, one of the most illustrious medical historians of the century, found among the many scraps of writing which are attributed to Valentine the following declamatory remarks against the unscrupulous doctors of his period.

"And whensoever," Valentine writes in the second of these works, "I shall have occasion to contend in the School with such a Doctor who knows not how to prepare his own medicine but commits that business to another I am sure I shall obtain the Palm from him; For indeed that good man knows not what medicine he prescribes for the sick, whether the color of which be white, black, gray or blew he cannot tell; nor doth this wretched man know whether the medicine he gives be dry or hot, cold or humid; but he only knows that he found it so written in books, and then pretends to knowledge or as it were a Possession of Prescription of a very long time. Yet he desires to further information. Here again let it be lawful to exclaim, Good God, to what a state is the matter brought! Wo Wo to them! In the day of Judgement they will find the fruit of their Ignorance and Rashness, then they will see Him Whom they pierced when they neglected neighbors, sought after the money and nothing else; whereas were they cordial in their profession they would spend Nights and Days in Labour that they might become more learned in their Art, whence more certain health would accrue to the sick with their estimation and greater glory to themselves. But since Labour is tedious to them they commit the matter to Chance and being secure of their Honor and Content with their Fame, they like brawlers defend themselves with a certain garrulity without any respect had to Confidence or Truth."

An English translation of Valentine's book published in London in 1678, which may be seen in the British Museum, contains the following paragraph: "Basil Valentine's *The Triumphant Chariot of Antimony.* Since I by religious rules am bound to live according to the vows of the Saint Benedict that requires another manner of spirit of Holiness than the common state of mortals exercised in the profane business of the world, I thought it my duty, above all things, in this little book to disclose what is necessary to be known by the pious Spagyrist influenced with an ardent desire of this art, and what he ought to do and whereunto to direct his striving that he may lay such foundations of the whole matter as may be stable lest his building shaken with the words happen to fall and the whole edifice to be involved in a shameful ruin which otherwise being founded on more firm and solid principles might have remained for a long series of time. Which admonition I judged was, is and always will be a necessary part of my religious office; especially since we must all die, and no one of us which are now, whether high or low, shall long be among the numbers of men. For it concerns me to recommend these meditations of Mortality to Posterity, leaving them behind me that honor may be given to the Divine Majesty, but also that men may obey Him sincerely in all things."

Basil Valentine freely admits in this little volume that he is in search of the philosophers' stone. This, he declared, was the aim which directed him into a consideration of all known metals. He first began experimenting with copper pyrites, which he found changed to copper sulphate after applying oil of vitriol. The copper, he noted, was precipitated from the solution when he plunged iron into it. Immediately he recognized in it a certain similarity to the appearance of gold, and much of his book gives theoretical reasons why baser metals may be changed into gold. It was during one of these experiments that he stumbled upon antimony, which he obtained by melting stibnite and iron with metallic sulphides. This gave him a white, lustrous, crystalline metallic element which he found would form alloys with various other metals. So interesting to him were the possibilities of obtaining these alloys that he devoted a greater part of his time to experiments of this nature, and so many new substances did he claim to discover that he said it would take a chariot to move them away, and thus was the title, *The Triumphant Chariot of Antimony,* arrived at.

It was the habit of the alchemists to admonish each other that the secret of the philosophers' stone, when once discovered, must be hidden from everyone. An alchemist of the fifteenth century is said to have warned his disciples that to divulge the secret of how gold may be made from the baser metals would so cheapen the value of the precious metal that it would become as worthless as the glass made in the bazaars, so he said, "Divulge to no one the process, not even to your wife or cherished child. To fail to do this will cause great repentance at a time when repentance would be too late." We have an echo of this in the fear expressed by England that the success of the alchemists would overrun the country with alchemic gold and thus upset the nation's economy. This became so great that England passed a law prohibiting the manufacture of alchemic gold. This law was later set aside by Henry IV, who ruled that gold might be transmuted only by persons appointed by the crown. He, therefore, designated certain influential and scientific persons to study the transmutation of metals, and he ordered that when they succeeded they should report to him for further instructions. In 1445 two alchemists, Trafford and Asherton, were granted permission to produce gold artificially. Some coins which passed as gold were actually minted, but they were later found to be alloys of gold, mercury, and copper.

At about this time frauds first crept into the process of transmuting baser metals into gold, and the public experienced concern that they already might have succeeded, thus rendering of little value the coins they had in their pockets. This unrest continued for decades. As late as 1867 a Spanish grandee and an alchemist from Naples imposed their deception upon Emperor Francis Joseph of Austria and received advance payment of what in our money would be ten thousand dollars to further an experiment in producing gold artificially. In October of that year this pair of charlatans began operations which they declared would take a period of four months to complete. Leaving subordinates to keep their retorts burning, they soon disappeared and the Austrian emperor's dream of acquiring great wealth vanished with them.

In Geneva Francis Taussaud demanded still a greater initial payment for producing gold and so deceived leading German financiers that the money was soon forthcoming. These same financiers, growing suspicious before the culmination of the experiments, had Taussaud arrested. Lodged in jail, this impostor asked for permission to prove to his accusers that they were mistaken. He was then permitted to proceed with his experiments and, to the astonishment of all, he produced from his cauldron, which had been previously examined and which he had not been allowed to touch, one-tenth gram of pure gold. After careful examination had uncovered no fraud, Taussaud was liberated. Later, the director of the mint, and one of the committee to investigate Taussaud, discovered that the gold had been dropped into the cauldron from the cigarette of the experimenter, for another partially charred cigarette which had fallen from the trembling fingers of the presumed transmuter was found to contain a similar amount of gold to that found in the cauldron.

Some who doubt that Valentine ever was a monk refer to the fact that he was not confined to a cloister, as notes from his works mention that he was in England when they were written. There also seems to be evidence that he resided for a time in France and Spain. In the books attributed to him, the names of which follow, are given the places where each was written. *The World in Miniature or the Mystery of the World and of Human Science,* Mayburg, 1609; *The Clinical Apocalypse or the Manifestations of Artificial Chemical Compounds,* Erfurt, 1624; *Alchemico-Philosophic Treatises Concerning Things Natural and Preternatural, Especially Relating to the Metals and Minerals,* Frankfurt, 1676; *The Science of Salts, a Treatise of the Preparation, Use and Chemical Properties of all Mineral, Animal and Vegetable Salts,* Bologna, 1644.

The patient search for knowledge by the alchemists led to the discovery of oxygen by Scheele of Sweden in 1773 and to a similar discovery in the same year by Priestley of England, a nonconformist minister. Scheele and Priestley have since remained great names in chemistry. From the ancient spirit of delving into matters of the unknown world much good has resulted, for we cannot forget that it was just such a spirit that motivated Madame Curie, who after many years in search of the illusive unknown, was able to announce, one day in July 1898, in the amphitheater of the Sorbonne, the discovery of radium, a new element which since has brought undreamed-of good to a suffering world.

But while the searches for artificial gold by Basil Valentine and the alchemists failed, by patient experiments they succeeded in adding some valuable facts to the then slender knowledge of chemistry. Antimony, as already noted, as well as phosphorus and bismuth, is the direct result of the labors of early alchemists. That these men paved the way for the promotion of medical science through modern chemotherapy is undisputed. Scientists from all over the world had occasion to remember the work of the humble alchemists when the tremendous announcement was made by Paul Ehrlich before the Congress of Internal Medicine at Wiesbaden, April 19, 1910, that in an arsenical preparation, which he termed 606 because its discovery occasioned that number of laboratory experiments, he had found a cure for syphilis. It was also tests originating with alchemy and culminating in the science of chemistry which in recent years have given us a great number of antibiotics or so-called miracle drugs. These have already caused the insurance companies to add years to their tables on the expectancy of human life.

14.

Ambrose Paré, the Great Barber Surgeon

The Babylonians, according to Herodotus, who extols the surgical skill of their priests, had made much progress in surgery as far back as the second millennium before Christ. A clay tablet from the Royal Library at Nineveh, telling of the surgical practice of Izdubar, the founder of the United Babylonian Empire, seems to lend some dignity to this claim of the great historian. As a further indication of the careful knowledge of surgery possessed by the Babylonians, we find in the writings of Hammurabi the suggestion that surgical instruments should be cleaned before they are used. It is interesting to recall that no further mention is made of this important technique until Lister emphasized the necessity for it many centuries afterward.

In the fifth century before Christ, Democritus supplied another interesting fact now recognized by modern surgery, by teaching that small living particles were the cause of disease, thus anticipating Pasteur about 2,300 years. These two instances of old ideas being reborn give a modern emphasis to the wisdom of the sage who proclaimed that under the sun there was nothing new.

India seems to have attained a high degree of surgical skill at an early date in her history. A commentary on the work of Sashruta explains the various steps necessary in performing an operation for hysterectomy and gives the technique employed in opening the abdomen. Surgery later was put under the ban of the Brahmanic castes in India and declined so rapidly that in the seventh century, though we find a chain of hospitals reaching across the country, no surgery was performed, the hospitals being given over to the treatment of the poor and the care of the sick and helpless animals. This all may be considered as no more than a prelude to surgery as we know it today, serving only as a foundation for the great work of Ambrose Paré, who was to follow.

Ambrose Paré has been called the father of modern surgery. He lived at the time when the wheels of progress that had spun steadily backward for many hundred years had only begun to reverse themselves. Paré had as a foundation for his science an erroneous anatomy, a physiology of pure fiction, a chemistry made up of absurdities, and just enough knowledge of surgery to act at times as a handicap. During the most active part of his career the *De Fabrica Humani Corporis* of Vesalius was in its making. Paré's anatomy, then, was the anatomy of Galen. He believed that there was a porous wall between the ventricles of the heart through which the blood circulated, that the sternum or breastbone was really composed of six bones, that the largest vein in the body had its origin in the liver, that the skin was supplied by muscles, and that the human heart was provided with an "imputrecible" bone.

Paré's physiology was also the physiology of Galen. Galen taught that life, both physical and mental, was controlled by four elements. These elements were spoken of as humors and consisted of yellow bile, black bile, blood, and phlegm. They were again subdivided into hot and cold, and dry and moist. By these elements a person's characteristics and disposition were formed. An echo of this belief is found in our own language; hence we speak of a high-tempered person as hot-blooded and of a cruel person as cold-blooded. One with a good disposition is good-humored and the opposite is bad-humored. Yellow bile causes one to be dull or choleric; good blood makes him hopeful or sanguine, and too much phlegm leads him to be phlegmatic. Our phrases, good-hearted, hardhearted, heartsick, and tender-hearted, have their origin in the physiology of Galen.

Physiology during Paré's time was greatly influenced by the *Physiologus* and later bestiaries. With much gravity these treatises describe why the lion sleeps with its eyes open, why the elephant cannot lie down, how the pelican is able to bring her young back to life by sprinkling them with her own blood, and the reason why the crocodile weeps after he has eaten a man. These writings so affected medieval thought that they supplied the imagery which gave origin to the animal heads seen on antique furniture, animal appendages on ancient European churches, and grotesque embellishments of medieval architecture generally.

Ambrose Paré was born in Bourg Hersent, France, in 1510, the son of a common servant, though to chronicle this fact is irrelevant. No one is born great. One may be born with characteristics which lead to greatness, but these have to be developed by the individual himself. Who saw greatness in Lincoln in his homespun pinafores or in Garfield sleeping upon a corn-shuck mattress in a log cabin? Their greatness came only after they had transformed their natural characteristics into character. Paré lived to revolutionize surgery and to place it upon a scientific foundation, to transform it from a shameful occupation to a respectable science, and, incidentally, to hew out a place for himself among the great.

Paré did not have the advantage of an early education. Whether he gained or lost by this will always remain a matter of opinion. A certain amount of mental discipline, we believe, is good for the youthful mind, but if we take Humboldt seriously we will conclude that more than one year in a university will "constrict rather than expand the intellect." Many pebbles have been polished by a college curriculum. Of this there can be no doubt, but what of the diamonds that have lost their luster by the same process?

Paré's schooling was given him at the hands of kind old Nature. As a boy he knew the habits of all the birds in his community, was acquainted with the plants and flowers of the adjacent country, and stored up many things regarding these in his mental granary. In thus developing his powers of observation, he was learning to appreciate firsthand knowledge. Without this gift he would never have been known to us.

Paré placed his foot on the first step of the ladder of fame in the capacity of village barber, and while shaving chins he also did the surgery that came his way. Popular superstition had long since made of surgery a despised calling. The physicians of the time dealt with the treatment of wounds only. Aside from the practice of phlebotomy, or opening a vein, they abhorred the shedding of blood and despised those who practiced any form of operative surgery. Naturally, the practice fell into the hands of the lowly and the unlearned. Historians tell us that "till the time of John Hunter surgical practitioners consisted generally of barbers, furriers, and even cobblers and tinkers." Usually, however, surgery was the prerogative of barbers, then an ignorant and despised class, and those practicing it were known as barber surgeons. This was Paré's status in the society of his native village.

The familiar barber pole seen everywhere in Europe and North America is reminiscent of the time when the barber was the only surgeon. The white band of this emblem represents the bandages used by the surgeons; the red stripes indicate the arterial blood.

In the Tower of London is a life-size figure of a surgeon clad in armor, astride a horse also protected by armor plates, and resting upon his knee is the emblem of his calling, the striped barber pole. The surgeon is represented as being entirely unarmed. This would indicate that in medieval warfare the calling of the surgeon was so respected that arms for him were not thought necessary. But that he sometimes suffered the fate of other warriors is represented by a painting in the Louvre which depicts a fallen surgeon, also unarmed, lying beside a prostrate horse; extending from his hand is the broken barber pole of his calling.

The medieval surgeon seemed to have dressed his patients'

wounds with the cheapest material then known to warfare, linen. This economical practice no doubt was responsible for the saving of many lives. The linen dressings prepared by thousands of housewives were, of course, washed and ironed in order to make the product more marketable. This process, the advantages of which were then entirely unknown even to the medieval surgeons, made these partially sterilized dressings safer than wool, which was the only other available material in use at that time.

In 1533 the bubonic plague was raging in Paris and innumerable buboes were awaiting the touch of the surgeon's razor. In a little while Paré was in the city, carried there no doubt by the enthusiasm and devotion to his work which was to make his name immortal. We hear nothing more from him until the epidemic subsided, at which time we find him a dresser of wounds at the hospital, Hôtel Dieu. In this capacity he served several years during which, not being content with the surgery as practiced by his colleagues, he made application to the then great anatomist, Sylvius, for a course in anatomy and was duly installed as a member of his classes. To take a barber under his pedagogic wing was an innovation with Sylvius and was brought about, it is thought, through the influence of some person now unknown. Probably the name of Paré's benefactor was withheld in order to escape reproach.

Paré's work at the Hôtel Dieu created for him an acknowledged reputation, and when Francis I invaded Piedmont he accompanied the army as a surgeon. Surgery at this time was crude and cruel in the extreme. Anesthesia, of course, was unknown. Patients to be operated upon were bound upon a table, and the surgeon proceeded with no regard for the cries and screams of the victim. Boiling oil used without mercy was the principal surgical dressing. Spurting vessels were closed by being seared with a red-hot iron, instead of with the ligature. The more courageous patients held bullets between their teeth and allowed the surgeon to proceed, while the more timid, rather than submit to surgical operations, often chose death by suicide.

Green vitriol stood next in popularity to boiling oil as a surgical dressing, and its use at that time suggests the faith cures of the present day. John Cordo Jefferson states that this treatment was used in England as late as the seventeenth century. "Good for many things," he writes, "it was especially efficacious for the cure of wounds. If a piece of a wounded man's raiment, stained with blood from the wound, were dipped in water holding some of this miraculous powder in solution, the wound of the injured person forthwith began to heal. It mattered not how long a time had elapsed since the infliction of the wound or how far the sufferer was away from the place when the bit of blood-stained raiment was placed in the sympathetic solution. The patient might be dying in Paris or Madrid, and the piece of stained velvet or linen might be operated on in London."

After the close of one of the bloody battles of the campaign the young surgeon Paré found, to his dismay, that the supply of boiling oil and the green vitriol had run short while there were still many wounds to be dressed. The story of how during this emergency he substituted a simple ointment—containing, among other things, the fat of puppy dogs—and, finding this method superior to the established treatment, succeeded in introducing it into the French Army, thus revolutionizing the treatment of gunshot wounds, is well known.

Paré's next innovation was the use of the ligature as a means of checking hemorrhage from large arteries during amputation. Previous to this time, as already mentioned, bleeding vessels were seared with hot irons. Other innovations followed in rapid succession. He was the first surgeon to use the suture in hare lip, the first to employ successfully the truss in hernia, and the first to amputate at the elbow joint. He introduced the practice of massage, made artificial eyes from silver, and originated a method for re-implanting teeth. He described fractures of the neck of the femur and treated these fractures by extension. He described the advantage of podalic version in obstetrics and discovered the part played by syphilis in the establishment of aneurism.

As just noted, Paré was with the French Army when it invaded Piedmont, Italy, where several of the interesting incidents of his career are supposed to have occurred. I have been on this historic battlefield. It consists of a plain surrounded on three sides by the Alps. The French had come through the pass early in the morning and were met by the enemy. The battle raged all day. Toward night a truce was called to enable each force to take care of its wounded. It was supposed to have been on this battlefield that Paré gave up the practice of using heated irons to control bleeding. The older surgeons may remember having seen the original, or at least a copy, of a painting put out many years ago by a pharmaceutical house. It depicts Paré waving aside an assistant who endeavors to hand him a red-hot iron while he prepares to stop spurting blood by means of a ligature held in his hand.

It was possibly at Piedmont that an event occurred which caused the following anecdote to find its way into his book: Paré had just undergone the experience of finding two men maimed, blinded, and past all help of his services. At this moment an old soldier came up and asked him if the wounded men had any chance of recovery. Paré assured him that they had not. "When, in turning, I saw that the old soldier had without malice and quite gently cut both their throats." Shocked at this performance, Paré was vehemently protesting such a cruel action, when the soldier replied, "I pray God, if I am ever in similar circumstances, someone will be good enough to do for me what I have just done for these men."

Paré was continually with the army in time of war during a period of thirty years. In the intervals of peace he lived in Paris where he served as surgeon to the French kings Henry II, Francis II, Charles IX, and Henry III. Between his army campaigns he wrote voluminously, his principal works being *Journeys in Diverse Places, An Essay on Gunshot Wounds, A Discourse on Podalic Version,* and *A Treatise on the Unicorn.* In the latter work he attacked the then popular superstition regarding this fabled animal. Filings from the unicorn's horn had long been a favorite remedy with medieval physicians, which fact illustrates the charlatanry associated with early medicine, for this supposed quadruped with a gigantic horn on its forehead in reality never did exist. Paré's essay, however, failed to banish the superstition at once for we find Sir Thomas Browne of England combating the "insufferable delusion" in his *Religio Medici* written fifty-three years after Paré's treatise was published.

Paré was the first man of his century to enter a protest against indiscriminate bleeding. "When in doubt, out with your lancet" was then a familiar maxim. The written works of the medieval and later surgeons indicate the extent to which this practice was carried during and long after the Middle Ages. Guy Patin, Dean of the Paris Faculty in the seventeenth century, described the surgeons of his time as "a race of evil, extravagant coxcombs, who wore mustaches and flourished razors." From his writings it may be supposed he was conservative for his time; yet we find him bleeding his wife twelve times for a "fluxion in the chest," his son twenty times for a continued fever, himself seven times for a cold in the head, while his friends, M. Mantel and M. Consino, were bled thirty-six times and sixty-four times for a fever and a rheumatism, respectively. Sir Edmond King of London, received a thousand pounds for bleeding Charles II "with the courageous promptitude that prolonged the king's life for a few days." And when we remember that the good king had been bled by twelve other surgeons previous to this, these words from the record, "And so he died," do not appear to indicate a very marvelous termination.

The following verses from the pen of a phlebotomist of this period extol the virtue of his art:

Of bleeding many profits grow, and great,
The spirits and the senses are renewed thereby,
Tho these men slowly by the strength of mate
But these by wine restored are bye and bye:
By bleeding to the marrow cometh health.

It maketh clene your brane, releeves your eie,
It mendeth appetite, restoreth sleepe,
Correcting humors, that do waking keepe
All inward parts, and senses also clearing.
It mends the voice, the smell, the hearing.

Paré emphasized the fact that the meddling surgeons, appearing at the time when Nature was making her greatest fight, when every ounce of blood was needed, instead of doing good, drove the patient beyond all hope of recovery.

In keeping with the spirit of the time, Paré met with vituperation on every hand. His colleagues denounced him for the use of the ligature, which they characterized as "hanging the life of a man on a string" when red-hot irons were always available, and for blinding himself to the virtue of boiling oil as a surgical dressing. Medical men also took a hand against him and were particularly bitter because of his ridiculing their popular remedies. Notwithstanding the enmity of the profession, he retained his position in royal circles and was a popular hero with the army until the last. He died, in 1590, a peaceful and natural death.

15.

Vesalius and Human Anatomy

Humanity moves in a dull procession but its ultimate goal is progress. Since the dawn of history the world's institutions have been in constant change. Every step forward has been paved by the sacrifice of someone who possessed sufficient courage to cast aside the intellectual dross of his age to cling to what his senses demonstrated. For thousands of years, reason, investigation and common sense, anything in fact which interfered with the prejudice of the past, was greeted with disfavor. As a result of that liberty of thought which was born with political liberty, science has advanced more during the past one hundred years than it did in the preceding four thousand years. We owe much of this advancement to isolated individuals who failed, but who attained in their defeat more than they could ever have hoped to accomplish by victory. The saviors of medicine have been those who, with a heel upon prejudice, have been unafraid to face persecution and, with truth as their guide, have been unappalled even by death. Such men have transformed a medieval superstition into a science.

In the year 1543 it was reported that Vesalius, a young surgeon of Padua, had come forward heretically proclaiming that anatomy as taught by his contemporaries was a maze of inaccuracies founded upon the mistakes and superstitions of the ancients. For thirteen hundred years all disputes in anatomy had been referred back to Galen, and during that period everything not in harmony with Galenic teaching had been cast aside. From Galen, as from a supreme court, there had been no appeal.

For centuries Galen's anatomy had been maintained by a reverence for the past which had seemed to block all progress in anatomical study. Let us not blame Galen for this. Not a line appears in his writings tending to uphold a veneration for the teachings of antiquity. Galen was himself an iconoclast, and for his innovations in medicine was compelled to leave Rome in haste, after crouching in the dark alleys so as to escape the fury of the mob. Galen's studies in anatomy were carried far in advance of his time, and while he dissected Barbary apes it is doubtful if he ever performed a human dissection. Shaping his deductions as he did, in the light of theory, it is nothing but natural that some of his conclusions should have been visionary and unsound. The many mistakes which appear in his works would not have been there had his opportunities been greater.

According to Galen, the function of the left ventricle of the heart is to produce "vital spirits" which are changed to "animal spirits" by the blood; the blood passes from the left to the right ventricle of the heart through an imperceptible opening and the function of the veins is not to carry blood but chyle. Galen believed that man possessed an intermaxillary bone and that the human eye has three humors and seven coats. He held a number of fanciful ideas in regard to humors and spirits of the body, and some of them have lived on in modern languages, though the mistakes on which they were founded have long since passed away. Since the days of Vesalius the pendulum of opinion regarding the work of Galen has swung so in the opposite direction that reverence has given way to an unjust disparagement. In speaking of the mistakes of Galen, then, we should not forget that his progress in anatomy was impeded by the same spirit which held Vesalius in check and that Galen lived centuries before the time of Vesalius.

Andreas Vesalius was born in Brussels in 1514. In the same city he began his anatomical studies some seventeen years later, guided by the Galenic text and the dissection of animals. At that time dissection of the dead human body was forbidden by law. Vesalius was just rounding off his nineteenth year when it came to his ears that over in Paris a certain Sylvius had received permission to dissect the bodies of criminals. Soon we find him duly installed as one of Sylvius' pupils. What part he had in demonstrating the fissure of Sylvius we do not know, but we do know that he was an earnest student. That merit does not always win praise is made evident by the fact that Sylvius later denounced him for intimating that Galen had made mistakes.

Sylvius, a teacher de luxe, did not soil his hands with a cadaver. The actual dissection was done by barbers with that primitive instrument, the razor, and as the parts were exposed Sylvius clumsily demonstrated them at the point of a cane. It is said that Vesalius became so impatient with this bungling method that he often grasped the razor to expose the dissected parts more thoroughly.

Clinging to the ideas of Galen with a persistence characteristic of his age, Sylvius sought to bridge over the mistakes of the master with arguments to the effect that modern observation should have no weight as compared with infallible teachings. It began to dawn upon the young student that a man whose reason was submerged in traditional orthodoxy was not a safe teacher; so he left Paris and next we hear of him in Italy.

Vesalius arrived in Padua in 1537. It appears that his genius was soon recognized, for the same year he was tendered the chair of surgery and anatomy in the university. Here he began the preparation of his great book, *De Fabrica Humani Corporis*, a work which was to make anatomy a science and bring upon its author's head the condemnation of the scientific world of that day. To produce material for his plates he was a habitual haunter of gibbets. He bribed dead-house keepers and on more than one occasion became a grave robber. His book, richly illustrated with woodcuts, appeared in 1543. With surpassing ability the old mistakes of anatomy were swept away and structures never before discovered were dealt with with marvelous accuracy.

From a modern point of view one would think that such a work would be greeted with approval, but the reverse is true. Vesalius was at once denounced as an impostor and a heretic. Sylvius, his old master, hurled invective at him in Paris, and his friends and students, swayed by popular sentiment, were human enough to hold him in derision and forsake him. Greeted upon every hand with calumny and vituperation, with prejudice gaining and the law beginning to frown, Vesalius lost no time in leaving Padua. What fate might have befallen him had he remained is suggested by the case of Michael Servetus, who anticipated Harvey seventy-five years by the following description of the circulation of the blood through the lungs:

"The vital spirit is generated by the mixture in the lungs of the inspired air with subtly elaborated blood, which the right ventricle sends to the left. The communication between the ventricles, however, is not made through the midwall of the heart, but in a wonderful way the fluid blood is conducted by a long detour from the right ventricle through the lungs and when it is acted upon by the lungs and becomes red in color passes from the Arteria Venosa into the Vena Arteriosa, whence it is finally carried by the diastole into the left ventricle."

The work of Servetus containing this extract, with certain theological opinions, was construed as an attack upon established order. When published in Paris it awakened a series of denunciations against its author so virulent that he was forced to flee from Paris. On his way to Italy he passed through Geneva, then the stronghold of John Calvin and the Reformation, where he was arrested and charged with heresy. Calvin was then the central political figure of Geneva, but what part he had to do with the undoing of Servetus is controversial; there cannot, however, be any controversy regarding the following verdict of the court at Geneva: "We condemn thee, Michael Servetus, to be bound and to be led to the place of Shampell, there to be fastened to a stake and burned alive, together with thy heretical book, as well written by hand as printed, even until they be reduced to ashes, and thus wilt thou finish thy days to furnish an example to others who might wish to commit the like." In July 1953 I stood on what is thought to have been the exact spot where Servetus was burned. Calvin was present at the burning of Michael Servetus, which indicates the fanatical spirit of the age.

Vesalius, by interfering with conventional thought, had made many enemies, and repercussions were soon to follow. The next year he was carried before the Inquisition on the charge of dissecting a living body. Through the influence of the court, he escaped with a promise to atone for his crime by making a pilgrimage to the Holy Land. On his way back from Jerusalem he was shipwrecked and died on the island of Zante, the victim of privation and despondency.

The world has been blest and hampered simultaneously by two classes of thinkers: those who, lacking the courage of conviction, have built a wall of silence about themselves, and those in whom the desire for self-expression has risen above both fear and personal aggrandizement. To the latter class belongs Vesalius. Restive under venerable restraint, he dared to express his honest thoughts. He was an observer of the highest order. He believed in evidence and was willing to stand behind what his senses demonstrated. He found anatomy a superstition; he left it a rational science. His work paved the way for Highmore, Glisson, Wharton, Malpighi, Peyer, Meibom, and Billini, names familiar to every student of anatomy.

Vesalius died long before he was appreciated, but in life he won this victory—the supreme satisfaction which only the search for truth can bring.

16.

William Harvey Discovers the Circulation of the Blood

William Harvey, who first unraveled the enigma of the circulation of the blood, is considered by the British nation as one of its two greatest scientific geniuses, the other being Sir Isaac Newton, the discoverer of the law of gravitation. Harvey was born in Folkestone, England in 1578. When twenty-four years of age he was sent to grammar school in Canterbury, where he was an average pupil. After graduating from grammar school he proceeded to Caius College, Cambridge. He then went to Padua, Italy, for the study of medicine, where he received his M.D. degree in 1602. One of his teachers in Padua was Hieronymus Fabricius, who had been a pupil of Vesalius and who had just published a brochure entitled *De Venarum Ostiolis,* which means "on the doors of the veins." Fabricius, as Harvey later proved, did not have a true conception of these doors (valves), believing them to be meant only as a means of preventing overdistention of the veins. The very fact that there were valves in the veins, however, set Harvey's mental machinery into motion. He was to work continuously on the subject of the blood until he determined that the real purpose of these valves was to prevent a backflow of the blood toward the extremities, thus keeping the blood in motion.

This conception was finally used as an argument by Harvey to prove his theory of how the blood circulates.

Shortly after taking his medical degree in Padua, Harvey received an appointment as Lumleian lecturer on anatomy and surgery in the College of Physicians in London. This course prescribed two lectures a week on anatomy which were to continue throughout the year, together with the dissection of a human body for five continuous days, and longer if the bodies were still not sufficiently decomposed to prevent further study. At this same College of Physicians Harvey continued to give these lectures and to make these dissections for the next forty years, and in the British Museum may be seen the notes which comprised the first year of his lecture work. Anatomists poring over these notes have concluded that it was at the College of Physicians of London during this first year that Harvey hit upon his discovery, though it took many years of further study and experiments before he was ready to give to the world his conclusions relative to the circulation of the blood. But these notes in the British Museum clearly indicate the conclusions which were to follow later, for in them he incorporated the following statement: "The movement of the blood occurs constantly in a circular manner and is the result of the beating of the heart."

It is quite possible that Harvey in his conclusions on the circulation of the blood was impelled in the right direction by having had the privilege of studying the drawings of Fabricius, his former teacher, which show the veins of the left arm with the valves therein outlined, as well as suggesting the function of the valves of the veins. Harvey had begun to think of the heart as a kind of pump, a never-ending pulsating organ until death stills it, which continuously uses over and over again the same blood at each cycle, and the blood being purified in the lungs serves to keep the body living. More than this Harvey would not venture to assert, and he died still contemplating whether the blood supplied the body with nourishment or whether its function was to provide body warmth. Neither was he able to determine how the blood gets from the arteries to the veins in surfaces and extremities of the body. Had he theorized on this it might have weakened the greatness of his discovery, for his conclusions could not have been more than conjecture, as the microscope had not yet been perfected and the free passage of the blood from the arteries to the veins through the capillaries, which a student today can see in a frog's foot even through a low-powered microscope, would not likely have been accepted as fact at that time. This tremendous conception of how the blood circulates, second only to that of Newton's discovery of the law of gravitation, came to Harvey by degrees; nothing was taken for granted until proven.

After Harvey returned to London the subject of the movement of the blood continued to occupy his attention, and an anecdote tells that one day as he sat in a contemplative mood, stroking the back of one hand with the finger of the other, he noted that when stroking downward over the basilic vein the blood was in some manner prevented from following the course of his finger, but that on releasing it the blood immediately rushed up to fill the empty vein. Reasoning on the cause of this, it occurred to him that there was some kind of wall or valve other than the one described by Fabricius, which had prevented the blood's immediate return. During the reverie Harvey had occasion to recall Fabricius' sketch showing the veins to have valves that Fabricius claimed were meant to prevent a bursting of the veins during strenuous exertion. But it dawned upon Harvey that Fabricius, great as he was as a teacher, had the wrong impression of these valves, that he had failed to grasp the fact that the valves were placed in such a position that they would not serve a useful purpose if the venous blood had its origin in the liver and flowed toward the extremities, as Galen had taught.

Many writers have suggested that the work of Galen, Realdus Columbus, Fabricius, and Michael Servetus had much to do with putting Harvey on the right track regarding the circulation of the blood. In the case of the former two authors nothing could be further from the truth, for had Harvey been swayed in his judgment by the supposed infallible conclusions of Galen, which conclusions were also the basis of the opinion of Columbus and Fabricius, his great discovery would never have been made.

It has been suggested that Realdus Columbus came near to discovering the complete circulation of the blood in his treatise, written in Venice, in which he attempted to explain the pulmonary circulation. Just how this is achieved he points out by the following: "As the heart dilates, the blood passes from the vena cava into the right ventricle where by contraction of the heart it is forced into the 'arterial vein' [*sic*] and is thereby carried to the lungs where it is thinned out and becomes mixed with air. From here it is passed into the venous artery [*sic*] which carries this blood, now thinned by air, into the left ventricle of the heart." It has also been claimed that the important conclusions of Michael Servetus in reference to the pulmonary circulation of the blood had much to do with Harvey's great discovery of the total circulation of the blood. Those who advance this claim fail to take note that the conclusions of Servetus were purely theological, and Harvey, being absorbed in scientific anatomy and medicine, devoted no time to theological discussions. The following note from Servetus' book indicates what he was attempting to prove:

" 'The soul,' says Holy Writ, 'is in the blood.' More than this the soul is the blood. Then if the soul is the blood one must know how the blood is formed before arriving at any conclusion as to how the soul is formed, and in order to understand how the blood is formed we must first know how it moves."

Even with this confusion in his mind Servetus was able to demonstrate how the blood circulates from the heart through the lungs.

Of all these great investigators it is only fair to conclude that it was Fabricius who first opened the eyes of William Harvey as to how the blood circulates, by emphasizing the importance of studying the human body not from books but from Nature herself.

As a member of the College of Physicians, the chair of anatomy and surgery of which Harvey was given in 1615, he devoted all his available time to organizing his theory of the circulation of the blood. The manuscript, *Exercitatio Anatomica de Motu Cordis et Sanguinis,* now in the British Museum, was written during this period. In this paper Harvey demonstrates that the blood enters the left ventricle from the lungs, and he describes the systole and the diastole of the heart. Columbus, Vesalius, and Servetus might have reached the same conclusions and thus would have been able to arrive at an explanation of the total circulation of the blood before Harvey's time, except at that time the anatomical world was so imbued with the teaching of Galen that while these three earlier anatomists did branch out into new fields of thought regarding the circulation of the blood, they were still under the influence, to a certain degree, of what they had been taught regarding the infallibility of Galen.

Then just how did Harvey happen to grasp the truth that long eluded anatomists and physiologists? Harvey's demonstration that the heart is a muscle containing four chambers was a logical conclusion of a long series of experiments in which he noted that the pulse was due to the bounding movement of the heart itself and not to the throbbing of the veins as was once supposed. Harvey ligated the arteries and then divided them to prove that the arterial blood flowed away from the heart. After a great number of experiments occupying several years, he learned that the auricles and ventricles on each side of the heart do not contract in unison, but one contraction succeeds the other.

It was not until 1628 that Harvey saw fit to give his great discovery to the press. In this year in Frankfurt, Germany he had published *Exercitatio Anatomica de Motu Cordis et Sanguinis,* "anatomical treatise on the movement of the heart and blood." The book created a sensation. In this work he established a fact now familiar to all students of anatomy, that the movement of the heart could be better observed in amphibians, such as in the frog, than in warm-blooded animals. In the frog he demonstrated the fact that the blood went continuously in a circle, and gave the scientific world the first positive proof of the function of the heart.

While the discovery of Harvey may be considered as the most momentous single achievement in the history of medicine, it brought him a storm of abuse. Invective was hurled at him by anatomists from all quarters of the globe, but he never wavered in his decisions and had sufficient courage to stick by what his senses demonstrated, even at a time when to disagree with Galen was considered to be heretical. It is gratifying to realize, however, that his discovery was universally accepted during his lifetime. Harvey at no time advanced any reason for the circular motion of the blood. This was found only after development of the microscope, which enabled the anatomist to see the capillaries between the terminals of the veins and arteries.

17.

The Discovery of Obstetrical Forceps for Delivering Women in Difficult Labor

In the year 1569, there being much political and religious unrest in the city of Paris, an accomplished obstetrician by the name of Chamberlen, who had resided in France from infancy, decided to seek asylum elsewhere. Accordingly, he secretly made his way to the coast and took passage in a vessel for Southampton, England. Arriving in this city he established himself as an obstetrician and soon, as in the city of his birth, became widely known as being skilled in delivering women in difficult labor, in which all local physicians had failed. Here he married and reared a large family, the eldest of whom, a son named Peter, followed in the footsteps of his father, studying medicine and devoting himself to the relief of women who failed to deliver their children normally and whose physicians, to save the lives of their patients, had called for help from the Chamberlen family.

In these trying labor cases it was the practice of both father and son that the attending physicians must relinquish charge of their patient before any assistance would be given them. Soon it was surmised by these physicians that a valuable secret was in the hands of this family, and all manner of conjectures were advanced as reasons for their success. Many claimed that a secret powder was used by them to be insufflated into the pelvic canal of the prospective mother, which lubricated the tract so thoroughly that the child could then be born normally.

In 1616 Peter, the younger Chamberlen, moved up to London where he soon acquired a tremendous reputation and became wealthy, but the secret belonging to the Chamberlen family was not revealed. As was the case in Southampton, all kinds of vague rumors were advanced to explain the success of this London obstetrician, but the secret held.

Peter of London had a son named Hugh, who studied medicine and soon was possessor of his father's secret and, as his father grew older, capitalized on it and also became wealthy. After his father's death Hugh, in attempting to sell his secret to a French obstetrician for the equivalent of ten thousand dollars in our money, is said to have attempted his operation on the person of a rachitic dwarf with a small pelvis and lost both the mother and the child as a result. Hugh then proceeded to Holland, where he finally succeeded in selling what he claimed was his secret to the College of Physicians in Amsterdam, and the college also kept this method of delivery secret except for its own graduates, who were pledged not to reveal it.

At about this time two young public-spirited citizens of Amsterdam, believing it was criminal to withhold a secret from the world which could be made the means of saving many lives, took courses in the University of Amsterdam, graduated in medicine, and then made the secret, as the university had acquired it, available to all physicians who would promise to use it properly. It therefore became public property. Later it was revealed that the secret which Hugh Chamberlen, now deceased, had sold to the University of Amsterdam was simply a single blade of the original Chamberlen obstetrical forceps. Many physicians now began to experiment with the single blade, and they learned that when an opposing blade was added it became a phenomenal instrument in delivering women with contracted pelves.

News at that period was slow in travel, but it leaked out finally that a new method was in the hands of obstetricians which, if in general use throughout the world, would be capable of saving hundreds of lives annually. As a result there grew up in the minds of the physicians of the period a bitterness toward the Chamberlen family, all of whom were now deceased, who for gain through three generations had kept their method undivulged and by so doing sacrificed thousands of mothers and unborn children. Other skeptical physicians now claimed that the Chamberlen reputation of almost miraculously relieving pregnant women was a mere myth, and this conclusion slowly took hold of the profession of medicine until the so-called myth was about exploded. And then a single incident occurred to revive the old Chamberlen claim. In 1813, at Mortimer Hall in Essex, England, a palatial residence once owned by Peter Chamberlen, a chest was found containing four rusty instruments, now known to be those invented by the Chamberlen family. These instruments contained no pelvic curve and no locks.

Improvements on the Chamberlen Forceps

Many improvements were later made in the Chamberlen invention. In 1750 Smellie in England added a pelvic curve, and at about the same time Levret in France created a locking device which did away with the old method of wrapping the handles. Soon after this Buech of Germany added to the handles a shoulder, thus enabling the operator to take a firmer grip. Thompson of Edinburgh then put out his modification and improved upon the lock as well as the pelvic curve of the instrument. Later Davis, by making a large number of models of the fetal head and applying to them forceps of various shapes, was enabled to create an instrument which would fit almost any type of fetal head. So far as I am able to learn, no further improvements have been made in this instrument since the time of Davis, except in an adjustment on some later forceps which enables the physician to create traction in the direction that the head has to move to be delivered. All of these additions have served to increase the effectiveness of this remarkable instrument.

There can be no doubt that the work of the Chamberlens saved the lives of many women and their unborn children. But the fact that the Chamberlens had a secret which made this result possible and that they failed for almost a century to reveal it to the world awakened in the minds of everyone, so soon as the secret was made known, a feeling of crying resentment. Thus the Chamberlens have been subjected to a reproach which is as keen today as it was at the time when the secret first leaked out. Had this effective method been made known when it was discovered, thousands of women at the most critical time of their lives, as well as their unborn children, would not have been allowed to perish to provide gain for the Chamberlens. This fact when recalled today places a stigma upon these skillful, though cruel and crafty, obstetricians, and instead of being honored, they shall ever bear the blame of right-thinking people.

18.

The Early Knowledge of the Eye

In the Bible occur these sentences: "Let there be light, and there was light," and "He who has eyes to see, let him see." It must be said, however, that those who received these messages and for centuries translated and quoted them had no true conception of how we see. Vision was then thought to be due to light emitted from the eyes, and anything that obstructed this light would keep the subject from seeing. An evidence of this is the ancients' belief that the film sometimes seen through the pupil of the eye was in reality a fluid within the eye, which fell behind the pupil and obstructed the rays emanating from the eye, thus causing blindness. They called this suspected fluid a cataract, and this mistaken term still persists even in scientific literature.

Johann Kepler, the German astronomer, left the world with a knowledge of the true laws of planetary motion which guided Newton to his discovery of the law of gravitation. His *Dioptrice,* published in 1611, contains the first information on how the retina within the eye is responsible for vision. This and other essays demonstrated that the crystalline lens is an elastic body which by refracting the rays of light upon the retina causes them to reach a focal point on the most sensitive retinal spot, giving us a clear picture of what is before us. He also demonstrated in various essays that the two greatest impediments to good sight, in the average eye, resulted from the failure of the eye to conform to a given standard; if the eye is too long, one is shortsighted, and if it is too short, the subject will be farsighted. There the matter rested until René Descartes, in 1637, took up the question of how vision occurs and further clarified it.

Descartes compared the eye to a camera obscura, then still a novelty, but the comparison was so apt that the camera as an illustration of the organ of vision has never lost its place in the teaching of the physiology of the eye. He also taught that the normal organ of vision is a globular body placed in the orbit which protects it, and that, reduced to its simplest part, it consists, in front, of the cornea, which was long spoken of as the glassy part of the eye. This cornea he described as being tough and transparent and slightly more convex than the other coats of the eye. The side and back walls of the eye he described as being formed by the sclera, a very dense membrane. He further describes this membrane as being opaque and perforated behind by an opening through which the optic nerve enters. Just within the sclera and attached to it, he states, nature has set the choroid, a layer of pigment in which are most of the blood vessels of the interior of the eye. This black coating of the eye he described as having its counterpart in the black paint inside the camera. He determined that as this coat extends forward there is a gradual change in the arrangement of its cells and fibers until it reaches the front of the eye, where it goes to form the iris, a delicate curtain which regulates the amount of light that the eye needs. In the camera this curtain is supplied by the shutter. The curtain or iris, he noted, is of a different color in different individuals. In the blond it ranges all the way from a hazel to a blue; in the brunette it is medium or dark brown. When one looks into the eyes of his friend, Descartes stated, it is this iris which he sees, and he suspected that the "expression" of the eye was due to the color and markings of the iris.

The light he described as entering the eye through an opening, the pupil, which is seen as a black spot, the "sight," in the middle of the iris. The pupil contracts and expands in order to regulate the amount of light which the eye needs. The action of the pupil he arrived at by watching an eye closely while it rested upon a light and then was turned to a dark corner of the room. In the former position it was seen to contract in order to shut out an excess of light; in the latter position he described it as gradually expanding. He also took note of the fact that in going from the light into a dark room, objects are obscured at first and then gradually appear. This phenomenon, he declared, was due to the fact that on entering the room the pupil was contracted. Later, acting under the influence of the diminished light, its gradual dilation occurred.

Descartes found that the optic nerve, after it enters the globe, spreads out over its walls and forms the retina, which is the receptive apparatus of the eye. Upon the retina the image is focused and the picture thus formed is transmitted to the brain. Its most sensitive portion he termed the fovea. He discovered that the focusing apparatus of the eye directs the light rays so that they fall upon this sensitive spot.

Other early students of the eye demonstrated that the crystalline lens is a flexible, transparent body contained in a capsule, and that it is placed directly behind the iris with an attachment to the focusing muscle. Its function, they discovered, is to contract rays of light and cause them to fall upon the retina, where they are received and carried to the brain in what we call sight. When we look at objects near at hand this focusing muscle comes into play and contracts the lens, making the short rays of light fall on the retina at the necessary point, and the result is that we see.

It had long been known that the various excursions of the eye within its orbit are controlled by a set of six muscles. Four of these muscles are used in directing the eye from side to side and up and down. These are called the recti muscles. Two other muscles, the "obliques," are used to give the eye a rotary motion. The action of these muscles is such that rays of light coming into the eyes from different distances are focused without the consciousness of their possessor. The closer an object is to the eye, the more must the light converge, and by these muscles the act of convergence is produced.

The amount of light entering the eye is regulated by the iris; in Descartes' hands the sliding screen of the camera served the same purpose. The crystalline lens and the camera lens have the same function, to focus the rays of light and thus form an inverted image on the screen behind. As we have seen, in the eye this screen is the retina; in the camera it is the sensitive plate, or film. The film of the camera receives the rays of light, after which they are transferred to the photograph; the retina takes the impression and transfers it to the brain and a visual image is made. One who wishes to receive a valuable lesson on the eye might spend a quarter of an hour in taking a camera to pieces and examining its parts.

While the camera is a mathematically correct instrument, the eye unfortunately is rarely so. The majority of eyes met with in actual life vary considerably from a mathematical standard and are poorly adapted for close vision or for seeing at a distance without strain. The reason for this is that at birth the eye is more or less flattened and will remain so unless circumstances are favorable to its developing a normal shape. Among nomadic peoples the eye is usually perfectly developed, but in civilized man the normal eye is so rare as to be abnormal.

In 1671 Edme Mariotte demonstrated that the luminosity of the eyes of animals at night was due entirely to reflection of light, and found that in a totally darkened room no light was emitted from the eye. His conclusions did away for all time with the old belief that the eye was the cause of light. Christoph Scheiner of Vienna in 1619 demonstrated how images fall on the retina and that vision in the normal eye depended on the elasticity of the lens, thickening in the center while looking at objects close at hand and flattening when no effort is made by the subject. His paper on this subject, put into its simplest form, is about as follows:

The most common eye defect from the standpoint of light refraction, as Descartes pointed out, is "far sight." The farsighted eye has its axis from front to back shorter than normal. A picture falling on the retina in such an eye will make a blurred image without the help of the focusing muscle. When the eye looks at distant objects, this muscle acts or "accommodates" in order to correct the focus so that the object will be seen clearly. But now should the eye attempt to see objects near at hand, it cannot possibly get a distinct image. The object looks blurred because the eye has used up all of the focusing power or accommodation in viewing distant ones. What the more fortunate see clearly, the subject now fails to see. During the weary hours of the day his focusing muscles are tugging and straining at the crystalline lens in an effort to make the light rays focus. He soon uses up his reserve nervous energy, the eyes act for a few minutes and then "let go," and the print blurs. Today the refractionist examining a farsighted patient with headache puts a convex lens in front of the patient's eye. This lens concentrates the light rays and causes them to focus on the retina in the proper manner without any effort upon the focusing muscles. A wonderful change is brought about. The headache ceases and the nervousness disappears, because the leakage of nerve force caused by ineffectual attempts at focusing is stopped.

It took many more years of observation and study before the refractionist discovered that in neglected cases of far sight, strabismus, or crossed eyes, is apt to result. It was found to be a law of nature that the more the focusing muscle is needed in "accommodation," the more convergence occurs in the eye. In other words, a very strong impulse is given to turn the eye in when far sight exists. In cases of this character the drawing in of the recti or converging muscles goes on until the subject develops double vision. When he looks at one object, two objects are seen, a very confusing phenomenon. Eventually he learns to disregard one object. In other words, he finds, unconsciously, that he can see better with one eye than with two, and the unused eye follows the course of least resistance, which is a turning inward toward the nose.

All refractionists now know that this very unsightly and injurious defect may often be prevented, or corrected when once established, by wearing correctly adjusted lenses. It is very important that these cases be attended to as soon as discovered; otherwise the retinal fibers of the unused eye will atrophy or waste away from disuse. This disfigurement was for centuries believed to be permanent, and it was only in 1829 that Frederick Diffenbach of Berlin demonstrated that the unsightly crossed eye could nearly always be corrected by surgery. Such correction, by which the subject is usually relieved of a depressing feeling of inferiority, is now almost a daily occurrence in any larger hospital.

Cases of nearsightedness are all due to an elongation of the eyeball, in which light rays from a distance, instead of focusing on the retina, come to a point in front of it and cross, thus making a blurred image. Eyes which have a tendency to short sight, by long continued overexertion, gradually pass to the elongated type and become myopic or shortsighted. When close vision is encouraged in infancy and when excessive use of the eye is permitted in early childhood, the elongation of the globe may be hastened and the child will sooner than otherwise become shortsighted. Correction of uncomplicated short sight is a simple matter and consists of the adjustment of concave lenses which spread light rays and in the careful regulation of the amount of work that should be done.

Astigmatism is a condition which gives rise to a great deal of discomfort and one which has only more recently been understood. In this disorder the eye has what may be termed a double focus. The horizontal light rays, for instance, may focus on the retina, while those in the perpendicular meridian come to a point in front of the retina. This is due to the lack of correct curvature of either the cornea or crystalline lens. If one should look into the bowl of a highly polished spoon he may be helped to understand this phenomenon. If the spoon is held in one direction the focus is lengthened; if it is held in the opposite direction the opposite occurs. In either position the face of the observer in the spoon is more or less distorted, depending upon the depth or the length of the spoon. In both there is an over-focus in one direction and an under-focus in the other. Now this is just what happens in the astigmatic eye. The rays of light as they pass through the cornea and lens are not brought to one point, and a blurred image falls on the retina, a condition which necessitates muscular strain before it can be equalized.

Christoph Scheiner also demonstrated the power of accommodation of the eye. He proved that the normal eye has the power to direct its attention to a far object and see clearly, and it also has the power to direct its attention to a near object and still see clearly. This is due to altering the convexity of the lens. He called this power "accommodation," and his term is still in use.

The physiology of the eye being better understood, a great change was to take place in eye surgery, which was then in the hands of "eye destroyers," as Bartisch, one of the world's first scientific eye surgeons, called those pretending surgeons who in cases of cataract temporarily restored vision by pushing the crystalline lens back into the eye, thus improvidently freeing the pupil from obstruction, but it almost always ended in the total destruction of vision.

The Development of Modern Ophthalmology

The sage who said that "an ounce of prevention is worth a pound of cure" was voicing a sentiment now generally accepted by the medical profession and more particularly perhaps by those engaged in the treatment of the eye. As an example, fifty years or so ago, before the tonometer instrument was devised to measure the tension of the human eye, nearly all cases thought to have glaucoma were immediately operated upon. In view of the frightful consequences in certain cases of glaucoma, all suspected cases were given the benefit of the doubt and forthwith sent to the operating room. In this the surgeon was proceeding in an entirely conservative manner, for with no gauge to the tension of the eye except that of his fingers—and these, as we now know, often erred—he was frequently led into error.

During late years this precipitant method of treating glaucoma, except in the acute stages, has been entirely given up, and the patient of today suffering from so-called chronic glaucoma is usually subjected to a long period of observation and treatment before any surgical course is decided upon. Very often, in chronic glaucoma the operation, especially in the aging patient, may be deferred throughout the remaining years of his life, and by careful periodic observations in the eye physician's office the patient may in reality be safer without surgery than he would be if the operation had been done at the moment the disease was discovered. Conservatism with the modern eye surgeon has been a part of his training, and no patient need fear that his eye may be the subject of an ill-advised operation.

The Early Treatment of Glaucoma

Primary glaucoma stands foremost among eye diseases fatal to vision. There are phases of the disease which are still obscure though they have been the subject of intense study for many years. It is generally held by the average eye physician that increased tension in the eyeball, or glaucoma, is due to some manner of obstruction to the normal drainage from the eye, predisposed to by a shallowness of the anterior chamber of the eye, together with a hypersecretion of the fluid within the eye itself resulting from disturbance of the sympathetic nervous system. Other academic causes often discussed are thrombosis, or plugging of the central vein of the retina, and loss of normal elasticity of the walls of the eyeball. Theories to this effect may have some truth, but, as noted by Priestly Smith, a great English eye surgeon of the last century, such causes, if they exist, all lead to improper drainage from the eye, a condition which is glaucoma.

In this disease there is always a lack of balance between the secretion of the fluids and their normal escape from the eye. It is an often-noted fact that the fluid within the eye is in continuous circulation. This is well illustrated by the manner in which a wounded crystalline lens is dissolved and removed from the eye following a puncture of the capsule of the crystalline lens.

The normal fluids from within the eye escape through a structure formerly a vein, which nature has transformed into a canal. The anatomist knows it as the Canal of Schlemm. This evolutionary structure no longer contains blood and it always remains open, while all other veins collapse. It has also a greater caliber than that of other veins in the eye and, in the normal state, filters out of the eye sufficient fluid to maintain a balance. But when this vein becomes obstructed so as to prevent normal outflow of fluid from the eye, glaucoma is established. In the mechanics of glaucoma the most common cause for an occlusion of the opening of Schlemm's Canal is pressure upon it by the thickened root of the iris. The process of occlusion is apt to come on in advanced age, and this unfortunate tendency leads to the crowding of Schlemm's Canal and often to its complete obstruction.

In attempting to work out the reason for the phenomenon of glaucoma, we must start with the premise that in the normal eye at birth there is maintained a complete balance between the pressure of the contents of both the front and back chambers of the eye. This in the more fortunate person continues throughout life, but in all eyes a physiological process goes on by which the crystalline lens becomes gradually larger because it is being added to by cells which form around its nucleus. A shallowing of the front chamber gradually takes place in the average eye as the years pass, and as the crystalline lens enlarges, it in its longitudinal diameter presses the base of the iris against Schlemm's Canal. In most instances, drainage sufficient to maintain a balance may continue for long periods after this happens, and then, suddenly, adhesions may occur so that normal drainage becomes completely closed off. This is the dread disease of glaucoma. This is, as well as I can give it, a brief synopsis of the general events leading up to the development of increased intraocular tension and, finally, to glaucoma.

As already noted, since the days of Priestly Smith, all theories relative to the cause of glaucoma in the final analysis lead to compression of the drainage canal. Our objective of surgical attack in cases of glaucoma must necessarily be directed toward this area.

Therefore, if this description of glaucoma is to be of practical value, the various procedures for overcoming the retention which leads to glaucoma should be briefly reviewed.

Operation for Glaucoma

It is generally agreed that there are three practical methods for the surgical relief of glaucoma. The first consists in an attempt to re-establish the normal drainage through the Canal of Schlemm. The cure of glaucoma has been accomplished most often, perhaps, by removing a piece of iris at its base where it crowds Schlemm's Canal. Of the various methods directed toward the restoration of drainage through this normal route, the broad iridectomy, or removal of a segment of the iris, as done by von Graefe stands first so far as good results are concerned. The operation, as performed by this great surgeon, was the only recognized surgical procedure for any type of glaucoma for many years. Later, except in cases of acute congestive glaucoma, the operation fell into disuse, largely because the results began to fail to come up to formerly accepted standards. This, I am convinced, was partly due to an alteration in technique upon the part of later eye surgeons. During forty years I have had occasion to follow the development of this operation as I have seen it done by German and Austrian surgeons who meticulously followed the technique of von Graefe. I have also noted that today the iridectomy as usually done in America is performed through an incision frequently confined solely to the cornea, and the base of the iris is incised without due traction being made upon it. To a considerable extent an operation done in this manner defeats its own ends.

The mechanics of the second method of relieving glaucoma has as its purpose the re-establishment of the normal channels of drainage by creating a new channel by way of what is known as the supra-choroidal space. This undoubtedly has been accomplished in numerous instances by the operation of cyclodialysis, but this procedure is usually so much more unsatisfactory than other methods of overcoming glaucoma that no attempt will be made to describe its technique here.

The third method directed toward the relief of glaucoma consists in providing a new avenue for drainage through the wall of the eyeball. This has been brought about in innumerable instances by trephining the sclera, or wall of the eye, thus making an opening through which excess fluids can escape. The surgeon has great latitude in selecting an operation for the relief of glaucoma, but in all the many procedures, too technical to be dealt with here, he has this purpose in mind: the establishment of sufficient drainage from the interior of the eye to promote a condition of normal balance between the fluids forming within the eye and those escaping from the eye. By this procedure thousands of eyes with increased intraocular tension have been saved from blindness.

Treatment to Retard the Development of Early Cataract

Perhaps in no department of ophthalmic practice has conservatism done more to protect the patient from premature operations than in the condition of incipient cataract. It is apparent during recent years that a change of attitude toward the patient just beginning to develop cataract has come about. The Scotch surgeon, George A. Berry, in his book, *Diseases of the Eye,* wrote in 1893 that "the main cause of opacity (of the crystalline lens) appears to be, then, a too rapid abstraction of the fluid from the lens," and that in incipient cataract cases dehydration associated with opacification is in no sense dependent upon changes which are the result of age, and it has no relation to the "ordinary senile lens." Later Collins and Mayou of London in their book, *Pathology and Bacteriology of the Eye,* while discussing the question of diabetic cataracts which they believed were due to loss of normal fluid from the lens, said that where the opacity of the lens has been only of short duration, it has been observed to decrease in amount or even to clear up altogether as the result of improvement in the patient's general condition.

Another renowned London authority, Robert Brindel Carter, chief surgeon of St. George's Hospital, taught that "there are undoubtedly certain forms of cataract such as those due to malassimilation in which peripheral strias are present in the lens" and "there can be no doubt that under the influence of a suitable diet and regimen such a person may preserve his eyesight, just as he will preserve life longer than he would if he continued in his unphysiological course." These conclusions agree with those of many other authorities on the eye who have since expressed their opinions regarding the subject of the beginning cataract, including the renowned American eye surgeon, George E. DeSchweintz, who wrote in 1899 that "the etiology of cataract is by no means clear" but "often there are extraocular reasons and the cataract results from nutritive causes."

Davis, a noted eye surgeon and long a teacher of ophthalmology in the New York Postgraduate Medical School, Columbia University, later stated that early cataract was often due to a lack of proper food and believed that "it is most important, therefore, that senile cataract . . . be diagnosticated early and the patient treated as well as the disease."

Formerly, it was believed that so-called senile cataract was due entirely to aging of the patient. This idea was not controverted until it was seen that in young patients a similar condition of the crystalline lens leading to cataract occasionally appeared. At this time there was a general agreement among eye physicians that the period between a beginning cataract and its maturity, or so-called ripening, which demanded operation, was on an average not more than from two to six years. If the patient follows a regimen of foods that are most nutritious and increases his intake of fluids, the time required for cataracts to reach the operation stage will be noticeably increased, and in many instances the cataracts may be arrested entirely.

This result was largely brought about by the discovery of Willstatter relative to the chemistry of chlorophyl. It was noticed that green plants had more nutritive qualities than had dried plants that had lost their chlorophyl and that animals which had been stunted during the winter throve as soon as they were turned out on green pastures. The reason for this is simple. The blades of grass are so placed that they absorb the orange, red, blue, and violet rays of the sun. The green in the spectrum is used less than any other color by the grass blades. The grass looks green to us only because little green is absorbed and therefore is registered in our retinas as this color. In the laboratory it was found that the chemical properties of chlorophyl and hemoglobin are much the same, the chlorophyl formula differing from the formula of hemoglobin only in the fact that the atom of iron in the hub of the hemoglobin molecule is replaced in the chlorophyl molecule by an atom of magnesium. It is a very engrossing fact, as it now appears, in the retardation of cataract that the formula of chlorophyl and hemoglobin are so nearly alike. Willstatter found carotin a type of chlorophyl in the body of fresh carrots, and he suspected that its administration had a wholesome effect on vision.

For many years the attention of eye physicians has been called to the fact that in patients whose diet is chiefly composed of foods poor in nutrition an unprecedented number of cataract cases are found. The reason for this remained obscure until 1885, when the Japanese physician Dr. Takaki, who had recently studied in London, lowered the high mortality rate among Japanese sailors caused by their exclusive diet of polished rice. By replacing the polished rice with barley that had not been deprived of the nutritious barley hulls, which we now know to contain vitamins in high degree, the Japanese Navy was able to overcome the disease of beriberi so fatal to the sailors.

The general routine in senile cataract cases now consists in increasing the amount of fluid taken by the patient and in adding to the diet of those with beginning cataract such selected green garden vegetables as contain the most chlorophyl. No vitamin is contraindicated in the treatment of early cataract, vitamin A and vitamin C being particularly useful. A patient with early cataract should have at least two eggs daily as well as a pint of milk. It should be borne in mind, however, that no patient should attempt to treat his own eye condition. To do so may lead to grave errors in diagnosis which might end in disaster. The patient with dimming vision who fears that he has glaucoma or an approaching cataract should at once apply to his own physician for advice. Only in this manner may he feel secure that everything possible to prolong his vision will be provided for him.

Creation of the Artificial Pupil

During all the early years of eye surgery, surgeons often failed to obtain vision in cataract and glaucoma cases, because as an aftermath of these diseases, even when an operation had taken place, the pupil became entirely sealed over, thus completely re-obscuring vision. In reviewing the history of the many attempts that were then made to provide artificial pupils, we cannot but be impressed by the perseverance of the many surgeons who first attempted to accomplish this result and who, in the face of repeated failures, kept steadfastly on in their efforts to win success. During this period there were several lapses of time due to discouragement, but most of the surgeons pioneering in this field returned to their labors and never gave up hope. Yet because of the frequency of cases of closed pupils, which meant permanent blindness, attempts to create such openings were made again and again until finally a method was worked out by which this result could occasionally be attained.

The early surgeons gave many reasons for failure in operations to create artificial pupils. It is well known now that the chief cause of these failures was infection, but no one at this time knew anything about the result of germ life in wounds. As the result of observation over a long period, it was considered hazardous to make an incision in the cornea, the glassy front of the eye, which is less protected from the invasion of bacteria than the sclera, the wall of the eye behind the cornea. For more than half a century no new openings in closed-over pupils were made in this area. The adherence to this rule laid down by former surgeons and the fact that such operations were usually made on eyes which already had undergone the operation of couching, or pushing back the cataract's lens, led almost invariably to disaster. In rare instances in which the operation resulted in some vision, the fact that the eye already had a crystalline lens floating in the posterior portion of the globe almost always caused a glaucoma to ensue, the process ending in complete loss of vision.

It is generally thought that the English surgeon Cheselden in 1728 first succeeded in creating new pupils in eyes in which the pupils had been sealed over, but Briggs, another English surgeon of the period, states that the several operations done by Cheselden at that time ended in complete failures. Briggs, however, gives the German surgeon G. Heuermann credit for the first success done by Cheselden's method and mentions the report of such a case, by Heuermann, as being made in Copenhagen and in Leipzig in 1756.

In 1792 Professor Joseph Beer, speaking in the auditorium of the University of Vienna, reported his celebrated case of artificial pupil done by a method which has transformed this type of surgery throughout the surgical world. Here Beer exhibited the case of a patient long blind from sealed-over pupils, who now could read print. Beer's success in regaining vision by means of this type of surgery, which had failed so many times at the hands of his predecessors, gave the operation for the creation of artificial pupils a new impetus, and it still remains one of the most important procedures in ophthalmic surgery.

The operation for the creation of new pupils has given hope to thousands to whom, without this type of surgery, permanent blindness is inevitable. In the hands of the expert eye surgeon of today this simple procedure originated by Beer, but now immensely improved upon, has brought vision, together with useful lives, to many victims of closed-over pupils throughout the world.

The Evolution of Cataract Surgery

That the ancient Greeks attempted to treat cataract is proven by the writings of historians of the time. Their greatest eye surgeons, however, lived not in Greece, but in Rome. During this early period there were no renowned Roman physicians. The patricians are known to have despised medical men, looking upon them as a class of wandering itinerants who preyed upon the misfortunes of the Romans, and it was even suggested by the Romans that to employ them was to invite disaster to one's health or even death itself. In a passage from the writings of Pliny the following warning is found: "The identity of the Roman does not permit him to make a profession of medicine, and the few Romans who do begin to study it are venal renegades to the Greeks." And to his son he gave the following advice: "The race of Greeks is very vicious; and, my son, believe this as the voice of an oracle, that Greece with its literature will spoil everything in Rome." It is no wonder that under these conditions, realizing that the Roman could do nothing for the blind, the Greek surgeon forsook his own country and took up the work of eye surgery in such a promising field for his labors.

The cataract operation performed by Greek surgeons was that of couching, a practice which they had learned from the Egyptians. This was a simple method of pushing the crystalline lens into the back chamber of the eye by means of a needle thrust through the cornea. The operation was done with the patient in a sitting position and was performed with no regard to cleanliness. The results, of course, were often disastrous, for if the eye was not lost from infection, a hardening of the eyeball or glaucoma sometimes presented itself and terminated vision. If the patient escaped glaucoma and if infection did not set in, the crystalline lens would sometimes rise to its former position in front of the pupils, thus re-obscuring vision. But regardless of these hazards many Romans operated upon recovered their eyesight.

Following the first Crusade in the late eleventh century, this method of operating for cataract became first known in Europe. Surgeons returning from the Crusades had been quick to observe that some cases of blindness could actually be relieved, for a time at least, by this method of forcing the crystalline lens back into the eye with a needle. Avicenna, an Arabian surgeon, in the year

1030 had published the fifth book of his great work on surgery, devoted exclusively to the eye. Though brief, it acquired great reputation in Mohammedan countries because of the accuracy of its descriptive matter. The work contains a clear description of the manner in which the operation for couching of cataracts was performed, and this concise description proved to be the chief source of the wave of cataract surgery which passed over Europe soon after the end of the first Crusade. However, in the hands of the unscrupulous and unlearned a degeneration of the operative technique of Avicenna soon took place, and the roving oculists of the time lost nearly all eyes they operated upon.

The first scientific European oculist of whom we have any definite knowledge was Georg Bartisch, who, beginning as a German barber surgeon, made several forward steps in the evolution of the cataract operation and published the results of his work, with illustrations which he himself had drawn and which appeared in his book as woodcuts. While crude, they show us, step by step, how his operation for cataract was performed. But Bartisch did not understand that cataract was an opacity of the crystalline lens itself. He believed instead that it was a "skin" or "pellicle" within the capsule of the lens. It was not until 1706 that it was discovered, while a barber surgeon was doing a post-mortem, that cataract was an opacity and hardening of the lens substance itself.

About this time Bartisch devised a substitute for couching, a method which he termed reclination. Bartisch performed this operation by introducing a needle through the wall of the eye behind the cornea. The point of the needle was then drawn across the back of the lens capsule, thus rupturing it. The needle was then slightly withdrawn and thrust between the iris and the crystalline lens itself. As soon as it was seen to appear behind the pupil, its handle was carried forward, thus turning the lens backward upon the floor of the eyeball. Frequently, the Bartisch operation caused a dislocation of the cataractous lens into the front chamber of the eye, where it rested against the iris. It was following an accident of this nature that Stephen Blaukaart, in 1688, removed the lens through an incision made in the cornea. This was the first cataract extraction on record, all other cataracts having been pushed back into the eye through a puncture made in the cornea. Jacques Daviel in 1748, taking his cue from Blaukaart, originated the treatment of cataract as it is done today, by extraction of the cataractous lens. In 1752 Daviel was able to report to the Royal Academy of Surgeons one hundred operations he had thus performed. Daviel died in 1762, and it is said that he had removed 434 cataracts with but fifty failures to restore vision.

Daviel's operation for cataract proved to be the greatest uplift given to eye surgery since the days of the old Greek surgeons. But he was bitterly attacked by all other eye surgeons everywhere, which points to the fact that surgical progress was often, then as now, retarded by conventional habits of surgical thought.

In 1851 Albert von Graefe introduced a method of combined iridectomy and cataract extraction; that is, in addition to a corneal incision, von Graefe cut out a small section of iris. This was a great step forward, for previous to this an iris prolapsed at the time of a cataract operation was placed in position, as far as that could be done, with only torn shreds being cut off.

Von Graefe during his life reported nine hundred extractions of cataract, of which only five per cent failed to restore vision, a record of which even the modern surgeon might be justly proud. Aside from a slight variation in technique and the observance of aseptic surgical rules, there have been few improvements made since the days of this great German ophthalmologist, unless the intracapsular operation should be regarded as such.

It is not known who was the first to perform this intracapsular cataract operation, the removal of cataract in its capsule. Sharp, an English surgeon, briefly described an operation in which he suggested a method of pushing the lens out of the eye by pressure with the thumb. He mentions the expulsion of the lens as a second step, and this has led many of us to believe that he practiced the intracapsular method of extraction.

The first man extensively to practice this method of extraction was the German surgeon, Herman Pagenstecher, his first operation of this character being done in the year 1866. His results were very brilliant, but because of the large number of eyes ruined by the loss of the contents of the eye which escaped as the cataract was pushed out, the operation was eventually abandoned by nearly all surgeons. Pagenstecher removed the opaque lens by introducing a small silver spoon behind the lens, after which, by exerting pressure upon the cornea with a smaller spoon, he caused the cataractous lens to glide upward into the bowl of the larger spoon. Following Pagenstecher, though differing with him in technique, many other surgeons performed and described in writing operations for the removal of the lens without opening the capsule, as the operation was formerly done.

In 1917 Colonel Henry Smith, operating under the auspices of the British Government in India, set the surgical world ablaze by reporting thirty thousand cases which had been operated by him in his Indian clinic.

The technique of the Smith operation was, in general, very similar to that done by the European and American surgeons, except in the method of expulsion of the crystalline lens. In spite of its apparent simplicity, it has proven not well adapted to the Occident and has now been relinquished by nearly all eye surgeons. Later, Barraquer of Barcelona removed the crystalline lens by suction applied to the front surface of the capsule of the lens by means of a tiny rubber suction cup. This operation is now being done by the majority of surgeons throughout the world, and it may be considered as the foremost step given the cataract extraction since the days of the old Greek surgeons.

19.

John Hunter, Master of Comparative Anatomy

John Hunter, the subject of this sketch, is said to have been born near Glasgow in 1728. No birth certificate of this event, however, has ever been found. His brother, William Hunter, had come into the world twenty years earlier. By some the date of John Hunter's birth is, therefore, assumed to be incorrect, as the interim between the births of these two brothers does not correspond to the average sequence of such events in Scotch families.

It is recorded that John Hunter as a raw youth shunned the schoolroom and spent most of his time exploring the country around Glasgow. Not until he was thirty-five did he enter Oxford University. Here he applied himself to Latin and Greek for two months and then left in disgust, declaring that the study of dead languages was contrary to his true instincts. This represented the entire amount of his university training. He also studied surgery with his brother, William Hunter, and became a member of the class of the renowned English surgeon, William Cheselden. Regardless of the fact that his studies seem erratic and disconnected, he became one of the greatest of English anatomists. This was, no doubt, due to the fact that he had as friends many grave robbers or "resurrection men," as he called them, and was never at a loss for dissecting material. His bribing the guards for the body of

Harrison, famous giant of the time, and procuring it for a cash payment of five hundred pounds, showed his trend of thought and created for a time a great furor in London. This skeleton was articulated and hung among other specimens of anatomy in his private museum, which after Hunter's death became the Anatomical Museum of the Royal College of Surgeons. The skeleton still adorns a dark corner of this institution.

John Hunter is considered to be the greatest anatomist of the eighteenth century. He was also looked upon as an authority on comparative physiology. By many he was believed to be the greatest factor of his age in furthering science.

Hunter was also a lifelong friend of Edward Jenner, the discoverer of vaccination against smallpox with cowpox vaccine, and his encouragement of this young scientist probably had much to do with the establishment of cowpox inoculation as a sure preventative against smallpox. A correspondence was carried on between the two men until the death of Hunter in 1793. Both were sincere naturalists and were fired with the ambition of proving their theories by actual experiment. They helped each other by a comparison of ideas and by obtaining specimens on any subject which they believed the other might be interested in. Much of the correspondence between Hunter and Jenner is still in existence. One interesting letter contains a request from Hunter for Jenner to procure for him, if possible, the body of a porpoise for dissection. Hunter had already determined that the whale was a mammal, breathing air like other mammals, which in prehistoric times had been driven from the land into the sea. He now suspected that the porpoise was a similar mammal and sought to prove it.

Hunter at about this time advised Jenner that a golden opportunity awaited him if he could discover and demonstrate the sex of bees, as this, he declared, had never been done. Jenner followed his advice and produced an essay on the subject. Jenner obtained for Hunter a hedgehog for dissection, and this Hunter gratefully accepted and warmly thanked him for in a letter. At about the time of this incident Jenner married, and Hunter wrote him the following strange congratulatory note: "I was glad to learn that you were married to a woman of fortune, but . . . never mind her, I shall employ you with hedgehogs." At a later time he again wrote to Jenner, saying, "Send me everything you can, whether vegetable, animal or mineral, or the compounds of the two."

During the next twenty years of Hunter's life he was occupied with the study of all manner of birds and animals and was in constant correspondence with friends abroad, seeking to procure specimens. These consisted of almost everything in the animal kingdom, from elephants to hummingbirds. During this period, however, he did not neglect the study of human anatomy but dissected hundreds of cadavers and described the anatomical parts of each.

John Hunter is of interest to surgeons chiefly because of his studies of aneurism, which term means a local dilatation of one or more of the blood vessels. His greatest fame, however, came from the fact that he was the founder of surgical pathology, something which the surgeon today comes into contact with, and woe to the patients of the surgeon who is not versed in this science, as upon it the related science of surgery rests.

To the comparative anatomist, John Hunter will always be remembered by the tremendous amount of dissection he made on the lower animals. His museum contained over thirteen thousand specimens, which included two thousand or more fossils. This great collection, with his relating description of each specimen, was inherited at his death by the Royal College of Surgeons. The collection comprises a greater variety of specimens relative to the science of comparative anatomy and physiology than ever has heretofore been brought together.

To humanity in general, John Hunter's studies on venereal diseases are of great interest, chiefly because for years he carried the profession of medicine and the general public down a blind alley, for he maintained until his last days that gonorrhea and syphilis were one and the same disease. To prove this, it is said, he purposely infected himself with the virus of syphilis.

Whether this be true or not, the fact remains that he refused to take any manner of treatment, so that he could better study the effects of the disease upon himself. Everything since Hunter's death points to the belief that he died as the result of this self-inflected inoculation. It was reported that while attending a meeting of the board of the St. George's Hospital, October 16, 1793, he became angered at a discussion and stepped into an adjoining room, where he was heard to fall with a dull thud upon the floor. Nothing has ever been added to the report that in this attack he was the subject of the intense pain which always accompanies death in angina pectoris, a disease which Hunter believed he had. This ending of his life, as seen by the scientists of today, points more to the rupture of an aneurism of the aorta, which is followed by almost instantaneous death devoid of characteristic pain such as that of angina pectoris. This is a condition not infrequently found in untreated syphilis, and, as John Hunter took no treatment for his infection, it is to be supposed that his sudden death resulted from his failure to counteract the poison of the disease with appropriate treatment.

A further evidence of Hunter's self-inflicted disease is that he became very irrational in his scientific conclusions and late in life incorporated into his writings some very fanciful ideas which prove today to be an interesting study for the modern psychiatrist. He went on record as believing that the fluid parts of the body were endowed with complete consciousness and "the blood's consciousness of its being a useful part of the body" cropped up after this in his later works. Hunter made one serious error in his *Natural History of the Human Teeth*, by which many have since lost their teeth. This was that the complete removal of the pulp of the teeth should be done before any fillings were inserted into the cavities by the dentist. It is thought now that a desensitized tooth becomes, in a sense, a foreign body and that abscesses at the roots of these teeth from which the pulp has been removed are no more than nature's method of attempting to get rid of a tooth no longer vital. I have but to glance into my own mouth to see results of this erroneous reasoning of John Hunter, for his conclusions were readily accepted by dentists everywhere and, until fifty years ago, pulp cavities were cleaned out of teeth before they were filled. But, on the other hand, the world should be grateful to him because of his studies in surgical pathology, shock, inflammations, and gunshot wounds, and for the rational treatment of diseases of the vascular system. That he became irritable in his later years and quarreled with so many of his colleagues may have been the result of a cerebral disturbance owing to syphilis.

While the growing irritability of John Hunter made him enemies, a circumstance arose in his own family which was to create enmity between him and his own brother, William Hunter, who had so greatly helped him, and which was to last until William's death. In 1780 John Hunter read a paper before the Royal Society in which he laid claim to the discovery of the circulation existing between the uterus and the placenta (afterbirth). His brother, William, had already described how this circulation occurred in his paper, "The Anatomy of the Gravid Uterus," and, activated by John Hunter's claim to the same discovery, wrote the Royal Society setting forth his prior claim, fully established by his former article. William Hunter's claim being on record, no possible controversy could occur. However, John Hunter failed to retract. Because of this, William refused to have anything further to do with his brother until a few days before his death, when he consented to accept a visit from John.

Ricord Clarifies the Nature of Venereal Disease

While Hunter with his erroneous belief regarding syphilis could not get a clear insight into the disease, Philippe Ricord of Baltimore, by close observation of many cases of the malady through a period of years, arrived at conclusions essentially the same as those of today. Syphilis, Ricord proved, has no relation to gonorrhea, except that it is possible to contract both diseases by a single exposure. The disease, he determined, begins as a lesion at the point of invasion, some spot in the body where the resistance given by the normal skin or mucous membrane has been broken down by an abrasion. Here the germs of the disease (the spirochetes) find lodgment, and in a period of days or sometimes weeks an ulcer forms. Hunter had already made these conclusions and described this initial lesion, as well as a minor lesion which is more or less a harmless ulcer, as it does not lead to systemic infection.

Ricord believed that if this disease were to end in the minor lesion it would have no serious effect. Unfortunately, this is not true, for in a space of from a few weeks to two months or more the secondary manifestations of the disease occur. Even then, Ricord observed, they are usually considered of little importance by the average patient, for they subside in a few months, leaving no apparent harmful results. It is only in the tertiary or third stage which Ricord described that the magnitude of the condition appears, and even this may be delayed for years. But Ricord did not know that diseases of the heart, the blood vessels, and the brain, leading to insanity, may be in store for all neglected cases of syphilis. Discoveries relative to this came at a much later time. Of these diseases paresis and locomotor ataxia are perhaps the most dreaded. The former consists of changes in the brain, leading to mental alterations of the severest form, which, when fully established, usually attend the unfortunate victim until death ensues. In cases which have been partially treated, locomotor ataxia, evidenced by a halting, shuffling gait but with no serious mental derangement, presents itself. This even under treatment may continue unabated throughout life.

The chief hope of all cases of syphilis, Ricord stressed, consisted of thorough and insistent treatment from the beginning of the condition, or as soon as the local lesion of the disease made its appearance. This with Ricord consisted of the administration of mercurial pills. This alone was a great step forward. Later Ricord added to the treatment the iodide of potassium, which constituted a great improvement over the treatment limited to mercury.

The outlook for the future of syphilis cases is vastly improved since the studies of John Hunter and Philippe Ricord were made. With the advent of Schaudinn and Wassermann and the use of arsenicals and bismuth preparations, the treatment has been improved. Then there came heat therapy, which was a great step forward. Finally, penicillin made the treatment and practical cure of syphilis almost a certain performance to those who are alert enough to avoid charlatans or advertising "specialists" and who select ethical physicians and follow their directions implicitly.

20.

Benjamin Rush, the First Accredited American Doctor

In 1745 a great event in American medicine occurred in Philadelphia. A lusty boy, Benjamin Rush, was born. From his first wail as he lay in the arms of the midwife until the time of his death in 1813, Benjamin Rush continued to raise his voice so it could be heard by all. That the voice was to be long remembered is evidenced by the fact that he transformed the care of the sick in early America, a practice then filled with superstition and crude and irrational ideas which had been responsible for many deaths among the early pioneers, into a science which saved and is still saving many lives. Benjamin Rush never admitted that he was accomplishing anything unusual. Years afterward, when the United States and the world began to recognize his greatness and there was erected as a result of popular subscription a monument to his memory, his name had been forgotten by many he had saved from untimely ends. This may have been due to his modesty. Once, it is said, someone in his presence referred to him as one born to be great. Immediately he turned on his heel and withdrew from the room with an exclamation of disapproval. This is one instance in which we may believe that his judgment failed.

Benjamin Rush, with appropriate humility, lived to transform the practice of medicine as he found it among the early pioneers into the respectable calling it is today among the descendants of these same pioneers and, incidentally, to hew out a place for himself among the renowned.

Benjamin Rush Pleads for More Digestible Foods

For the modern physician who has not had a term of practice among primitive people, it is difficult to realize what the early pioneer doctor had to contend with in the way of prejudice and mistaken ideas regarding the manner of living he was daily confronted with. One of the first evils Rush had to combat was overeating and the prevalent use of indigestible foods by the members of his community. People of Pennsylvania in all walks of life were then inveterate eaters of hot breads, a practice which, though somewhat reduced, exists to the present day in many parts of this country. This was the cause of dyspepsia, a malady which became known throughout the world as the great American disease. Another cause of ailing stomachs was an unwholesome meat supply. Salted hog meat was then used almost exclusively, in the form of hams, bacon, and what was humorously known as "sowbelly." The inordinate ingestion of salt from this type of diet was responsible for a tendency of the people to wash down all foods with enormous quantities of sweet milk, buttermilk, or strong coffee. Elimination was usually not attended to, and chronic constipation was accompanied by acute abdominal pain. Epsom salt was looked upon as a standard remedy for this disorder and was administered in huge quantities. This led to frequent cases of so-called "locked bowels," or what we now recognize as appendicitis. This practice frequently ended in ruptured appendices, which in the majority of instances resulted in death.

The infant mortality in Rush's community was high. Mothers usually nursed their babies, but often the mothers were ill-nourished themselves, being victims of the then current derangements owing to improper food. At such times they could not provide milk for their offspring, and their children were then "hand-fed" by the mothers or the relatives, who first chewed particles of food and then, often with unwashed fingers, placed them into the children's mouths. As a number of these family nurses had pyorrhea, their focal infections were passed on to their little charges, thus ending in intestinal derangements. Even when the children were to be milk-fed, the bottles used for this purpose were unsterilized and, because of the absence of ice, the milk generally was spoiled and in itself a source of intestinal infection. Physicians of the period noted that one out of every ten children succumbed to intestinal disease before it had reached the age of one year.

Benjamin Rush was graduated from Princeton University in 1760 and soon after this located in Philadelphia. One of his first crusades against the ill health of the community was that of urging patients with diseased teeth to have them removed. He was one of the first to suspect that much of the so-called gout of the world, as well as rheumatism, was due to chronic infections around teeth rather than to overeating, which was then accepted as the reason for the general incapacity of those affected with these diseases. But in his urge to have infected teeth removed he was confronted with opposition on every hand. His colleagues advanced the contention that the Creator had given us teeth to eat with and thus preserve our health, and that to remove them for any cause except that of severe pain was to thwart the design of the Deity Himself and thus slowly to pave the way for one's own destruction. The populace, fearing for their own teeth, readily fell into this idea. To substantiate his theory, Rush persuaded a number of known invalids from chronic rheumatism to submit to the operation of having all their infected teeth removed. Within two months nearly all of these former habitués of chimney corners were off their crutches, and the name of Rush thereby became a household word in Pennsylvania.

Rush Anticipates Pasteur by Heating Milk for Babies

In 1769 Rush was appointed professor of chemistry in the Medical College of Philadelphia. He had long pondered over the fate of infected children, so many of whom were destined to die from intestinal disease during their first year of life. By experiments in his chemical laboratory, he had learned that boiling milk for a short period lessened the likelihood of its becoming sour. It occurred to him that boiling the milk to be given to infants would likely decrease the high death rate of these children. As everyone knows now, Rush's idea was correct, but, though he attempted in every manner to convince the physicians of the country that they should adopt this method, his idea did not take root and become general until Pasteur verified and popularized it years later.

Rush's ideas were incorporated in a thesis, *On the Cholera Infantum,* which was presented to a Philadelphia medical society. This suggestion, directed toward the preservation of the child during its first and second years, was reluctantly received and seldom acted upon. If the practice of heating milk to the boiling point before feeding it to children had been taken up by the medical profession at that time and developed as it was later, it would, without doubt, have resulted in the saving of thousands of infants' lives.

In 1792 the yellow fever broke out in Pennsylvania. In a few weeks in the then small town of Philadelphia the disease had killed over three thousand people. There was general panic in the city. Those who could do so fled. Those obliged to remain held cloth saturated with garlic juice to their noses. Others smeared their clothing with tar, hoping thus to ward off infection.

It was generally believed that the disease was an importation from the South and that it came into Philadelphia from other cases in the form of fomites (articles which had been contaminated by former patients), and for this reason many ships from Southern ports were refused access to Philadelphia. Two co-workers with Rush, Dr. William Currie and Dr. Pinkhard, fought the idea of fomites conveying the disease. The former maintained that yellow fever needed no foreign source and was not communicable from infected bedding and similar articles, and Dr. Pinkhard wrote: "To look for it in ships and vessels or to strain the eye across the ocean is to overlook the reality for a phantom." Most Philadelphia doctors attempted to arrest the disease by fumigation of the sites where the disease had occurred and by copious bleeding of those infected. During this epidemic of yellow fever, Rush bled all infected persons he could prevail upon to submit to the procedure, claiming that bleeding cut short the disease and would prevent recurrences. He met all opposing arguments of his colleagues with an unsurmountable obstinacy. We know now that he was mistaken, but when we remember that bleeding was then and had been a standard treatment for nearly all diseases for over two thousand years, we can readily see how the fact that several hundred of his friends and neighbors who placed all responsibility for their welfare squarely upon his shoulders might during this emergency have unbalanced his judgment. Before long, however, a wave of calumny was to follow the great mortality occurring in his phlebotomy cases, which was met by him with disdain. But his obstinacy in reference to bleeding was soon to result in damage to his reputation, and he was thereby denied the privilege of becoming the chief physician to George Washington during his last illness. Rush, being then the leading medical authority of the country, would most likely have been selected to take charge of Washington's case, had it not been for this loss of public favor.

The Treatment and Disease of George Washington

In the early part of December 1799, George Washington was noticeably in failing health. He was awakened one night grasping at his throat, much in the attitude of a man being choked. Washington until that time had been a robust man, and his sudden illness created great alarm. A call by the whole country went up for the services of the nation's greatest physician. Benjamin Rush, for the reason mentioned, was not chosen, and a number of more or less noted physicians proceeded to take care of the former President's case. Hourly it was observed that the great man's condition grew worse. By the physicians in attendance he was purged and blistered and had leeches applied to his throat, but no improvement resulted from any of these attempts to save his life. The physicians in attendance all agreed that Washington was a victim of edema of the larynx. In this they were probably correct, but no one can be certain at this time what may have caused such edema. It is to be regretted that the Father of this country was allowed to die from a condition with which every general practitioner of medicine today is more or less familiar, and one which the greater percentage of modern doctors could have relieved. Yet George Washington had some of the most widely known physicians of the country in attendance. At this time there had not been devised any instrument for looking into the larynx or for passing through the larynx into the windpipe tubes for the purpose of promoting breathing. No one apparently had the courage or the initiative to suggest opening Washington's windpipe. Such an operation might have been done in an emergency with the familiar pocketknife. After incision the blade of the knife, if turned crosswise in the windpipe, would have permitted the entrance of air into the lungs, thus preventing suffocation. No physician of today could escape censure for permitting a patient to die from this kind of suffocation without having made an attempt to open the larynx or windpipe.

At the extremity of his illness, the treatment of Washington at the hands of the physicians in attendance had as its basis the letting of blood. This operation was repeated several times, when, as we now know, every ounce of blood was needed to sustain his strength. At last their patient, weakened by futile attempts to breathe and exhausted by the loss of blood, succumbed.

Regardless of his many shortcomings, Benjamin Rush will always be remembered by the medical profession as a man far in advance of his time. He was one of the founders of the University of Pennsylvania, and he was also the first to hold the chair of Professor of the Practice of Medicine in this institution. Rush was a public-spirited man and for a long period was associated with Washington, with whom it must be said he often disagreed on matters of policy and whom he deserted entirely at Valley Forge. But the breach between these two men was closed as Washington came to appreciate Rush as a sturdy character and remembered him as having been one of the most influential and forceful advocates of the Declaration of Independence.

Characteristic of the time, Rush arbitrarily held until his death more than one fanciful theory relative to the science of medicine. He claimed, for example, that inflammation was always a friend of the patient and was not the cause of any known disease. On the other hand, he believed that fevers often arose as a result of drinking cold water. He was bitterly fought in this, but we now know that thermal fever sometimes has its origin in the manner which Rush described. But Rush claimed that bloodletting "removed" fever and that "the more blood withdrawn, the more the fever would be dispelled."

Excessive bleeding of such patients was destined to live long after the time of Rush and result in much harm, but, on the other hand, by recognizing focal infections as a frequent cause of arthritis, Rush was responsible for taking great numbers of victims of this malady off their crutches, and he paved the way for the rescue of innumerable children from the grip of cholera infantum. Aside from the honor of having a monument standing in his memory, his name should be enshrined in the hearts of thousands of grateful mothers. If his work here is remembered, he needs little else to establish his name as one of America's greatest physicians.

21.

Jenner and Vaccination Against Smallpox

The practice of inoculation for smallpox was current in China a thousand years before Europe became acquainted with it. Next we hear of it in India. When the Hindus became familiar with it is unknown, but it was at a date sufficiently remote to permit reference to it in their sacred Vedas. There can be no doubt that the Hindus obtained the knowledge of this practice from the Chinese. Later, inoculation was adopted by Turkey, where it is known to have been in use for centuries. But for the keen insight of an English woman, the Western world might not yet have heard of the practice.

In 1716 Lady Mary Montagu, wife of the British Ambassador to Turkey, became acquainted with the Turkish methods of inoculation. The success of this method of warding off smallpox seemed so complete that she became convinced of its efficacy and is said to have submitted one of her children to inoculation. Soon after this she returned to England and found an epidemic of smallpox raging there. One of her children, a little girl who had not undergone inoculation in Turkey, was now submitted to the operation by a Dr. Maitland, who also inoculated his own child and is said to have been responsible for popularizing the practice in his section of England.

At this time smallpox was the world's greatest scourge. Macaulay in his *History of England* says that smallpox "was the most terrible of all the ministers of death. The havoc of the plague had been far more rapid, but plague has visited our shores only once or twice within living memory; and smallpox was always present, filling the churchyards with corpses, tormenting with constant fear all whom it had not yet stricken, leaving on those whose lives were spared the hideous traces of its power, turning the babe into a changeling at which the mother shuddered, making the eyes and cheeks of the betrothed maiden objects of horror to the lover."

Except locally, the new practice was slow in finding favor, because the virus used was taken from smallpox cases, and each case treated was found to be a focus from which the disease could be transmitted to others. Each person inoculated became, in reality, a modified case of smallpox, and as the mortality of these cases was found to be two per cent or more, the practice was soon vigorously condemned and its advocates ostracized. On this side of the Atlantic prejudice ran high against inoculation. Dr. Zabdiel Boylston, of Boston, who inoculated his own son as a demonstration of his belief in the new treatment, was forced to flee from the city for a time, and upon his return was forbidden by the selectmen to indulge further in the practice. The people of Boston became so infused with prejudice against the advocates of inoculation that the practice soon fell into disuse, stimulated, no doubt, by an attempt to burn the house of Cotton Mather, who had preached a sermon in favor of inoculation.

While the inoculation controversy, somewhat abated, was going on in Europe and America, a freckled-faced boy was growing up in an obscure village in England. This boy was Edward Jenner, destined to revolutionize the practice of inoculation against smallpox and to make it one of the greatest blessings of the world.

Jenner was born in 1749. His father was a minister and a lifelong friend of John Hunter, the great surgeon, physician, and natural philospher. Jenner's boyhood was spent in the village of Berkeley in Gloucestershire, a typical English hamlet composed of a group of cottages belonging to the landed gentry. A few dozen steps in either direction brought one into the country, with its brooks and dogfish, its hedges and hedgehogs. As a boy Jenner had none of the earmarks of genius; which goes to show that many stub-nosed, freckled-faced, and awkward boys of today may jump into greatness tomorrow. In observing the blemishes, we are apt to overlook the clear-cut mouths denoting initiative; and we fail to recognize the firmness in the eyes. We cannot place our fingers on these boys now, but they will be the Darwins, the Huxleys, and the Jenners of tomorrow.

It is said that Jenner was the village truant from school. This often brought up an analysis of the wisdom of a certain Solomon in reference to sparing the rod and spoiling the child. It goes without saying that the verdict was always given according to Solomon. Jenner's bucolic tendencies prevented him from learning many things which he might have had to unlearn in after years. It also taught him to depend upon his own powers of observation rather than on the precedents laid down by others. In other words, it enabled him to use his head, and his boyhood was spent in his own particular method of investigation and study.

Jenner was fond of making excursions into the country to study birds and gather a collection of bird nests. This collection, John Hunter insisted, was the most complete to be found in England, and John Hunter, it may be remembered, was himself a student of nature. His paper "On Bees," printed in the *Philosophical Transactions* of 1792, giving a minute description of the habits of the bee, is a masterpiece in bee culture. Naturally, a compliment from one of England's greatest physicians and philosophers encouraged the boy. It was also the means of obtaining for him, from a previously irate father, the liberty to roam and study at his will.

In time the boy became acquainted with the peasantry for miles around. He knew all their wise saws and their traditions, many of which bore the foolish fingerprints of superstition; but then, as now, ideas held by country people often bristle with common sense. A great financier once said that cities have no monopoly on wisdom, but, be that as it may, one fact remains: out of this heap of combined wisdom and intellectual rubbish Jenner was destined to draw forth a nugget which was to save the race from smallpox epidemics, then its most terrible scourge.

One day during his ramblings Jenner stopped to pass the time o'day with a dairymaid. Noticing a number of sores on her hands and arms, he drew back startled and asked, "Is that smallpox?" The girl laughingly replied, "Of course not. I can never have that disease now, for this is cowpox." It is very improbable that a remark of this nature would make more than a casual impression upon a country boy, but the idea stuck, nevertheless, and was pigeonholed, to be brought out a few years later at a time when he was growing his pinfeathers in medicine as an apprentice of Mr. Daniel Ludlow, a physician of Sudbury. A country patient made a remark in his presence in reference to cowpox warding off smallpox. This recalled to his mind the pustules on the dairymaid's fingers seen by him a few years before. It did more than this; it set his mental machinery into motion and gave him an idea: If this was true, why could not smallpox be controlled by substituting for it cowpox, a comparatively harmless ailment? The more he thought about it the more convinced he became that this method of prophylaxis against smallpox was feasible. As soon as possible he went to John Hunter and acquainted him with the idea, to which Hunter replied, "Do not dream, boy, experiment; either prove it or disprove it."

Regardless of this advice, the idea seems to have lain dormant for a time, as Jenner was busy preparing the thesis on the habits of the cuckoo and the hedgehog, which won him a fellowship in the Royal Society. After receiving this much coveted honor, he established himself at Berkeley, where his patients were so few that for a time failure seemed imminent. This threatened calamity was fortunate, for it provided the impetus for hard thinking and the leisure in which to revert to his almost forgotten prophylaxis idea. Misfortunes, after all, are often but blessings in disguise. There are few of us who have not seen the one-time discouragements and failures changed with the years into the pivotal points of our lives. The anticipated demand for the conventional plasters and bloodlettings would have been gratifying to Jenner, there can be no doubt, but it would have marked him for oblivion.

It is interesting to note that Jenner was threatened with expulsion from his medical society at about this time because of his insistence that smallpox could be prevented by inoculation with cowpox virus. The notion was an interference with the conventional order of things and was met in the conventional way, by protest. Conventional order as applied to science is and always has been vicious, because it impedes progress and because it does not take note of the fact that a thousand things in the darkness of the unknown today are about to spring into the light tomorrow.

In 1796 Jenner was called in the case of one Sarah Nelmes, a neighborhood dairymaid, who was suffering an attack of cowpox. With cowpox virus from her arm, he inoculated a lad, James Phipps, whose parents he had known years before. To prove the efficacy of this experiment, he received permission from the parents to inoculate the boy again, this time with the virus of smallpox. The inoculation failed to produce any symptoms of the disease. Jenner saw that, in this case at least, immunization was successful, and proposed other experiments which followed in rapid succession, all of which proved efficacious in combating subsequent inoculations with smallpox virus. His theory, so much laughed at, was about to assume the proportions of a demonstrated fact.

In 1798 Jenner published *Inquiry into the Cause and Effects of Variolae Vaccinae,* a book which eventually was to make the practice of vaccination with cowpox virus an accepted prophylactic against smallpox throughout the civilized world.

Previous to the practice of vaccination in England, the annual mortality of smallpox was seven hundred to each one hundred thousand people. At the beginning of the nineteenth century, it was thirty to one hundred thousand people. Before Jenner's time this disease was the chief cause of the nation's blindness. Moreover, thirty per cent of all English children died of smallpox before they were three years old.

Andrew D. White says that following Jenner's discovery "the diminution in the number of deaths before they were three years old from the terrible scourge was amazing." In Berlin during the eight years following 1783, over four thousand children died of the smallpox; while during the eight years following 1814, after vaccination had been largely adopted, out of a large number of deaths there were but five hundred and thirty-five from this disease. In Württemberg, during the twenty-four years following 1772, one in thirteen children died of smallpox while during the eleven years after 1822 the disease took only one in sixteen hundred. In London, formerly so afflicted by this scourge, only one person died of smallpox in 1890. As to the world at large, the result is summed up by one of the most honored English physicians of our time, in the declaration that "Jenner has saved, is now saving, and will continue to save, in all coming ages, more lives in one generation than were destroyed in all the wars of Napoleon."

One would think that a benefactor of humanity of this magnitude would not have had to run the gauntlet of bigotry, tyranny, and oppression, unless one chanced to remember that but for a few apostles of scientific truth, great and heroic men who have dared to keep their faces toward the light, medicine would yet be where it was during the Dark Ages. Just as bigotry in years past has been a menace to human progress, skulking and making its attacks from the dark corners, so did it give its usual welcome to vaccination. For several years Jenner was ostracized in England. That should not create surprise, but we would expect more liberality in America. However, we soon find Timothy Dwight, president of Yale College, denouncing the new practice; and we find in Boston an antivaccination society composed largely of physicians who favored the suppression of vaccination by law as a practice "in deference of Heaven itself, even unto the will of God."

Ignorance of itself does not merit reproach; it is odious only when allied with the prejudice which condemns investigation and despises facts. This combination has always carried and will always carry the black flag.

22.

Von Leber and the End of Legal Torture

The horrible practice during the Middle Ages and later of extracting by torture evidence from persons accused of crime was a part of the legal code of nearly all the countries of the Eastern Hemisphere. In medieval Europe it was an offshoot of the torture instituted by the Roman conquerors.

During the days of the Roman republic a master had the power to torture his slave, but later the *Lex Petronis* at least forbade the Roman master to punish his slave by entering him in the arena to fight with gladiators or with wild beasts. In France torture had been in existence for centuries and was not abolished until 1789. Italy, Spain, and Germany employed torture of varying degrees of severity ever since the days of their subjugation by the Roman Empire. In England the rack was introduced in the reign of Henry VI by the Duke of Exeter. Other varieties of torture employed in England were the "Scavenger's Daughter," an appliance which drew head and feet together, after which the prisoner was forced to the floor and left there until he expired. Pressing his body with iron weights until death ensued was the punishment administered to the prisoner who refused to plead, and it was a common legal practice until the reign of George III. In Scotland the iron boot was used for the purpose of torture.

Into this receptacle the foot was crowded and iron wedges were driven in at the sides until the foot was crushed. This method of inflicting punishment was in vogue chiefly to settle differences in ecclesiastical opinion and was used to convince the victim of religious truths.

In America torture to a large extent had spent itself before the days of English colonization and in New England had resolved itself into the ducking stool, though there is a record in early Massachusetts archives of one Giles Corey's suffering torture during the witch trials in Salem. He was slowly pressed to death after he had refused to plead. Further south in America, in the British colony of Trinidad, Sir Thomas Picton was convicted of applying torture to a prisoner as late as 1806, but he died before his sentence was pronounced.

During the Middle Ages wave after wave of plagues such as the black death in England, France, and Germany and the sweating sickness in Middle and Southern Europe for a time almost depopulated towns and cities, taking a total, it is estimated by later historians, of twenty-five million lives. Some of the more fanatical inhabitants believed that such epidemics were the result of the anger of the Deity because of the infringement of His laws. Others looked to natural causes and were convinced that the water supply as well as the walls of the homes of the people were being poisoned. Many residents, both Jewish and Christian, were accused of poisoning the wells and were subjected to torture unto death if they failed to name their imaginary accomplices. In the extremity of suffering they were driven to making false accusations and were for a time relieved of their torture, but in nearly all instances they were finally burned. The Jewish population suffered especially, many of them being burned to death, each one of them having been subjected to torture for varying periods in order to get names of supposed accomplices. The Jews at the time were not allowed to enter the professions in Europe or to compete with any non-Jewish person in business. Christians of the period were forbidden to take interest on money, so the Jews became the bankers of each country and made loans to

Christians. It was due to this that so many Jews were suspected of poisoning the wells. An accusation in those dark ages amounted in nearly every case to a conviction, and the plagues gave a golden opportunity to those indebted to the Jews for money to make accusations which would likely end in a conviction and a cancellation of their debts.

Then as now, the politicians of all countries had their enemies. In the Middle Ages many of these, though Christians, became the subject of torture brought about by the accusations of political enemies. In 1630, one of the plague years in Italy, a commissioner of public health, Guglielmo Piazza, finding that the horn in which he carried ink for use with his official seal had stained his fingers, sought to get rid of the fresh ink by wiping his fingers in passing on the walls of the houses. He was immediately taken before the city council and accused of spreading the plague by the use of some supposed poison carried in his inkhorn. Piazza was then made to undergo indescribable tortures. To save himself, he confessed and gave the names of accomplices who were also innocent of this imaginary crime, after which he was executed.

Legal torture as practiced in France during the reign of the Louis' consisted of what was known as drawing and quartering. To effect this, horses were attached to each of the prisoner's limbs and made to pull in opposite directions, the object being to draw the limbs from the body. Failing in this, the torture chief with a long knife would sever the limbs from the body. This method of inflicting punishment was a part of the legal code of France until the time of Napoleon.

The last legal torture to be committed in England occurred in 1594 when Dr. Lopez, physician to Queen Elizabeth, was put to death by being drawn and quartered, through suspicion of "encompassing the death" of the Queen.

In the illiteracy of the dark ages many who had charge of torture in Europe were unable to read. Pictorial forms were prepared to demonstrate how the torture might be conducted even by the most illiterate. A number of extant drawings demonstrate how

Empress Maria Theresa of Austria attempted to make clear to her torturers, most of whom were illiterate, various methods of manipulating torture implements.

The artists of Maria Theresa were expert in making their pictures divulge to the ignorant mind of the torture chief what was expected of him. One drawing of this code shows the thumbscrew, in which the thumbs of the victim were placed between crossbars of iron with sharp points. It is apparent that the operator was meant to turn the lever so as to bring the iron bars closer together and drive the sharp points into the thumbs of the victims. This minor torture was to be used only as a reminder of what remained for the prisoner if he failed to confess at once.

Another sketch from the *Constitutio criminalis Theresiana* depicts the method of using the rack and the lighted candle. The executioner could easily understand from this how the contrivance could be most effective. First the prisoner was to be placed on his back on a ladderlike appliance. His arms were bound to a rung of the ladder. His legs were then tied to a long cylinder, the turning of which by an assistant gradually dislocated both shoulders and knees. During this process the operator was to apply a lighted candle to the armpits. This famous document depicts other, even more horrible methods of torture, the descriptions of which I shall spare the reader.

In Austria at the time of Maria Theresa, no one accused of a crime was allowed to testify in his own behalf; nor could his seconds testify for him until they were subjected to torture.

During my early work as an advanced student in Vienna I became impressed with the influence physicians have exerted on law, which crops out in many places in the history of our profession. Nowhere has their influence been so pronounced in the cause of humanity as in the case of Dr. Ferdinand von Leber of Vienna University. His work in behalf of prisoners to be tortured for evidence was responsible to a great extent for freeing Austria, the last great torture nation, and all its dominions from this terrible practice. I became acquainted with the work of this great humanitarian. His portrait in dark court clothes with a golden chain about his neck hung in the laboratory of pathology in the university, and I often spent time before it pondering over the fact that the human mind is often a blind force when guided by precedent. In this case, conventional habits of thought going back to the darkest days of the Roman Empire, though relegated to the past elsewhere, had not changed in Austria. Torture in Von Leber's time was considered a necessary court procedure. Leber was court physician to Maria Theresa. It was his duty to examine prisoners about to testify, to determine whether or not they were amenable to torture; in other words, if they would survive torture without fatality. In these cases he developed a keen insight into clinical psychology and learned by something akin to instinct to differentiate the guilty from the innocent. He had also observed that the innocent, to obtain surcease from pain, often confessed to the most impossible deeds. At the time that he first realized this fact, his soul burned within him and he decided, at the possible risk of his own life, to help forever to banish legal torture from Austria and all the hereditary Hapsburg lands, including Hungary, Galicia, and Poland.

Two perplexing cases then occupied the Vienna docket of crimes, those of Eleanor Kermin and Franz Saches. From them no satisfactory confession of guilt had been obtained by the ordinary methods of torture. They were then about to be subjected to a reformed or "intercalary torture" as provided by law. This meant that torture only short of death should be applied on three successive days. Dr. Leber, overcome by grief at the plight of these two, appealed to Maria Theresa for a conference, which was granted. With tears in his eyes Leber pleaded with the empress to grant a verdict without this repeated torture. Maria Theresa, following the impulses of a woman's heart, granted his request. These prisoners were acquitted. Justice, as far as this case was concerned, was won over the ancient prejudice of darkness and ignorance. Soon the empress made this important decree: "The findings of the medical faculty move me to abolish the intercalated torture absolutely."

This case was as famous in its day as was that of the Dreyfus case in France a half century ago. The stirring of public opinion created by it served to abolish torture as a means of obtaining evidence among the Austrian dominions. But, for interfering with what they claimed as their special prerogative, the legal profession of Vienna was up in arms against Dr. Leber and demanded that he be expelled. Threats were also made upon his life, but it appears that no attempt was made to murder him.

Switzerland was for long afflicted by wholesale torture. At the time when the sinister hand of torture effectively obtained confessions of guilt, Switzerland was subject to Austria. No other people in the world suffered so much as the Swiss at the hands of medieval invaders and oppressors. The slightest suspicion of a desire for insurrection with a view to obtaining independence was at once acted upon. A system of spies was put in force, by which neighbor testified against neighbor. And before the accused was allowed to offer such testimony either for or against himself, it was the law of Austria to which Switzerland was subject that he should at first be given agonizing torture. If the evidence brought out was not in accord with the suspicions of the trial court, the testator was to be subjected to a reformed or intercalated torture, which could be repeated short of death. The memory of this period in Swiss history has been kept alive, and a feeling of coolness toward Austria remains to this day among the Swiss people.

In Vienna Dr. Adolph Wendle, a Swiss physician, explained to me how with her improved halberd Switzerland was able to rid herself of torture by throwing off the yoke of Austria. I have hanging in the loggia of my home a specimen of this improved Swiss halberd which for many years was in use by the Swiss guards in the Vatican. It is an interesting weapon, inasmuch as inserted in its handle are sixty-one Swiss coins of small denomination, many of them so worn that the dates are entirely obliterated. During the period of my audience with Pope Pius in 1951, I passed en route to the audience chamber a number of the Swiss guards, who for two hundred years or more have stood guard over the persons of the various popes. In the hands of each was a gleaming halberd, much like that with which the Swiss were enabled to regain freedom from the hated Hapsburg and thus to rid themselves of centuries of torture.

Dr. Leber died long before he was appreciated even by his own colleagues in the university, but he had the satisfaction of being led by his own convictions, a rare privilege in turbulent Austria. In our gratitude for his great achievement, we shall long remember a great man of science, the compassionate and just Dr. Ferdinand von Leber.

23.

Great Medical Innovators of the Eighteenth and Nineteenth Centuries

At this period of medical history six great innovators appeared on the horizon of Europe. The first of these was Sir Charles Bell, whose work on the anatomy and physiology of the nervous system is second in importance only to William Harvey's discovery of the circulation of the blood, and his greatness in this particular field is not preceded by the many suggestions of former anatomists, as in the case of Harvey. The pulmonary circulation of the blood had already been established by Michael Servetus, though it is not at all likely that Harvey was acquainted with it. Bell's discovery caused a startling effect in all anatomical circles, for no one had the slightest suspicion that there were two kinds of nerves, the sensory and the motor, until Bell demonstrated this fact and published his account of it.

Sir Charles Bell and Bell's Palsy

Charles Bell was born in 1774, the son of a clergyman in the Church of England. He is thought never to have attended school in his early youth, as he wrote later in one of his journals that he had been deprived of certain early advantages of education, which he thought of as a blessing, averring, "My mother was my only teacher." But he was an observant and talented youth, and early in life he became interested in anatomy and wrote a book meant for the use of artists, *On the Anatomy of Expression,* which received much favorable comment by artists as a work on a subject previously neglected and one which they could use to great advantage, especially in portraiture. In 1807 Bell opened a number of rooms for the study and the teaching of anatomy. Later he disposed of these and took on a greater venture, the Windmill School of Anatomy. Here he studied closely the anatomy of the nervous system. His discovery of the two kinds of nerves, sensory and motor, was the result of an experiment. During a vivisection of an animal, he opened its spinal column and pricked with a needle the posterior filaments of the nerves. He took notice that no responses of sensation were to be seen. Then he applied the same needle pricks to the anterior filaments of the nerves and the parts supplied by these nerves "were convulsed." "With this," he wrote, "I hope to prove that there are two classes of nerves." Numerous experiments followed in which he used the stimulus of a galvanic current to obtain responses, the use of the galvanic current being at this time a common practice in treating neuralgia. Bell noticed that after the division of the facial nerve was made, galvanization did not have any effect on facial neuralgia, and after long study in which all European surgeons became interested, he demonstrated that a division of the facial nerves would be for all time attended by a paralysis of the muscles of the face and the eyelids. This type of paralysis became known throughout the surgical world as Bell's palsy, which name is still in use.

Bell long studied art and conferred certificates containing appropriate and highly artistic engravings upon those who had attended his lectures. One such certificate was in 1912 hanging in the Royal College of Surgeons in Edinburgh, a copy of which I procured while visiting the postgraduate department in that institution.

As a recognition of his great work on the nervous system,

Bell was knighted in 1831, his fame having by this time encompassed the world. He died a peaceful and honored death in 1842.

Richard Bright, Discoverer of Bright's Disease

The second of these innovators was Richard Bright, who was born in 1789 and lived to become the most renowned physician of his time. Bright was born in Bristol, England, and attended medical school in Edinburgh, receiving his M.D. from that institution in 1813. He later settled in London and in 1824 became chief surgeon to Guy's Hospital, where, while he carried on a large private practice, he managed to spend six hours a day among the patients of his wards. Here he also had a private laboratory where he conducted experiments on a greatly puzzling condition, dropsy, then considered to be a special entity of disease. Daily he examined the urine of all dropsical patients in Guy's Hospital and was at first puzzled to learn that many of the samples contained more or less albumin. Suddenly it dawned upon him that dropsy was not a disease in itself but a symptom of either kidney or heart disease. In the former, he observed, the kidneys were at first involved and later were so damaged that the condition ended in death. Accordingly, he startled the medical world with a report of twenty-three cases of kidney disease accompanied by heavy amounts of albumin in the urine, which had ended fatally. The proof of this was given after a series of autopsies which in every case manifested a marked destruction of the kidney. These he described vividly with careful drawings of the kidney accompanying his whole series of cases. Following this report much of the scientific world was still doubtful, and Guy's Hospital set aside two wards for renal cases only for Bright's exclusive use, as well as a special laboratory for renal cases. Here Bright worked ten hours a day until shortly before his death in 1858. It was first thought that while this great investigator helped others he could not help himself, and it was suspected that he died of "his own disease," already known throughout the scientific world as "Bright's disease." An autopsy done on him as he had requested, however, proved that this report was incorrect. Bright had succumbed to a valvular disease of the heart, from which he had developed the so-called dropsy.

Thomas Addison: First to Understand Addison's Disease

The third innovator of this series was Thomas Addison, who gave his name to Addison's disease. Addison was born in 1793 and graduated, as did Bright, from the medical department of Edinburgh University. Very little is known of his early life except that he was born at Newcastle, on the Tyne. In 1824 he was first physician at Guy's Hospital, where he taught his classes with almost constant attendance until the year 1860. He has been remembered as a very shy and reserved man but one who inspired his students to put their hearts in their work. In collaboration with Bright he wrote a textbook, *On the Practice of Medicine,* in which he incorporated a chapter which bore a complete description of diseases attacking the vermiform appendix, a subject then almost unknown.

Addison later devoted much of his attention to the study of the various forms of anemia. One condition in particular was found by him to be an anemia always accompanied by a disease of the suprarenal capsule. He collected accounts of a large number of cases of this and later published them as *On the Constitutional and Local Effects of Diseases of the Supra Renal Capsule*. Among them was a description of numerous cases of anemia associated with darkened skins and with diseases of the suprarenal capsule. This has ever since been known in the scientific world as "Addison's disease."

Robert Graves, Who Discovered Graves' Disease

The fourth in this series of great innovators is one Robert Graves, born in 1797. He was the son of an Irish professor in Trinity College, Ireland, but he was sent to the University of Edinburgh for his medical course, this institution at that time being the most renowned center of medical education in the British Isles. After graduating and receiving his M.D. he spent much time on the Continent, most of which was passed in Italy. Being an accomplished linguist, he was so perfect in his German speech that in Austria he was once arrested as a German spy. This cut short the time he had planned to spend in Vienna, and he soon returned to Dublin where he became head physician to Meath Hospital. He was later appointed lecturer on physiology and became editor of the *Journal of Medical Sciences.* In 1843 he published his first brochure, *Clinical Lectures on the Practice of Medicine.* Therein he described so clearly the little-understood disease of exophthalmic goiter that his name has since been associated with it, and "Graves' disease" became known throughout the world as a synonym for ophthalmic goiter. Graves was a man who commanded attention wherever he went, and he greatly improved the standing of Irish medicine. He is said to have had an easy bearing which made him many friends, and he did much to make of Dublin a world-renowned medical center. He died in 1853 and his remains rest in a cemetery near Dublin, where he spent the greater part of his life.

Hermann von Helmholtz, Who First Saw the Fundus of the Eye

One of the greatest of these European innovators was Hermann von Helmholtz, who was born in 1821 at Potsdam, where his father was a teacher of philosophy. He later took up the study of medicine and after graduation was appointed professor of physiology at Königsberg University. Here he wrote his treatise *Physiological Optics* and invented the ophthalmoscope. Thus he was the first to see the fundus of the living eye. So great an impression was created by this new instrument that von Graefe, Germany's greatest ophthalmologist, wrote at this time, "Helmholtz has opened up a new world for all ophthalmologists, who before his time worked in the dark so far as the interior of the eye was concerned."

In 1871 Helmholtz became professor of physics in Berlin, where he labored continuously on the improvement of his ophthalmoscope until he died in 1894. Helmholtz was one of the most practical oculists who ever lived. His work made it possible for later generations to write and illustrate books, in all languages, dealing with the interior of the eye, one of which was the treatise *The Ocular Fundus in Diagnosis and Treatment* by this writer, which modest volume has found its way into all countries where ophthalmology is a science.

Louis Pasteur Studies Wine Diseases and Discovers Antisepsis

Louis Pasteur was born in 1822 at Dôle in eastern France, the son of a soldier in the army of Napoleon. Returning to Paris, he began a study of the cause of souring of wine, then a much-discussed condition which threatened to destroy the reputation of French wines. After a long period of intensive study in his laboratory, Pasteur was at last able to report that the fermentation which had for years destroyed great quantities of French wine was due to a special microorganism, and he outlined methods of combating it, which when put into use made France again one of the greatest exporters of good wine in the world. He now turned his attention to putrefaction in milk and discovered that by raising the temperature of milk to slightly less than the boiling point, it could be kept pure and unsoured for a much longer period than it was formerly believed. This has become known, and is practiced in all civilized nations, as "pasteurization," and it was because of this discovery of Pasteur's that Lister was enabled to bring into being his first antiseptic surgery.

In 1865 Pasteur began a study of the silkworm disease and finally discovered a means of controlling it which saved the silk industry of France. In 1885 he discovered a method of controlling the infection caused by the bites of rabid animals, which, under the name of hydrophobia, had for years been on the increase in France, causing a severe mortality. This was proved by his successful treatment of Joseph Meister, a boy who had been bitten by a mad dog, and who, without the injection of Pasteur's serum, would have died of hydrophobia. A second case, that of Jupille, who had received seven bites from a rabid dog and who had held the animal in an effort to save other children from being bitten, was given the serum and thereby prevented from contracting rabies. A statue of this famous case may be seen in the Royal College of Surgeons building in London, it being a replica of a similar statue which was erected in the gardens of the Pasteur Institute in Paris. The fame of Pasteur's discovery for protecting persons who had been bitten by rabid animals spread rapidly, and to the Pasteur treatment must be accredited the later saving of hundreds of lives in many parts of the world.

In a meeting of Pasteur and Lord Lister, both of whom were then internationally famous, Lister said, "Truly there does not exist a man in the entire world to whom medical science owes more than it does to you." Pasteur was said to have been so overcome by the tribute of this great surgeon that he could not reply.

24.

Daniel Drake Reconstructs Pioneer Medicine

Daniel Drake was one of the most picturesque of the pioneer physicians of early America. He first saw the light of day in 1785 in a small hamlet in New Jersey. His father was one of the class of individuals so numerous and improvident among the early pioneers. Finding that he was unable to keep his family from starvation, he joined a group of immigrants who traveled south for seven hundred miles and then, turning northward, passed through the Cumberland Gap and made their way into the hills of Kentucky. Here his father took up an allotment of land, proceeded with Daniel's help to build a log cabin on it, and then started to hew out a place for his family in the dense forest. First, the trees were "barked," that is, they were cut around so that the spring's sap could not ascend. This done, no foliage would appear to shut off the sunlight from their proposed crop. The rich soil was turned with a hoe, and seeds brought from New Jersey were pressed into the fertile ground. The results of these first efforts were an end to privation, and more food than the family could use.

Daniel grew up amid all the advantages which came to the country boy of the period. When the crop was "laid by" for the summer he attended the country school and soon became imbued with a passion to obtain a medical education. By honest effort and as a result of shrewd native ability he, as a pupil of Dr. William Goforth, made great progress in his studies and, having received a certificate to that effect from his preceptor, he moved to an adjacent community and proceeded to take up the practice of medicine.

Drake is but one of the many pioneer physicians who became successful in the practice of medicine and acquired many accomplishments and often fame before they were graduated from any institution of medical learning. Later, feeling the need for more clinical experience, he attended and was graduated from the University of Pennsylvania. Again he located far in the country and, not being satisfied with his progress, he moved and removed so many times that he became noted for his restlessness. Sir William Osler, later tracing his many ramifications, speaks of him as a "peripatetic" doctor. Time later proved that the numerous migrations for which he was so well known were to serve him well, for as the years passed he was continually gathering information about unusual cases, as well as incidents of general interest which were to be used in the career he had mapped out for himself, that of medical journalism. In this capacity he later was to charm both lay and professional readers with descriptions of many quaint situations which had befallen him in his various former locations and which he had jotted down while his memory of them was fresh. As a consequence of the newsiness of its pages and the excellency of its reported cases, his journal increased in popularity until it became the general favorite of the physicians in both the Mississippi basin and the East. While much of the material in his first attempt at journalism, the *Western Journal of the Medical and Physical Sciences,* was in a lighter vein, it contained a series of important essays on the subject of medical education, which future events were to prove he was master of. These essays appeared periodically in the journal for five years and were of a style so clear and forceful that their equal is not to be found anywhere else in medical journalism.

The early pioneer doctor as a rule wrote little, and the world has been the loser thereby. Not so Drake. His versatile pen touched upon every subject, trivial or otherwise, relative to conditions in early Kentucky, of the people living there, of their virtues and vices, of their strange manners and of their weird superstitions. His extensive practice, covering a period of twenty years in these primitive surroundings, and his gift for describing his relations with the interesting people he found there were sources of never-ending interest to his readers.

Drake Leaves a Record of Early American Medicine

Drake's book, *Pioneer Life in Kentucky,* appeared posthumously in 1870 and was one of his greatest achievements. It is so filled with humor that it strongly suggests the later writings of Mark Twain. Some have suggested that this author derived much of his style by reading Drake's book, but this cannot be verified.

The location in which Drake practiced was free from many of the evils of the more densely populated areas of the time, such as imperfect sewerage, bad milk and water supply, poor ventilation, and defective plumbing, or often no plumbing at all. But even in rural areas, conditions governing health were always bad. There was a great deal of malaria, and the inhabitants accepted chills and fever as a matter of course. They were thought to be the result of decomposing vegetation under and about dwellings. Night air was considered bad for the health, and families slept in houses with windows and doors tightly closed at night so as to avoid what was thought to be poisoned air. This deprived the occupants of needed oxygen, but was helpful in a way, for it kept out the anopheles mosquito which we now know to be the cause of malaria.

Drake noticed that there was less typhus fever in the country than there was in the city. The reason for this is now plain. Country people have fewer close contacts with others and, as typhus is caused by the bites of vermin which the early inhabitants of cities often had in abundance, the city folk succumbed to infections, whereas the country inhabitants were more likely to escape entirely. Drake never knew the reason for this, for the cause of typhus fever was not discovered for many years.

The country was beset with so-called catarrhs. Grouped together, they were all thought to be due to moisture in the atmosphere, or from going from warm rooms in which families had congregated for the night to the outside where the air was crisp and cool. For this reason fresh air was avoided as harmful, and there are extant some verses of the period filled with dramatic pathos, one of which describes a young girl with all hope gone and expecting death at any moment, who cries out "Open the window wider, Mother; air cannot harm me now."

The country was freer than the city from epidemics of disease. Smallpox was occasionally found in the rural districts of Kentucky where Drake practiced, but vaccination was by then generally practiced and the spread of the disease was thereby prevented. Diphtheria antitoxin had not yet been discovered, and diphtheria annually carried off a large toll from the younger generation. It was usually diagnosed as croup. The little patient with diphtheria was sometimes held up by the feet in a vain effort to force downward by gravitation what was recognized as some obstruction in the throat. The throat was also endlessly probed with feathers saturated with asafetida and "goose grease." This was meant to serve a double purpose, lubricating the air passages and producing vomiting, which it was observed was often helpful in freeing obstruction from the patient's throat.

In cases of acute sore throat it was believed that the uvula (the extremity of the soft palate) was apt to fall down in the air passage, thus causing difficulty in breathing. Many a patient mother spent hours over a sick child, gently pulling its hair upward in the belief that in this manner the "palate" could be kept from falling downward to obstruct breathing.

In cases of obstetrics where delivery was delayed, the practice of blowing tobacco snuff into the prospective mother's nose was often resorted to. It was thought that this would induce labor. The act of sneezing occasioned by the inhalation of snuff, it was observed, sometimes actually did produce pains, and in that way might occasionally have helped to promote delivery.

After the baby was born an unusual rite was, and often is still, performed in primitive communities, especially among those who can trace their lineage back to Oglethorpe's colony in Georgia. This is "smoking" both mother and child. In my early years as a general practitioner in the country I came across this practice often. After the infant had arrived and the umbilical cord had been tied and severed, the "grandmothers" customarily in attendance proceeded to carry out what was considered to be their important duty. This consisted of igniting some cotton rags previously laid by for that purpose, so that the smoke being diffused through the room would pass over both mother and child. I have never been able to trace the origin of this practice, but as a fledgling doctor when I attempted to discredit it and finally succeeded, my efforts in one instance ended in my own undoing.

Before *Pioneer Life in Kentucky,* Drake had written *Diseases of the Interior Valley of North America,* which book gives much of his experiences as a young untried doctor in Kentucky. It is a work distinctly American and was received in both America and Europe with enthusiastic applause. Soon after its publication Drake received an invitation to appear before British audiences as a lecturer. Anticipating, no doubt, the experiences which had come to several other pioneer doctors while abroad, he declined by saying, "I think too much of my country to place myself in so awkward a position."

Drake was a teacher of medicine for several years before he founded the Medical College of Ohio in 1821, but the school was not staffed as he believed it should have been, and in 1835 he organized still another medical institute, the Medical Department of Cincinnati College, in which he had associated with him some of the ablest lecturers of the Mississippi Valley.

Drake late in adult life was a commanding figure. Unlike his appearance in his early years, he was now meticulously dressed. As a lecturer he was superb, couching his thoughts as he did in picturesque words conveyed in a well-modulated voice. In the exercise of this gift and with occasional spurts of eloquence, he held his audiences spellbound. With his patients it is said he had a gentle sympathetic manner, so different from that of the average pioneer or, may we note, of certain of our modern doctors, and a charm of personality which made him beloved by all. Coming as he did from the lower walks of life, he ascended gradually in his profession until he was recognized as the most important medical figure of his age in America.

25.

William Beaumont and the Study of Digestion

The first important step in the understanding of the process of digestion was centered around the person of Alexis St. Martin, a *voyageur* of Indian and French descent. In 1822 we find St. Martin in the Canadian wilderness. Much of the time he was shooting rapids of otherwise placid streams. At this time, as with all *voyageurs,* he always asked the Blessed Mother to be his guide and felt secure as he kept his birch-bark canoe, with its heavy load of traps and provision, from the sharp ledges of rocks lying beneath; or as the sound of waterfalls ahead of him became more audible, he pulled the bow of his canoe up the bank and proceeded to make a portage. This may have been but a few yards, but too often it was miles ahead. Then some of his burden was placed on his shoulders, and he would run with it until his legs began to tire; then he would deposit it on the ground and return for another load. Soon all his goods had been carried to this first resting place. He would then pick up a part of his pack and run forward again until fatigue compelled him to put the piece of cargo down, and finally the long tiresome process of removing the total load to the second stop was finished. Once again he would seize a part of his load and run forward, this tedious process continuing until smoother waters were reached. Returning for his canoe, he would carry it to the point of a new embarkation, load his merchandise into it, and proceed on his journey. This tiresome method of making portages I learned in the Canadian wilds many years afterward as I ran behind French guides dogtrotting before me, loaded down by equipment and provisions often equal to their own weight.

The first trips of the French *voyageurs* began at Montreal. By following the streams northward and westward, paddling and portaging alternately, the *voyageurs* year after year found their way further and further up streams and into the heart of the best trapping grounds. But in due time the crop of pelts for this area became exhausted, and it was necessary for these hardy adventurers to move further west over streams beset by unfriendly Indians. Within the next few years the tips of their canoes touched sand banks on each of the Great Lakes, and the tributaries entering these lakes were beginning to undergo exploration. Montreal markets then were too far away to be reached at the end of each season, and the *voyageur* found to his delight that a new market was opening up on the island of Mackinac. Soon it became known that a certain Monsieur Astor would turn over to the *voyageur* more barter for his pelts than he could possibly get in Montreal. Mackinac Island was nearer the actual trapping grounds than Montreal, and before long all *voyageurs* learned to take their year's yield of pelts to this island village. Very little money passed into the hands of these trappers, but they soon accustomed themselves to the process of barter. Here a type of small-bore gun which would kill a fox or otter, with little expenditure of pelts for ammunition, was sold and became very popular. With this weapon the *voyageur* could almost double his output of furs at very little expense. Thus Mackinac Island for over a century was a permanent depot for the fur traders, as it still is to a limited extent. I learned on my visit to the island in 1944 that the French and Indian trappers still look to Mackinac as the best market place for their now limited catches of furs.

Around this trading post in those early years were encamped peaceful Indians, and in log cabins and hastily constructed shacks many *voyageurs* slept between seasons. The days were spent in the company store, where Indians and a stream of *voyageurs* continually passed in and out.

It was almost nightfall on an evening in the spring of 1820. Liquor had flowed freely all day. Wondrous stories were being told of portaging, of prowess in setting and baiting traps, of hair-raising encounters with bears and timber wolves, and of the manner of taking the moose, whose flesh for food and bait was a necessity to the trapper. Eagerly listening to these tall tales and anxious to learn all that he could about the profession he had adopted, in which he was still far from expert, was a youth of nineteen years, Alexis St. Martin. As an excited trapper whom Alexis admired and sought to emulate swung around the new Astor gun to demonstrate how he had killed otter and other fur-bearing animals, an accidental explosion of the gun took place and Alexis St. Martin lay writhing in his own blood. A drunken cry went up for the army doctor who for a few weeks had been stationed at Mackinac. William Beaumont responded, moved the patient to the side of the store, and made a temporary dressing.

"He can't live long," said Dr. Beaumont. "His stomach and part of his chest have been shot away, but I'll come back to see him later on in the evening."

William Beaumont was born in 1785 on a farm near Lebanon, Connecticut. The little village then had 150 inhabitants. In 1914 I attempted to find someone who could tell me something about the whereabouts of this farm. No one that I talked with had ever heard of William Beaumont. I inquired for the village doctor. So far as I could learn, no physician had lived there. Yet it was here that William Beaumont first purchased books and decided to become a surgeon. But he made no great progress until he moved to Vermont and became the pupil of Dr. Benjamin Chandler in St. Albans. In this same year, 1914, I went to St. Albans on a quest for Beaumont lore. The town then had six thousand people and a dozen doctors. I interviewed half of these, but though to some of them the name of William Beaumont seemed familiar they knew little about him. Not one I spoke with remembered anything of the Alexis St. Martin incident or of what Beaumont had really accomplished for the physiology of digestion.

Dr. William Beaumont read medicine here in St. Albans under the preceptorship of Dr. Chandler. Many modern physicians are surprised to learn that Dr. Beaumont, a surgeon in the United States Army, had never been to a medical school. The same may be said of his teacher. Few medical colleges were then available to young men who wished to become doctors. Those who had entered medical school often acquired a certain stiffness bordering on pomposity, which caused most backwoods boys to look toward some local physician who would act as teacher. We find then that Beaumont's schooling was given to him at the hands of kind old Nature, both on the farm in Connecticut and with his preceptor in rural Vermont.

Some time after the shooting of Alexis St. Martin, Beaumont returned to the scene of the accident, where he felt sure he would find his patient dead. In the meantime he had looked through his meager supply of medical books to learn, if possible, what might be done with a patient part of whose stomach was destroyed. He could find nothing about wounded stomachs, but he learned from this source something which is now known to be in error, that all gunshot wounds should be probed diligently in order to find and remove extraneous material. As he looked at his patient, he felt certain that he would soon expire, and he therefore decided not to probe the wound. Had he done so, a peritonitis would probably have set up, Alexis would have died, and a valuable lesson in physiology would not have been learned.

Long after this, when Beaumont had been recognized as the first man to study digestion in the human being by direct vision and by actual tests of stomach contents during digestion, he wrote in his journal, "When I first saw Alexis Saint Martin I considered, at this time, any attempt to save this patient's life as no use, but I considered it a duty to do what I could in any case, to relieve human suffering and to save life I therefore cleansed the wound and gave it a first dressing, not that I believed it possible that he would live more than a brief period. Later I attended more thoroughly to the dressing of the wound. I removed fragments of bone and other extraneous material which had extruded themselves from the wound and he amazed me with the fortitude with which he bore it without sinking." Later Beaumont wrote that he was obliged to remove a portion of Alexis' stomach which had been blown to fragments. As time passed, the opening in Alexis' stomach gradually began to get smaller by a process which surgeons know as the development of granulations. Slowly the skin crept over these granulated areas and the wound became smaller. Then for no reason which Beaumont was ever able to explain, a valvelike flap of tissue appeared over the orifice, closing the wound so that with a partially full stomach he could walk about without his semidigested food leaking out. But after a hearty meal, food was eliminated from the stomach. Beaumont made many attempts to overcome this, but his efforts were of no avail. Then suddenly, for a reason still unknown to us, the valve kept the opening closed and impervious to the exit of stomach contents even after the ingestion of alcohol together with a hearty meal.

Beaumont was not slow to realize that in his hands was an opportunity, which had not come to anyone else at any time, for the examination and study of digestion in the living subject. At various times he would elevate the flap to peer into the stomach, but the results were nil from the standpoint of learning anything about the process of digestion. He then began to put pieces of food, attached to strings, into the stomach and he made notes relative to the periods of time it took to digest each type of food. But he was still ignorant of the reasons why the pieces of food got smaller and smaller and then entirely disappeared. Not having studied physiology to any extent while an apprentice in medicine, he did not have an adequate knowledge of the subject or how to proceed farther.

At about this time he made application to General Lovell, his commanding officer, to be placed near some large city where scientific men might be able to assist him in his studies, but not realizing the importance of the study of digestion, General Lovell for a long time turned a deaf ear to his appeal. Finally, an order of transfer to Fort Niagara came to Beaumont and he was able to take his patient, still considered sick, with him. Here Beaumont continued for months to place in the stomach pieces of raw beef, cooked beef, cooked pork, bread, cabbage, and other vegetables, but St. Martin's attacks of nausea following this caused Beaumont to discontinue the experiments for a time. Soon he was again putting articles of food in the stomach, and then Alexis complained and begged that the experiments be stopped. Beaumont scolded and insisted that they continue. In the course of these trying events, Beaumont, it is believed, became very brusque. This domineering attitude antagonized Alexis, and he determined to make his escape to his native Canada. One morning Beaumont awakened and gave the order for Alexis to get up and get ready for a continuation of his experiments. There was no answer. Alexis had gone, no one knew where. Also, his few clothes were missing and the stick he used in walking during the early part of his illness could not be found. After many inquiries and after finding that no one had seen his "destiny," as Beaumont was pleased to call Alexis, Beaumont gave up in despair.

Beaumont remained at this post and proceeded to write up his experiments. These had resulted in many pertinent facts, but no idea was given as to why the food attached to various strings had disappeared in the stomach. However, the *Medical Recorder* gave space to an article written at this time, and the experiments stopped there for the time being, as Alexis St. Martin had now been given up as lost to him. At the time, the truant patient was slowly making his way back to Montreal with the vision of a pretty farm girl constantly before him. He had always loved her and meant to marry her as soon as he finished his second year as a *voyageur*. Whether or not she would be single when he returned was the question always before him as he plodded through the wilderness toward home. The journey took weeks. Finally arriving at the outskirts of Montreal, he crept Indian-like toward the house of his sweetheart and saw her through the window. No man was with her and no children's voices could be heard. Then timidly he rapped on the door. In a moment his love, Marie, was in his arms. In a few days they were married by the parish priest, Beaumont was almost forgotten by Alexis, and the world looked bright again for both of them. This season of bliss was soon to pass, for now a child was in promise and both realized that it took work to build a home, and the only work that Alexis had any inclination for was that of a *voyageur*. So within a few months he was following streams in the wilderness and making portages bound for a trapping center. Soon he learned that he was not equal to the tasks allotted to him by his fellow *voyageurs*. They called him lazy and tormented him about the hole in his stomach. Finally he could bear what he felt was disgrace no longer and he deserted. Before long, with his pride broken and almost in despair, he found Beaumont at Plattsburg, near Fort Niagara, and agreed to continue the experiments.

While Beaumont had made more experiments on the human stomach than any other scientist, he did not know how to analyze its contents. Realizing that the best physiologists were in Europe, he determined to go there and to take Alexis with him. But about that time the Black Hawk War broke out and, in consequence, his leave was cancelled.

Beaumont then gave samples of stomach contents to Silliman of Yale and Junglison of the University of Virginia. They both reported that the samples contained hydrochloric acid. There was something else he had noticed in the stomach but had failed to get samples of, which Beaumont suspected was an important factor in digestion. He died before realizing the nature of this substance. It is now known to be pepsin, and its nature is more or less understood even by laymen everywhere.

It is a long way from the work of this backwoods surgeon to modern physiology; yet his experiments conducted under such difficulties are the foundation of our present knowledge regarding digestion. And in giving due credit to Beaumont for his work which transformed the idea that digestion was due to a mechanical grinding of food in the stomach, to our present knowledge that the process is largely a chemical one, let us remember the humble *voyageur,* Alexis St. Martin, without whose co-operation the discovery of Beaumont regarding stomach physiology would never have been made.

26.

Ephraim McDowell, the First Pelvic Surgeon

Ephraim McDowell, who was for forty years or more to be the most controversial figure in the world of medicine, was the son of Samuel McDowell. He was born deep in the backwoods of Rockbridge County, Virginia, and until he became world-famous was still a backwoodsman with all the rustic traditions and prejudices of the early pioneer. Those were the days when the white man on the Eastern seaboard lived in constant apprehension of hostile Indians, and Ephraim, no doubt, was told often of the time when his grandfather was shot by the arrow of a skulking red man while he was placing a charge in the muzzle of his musket. The Indian menace to the white settlers' homes had only partially abated by November 1771, when Ephraim, the subject of this sketch, was born. The event of his birth rounded out a family of nine children, five brothers, and three sisters. Ephraim's father was a Scotch Presbyterian, and he is said to have ruled his family with an iron hand. But it was not possible at the same time for him to watch nine offspring scattered over a large neighborhood.

Ephraim had the amount of schooling which came to the average backwoods boy of the period. Reading, writing, and arithmetic were instilled into him by a teacher who boarded alternately with the parents of the school children. He seems to have taken a liking to Ephraim and neglected to report to the father if Ephraim, for any reason, was absent from his classes. A habit of truancy thus acquired by Ephraim the boy, was the means of paving the way for fame in Ephraim, the man, for while avoiding the drudgery of the schoolroom, he nevertheless had a passion for knowing things. There is a tradition, not so well substantiated, that at this time he, in one of his rambles about the countryside, witnessed the operation of removing the ovaries of a hog, as done by old-time sow-gelders. This, if it could be verified, would indicate the part a certain unknown pioneer of German lineage had in forming the future of a surgeon who became world-renowned. Be this as it may, Ephraim was a constant seeker of firsthand knowledge. His life in the open gave him an acquaintance with nature. It also created in him a desire to prove things for himself, and when we reflect, we will see that about everyone who has cut deep his niche in scientific history had the same desire for firsthand knowledge. Herbert Spencer was not voicing an idle sentiment when he said, "The man to whom, in boyhood, information comes in dreary tasks along with threats of punishment is unlikely to be a student in after years." To bear out this assertion we have but to remember the fact that at the time that Ephraim McDowell became the first man in the world who dared with his knife to invade one of the closed cavities of the body, he was not a graduate in medicine. While he studied anatomy and surgery in Edinburgh, he did not remain there long enough to take a degree. We may, therefore, conclude that while he lacked any evidence of the polish which might have come with a college degree, he made up for it by a knowledge of nature and a complete freedom from conventional thinking. Thomas H. Huxley and Alfred Russel Wallace always contended that what success they had achieved came in spite of, and not because of, their college degrees. Thoreau, one of the greatest naturalists of the world, is known to have refused his diploma from Harvard College because he believed the degree would not be worth the five dollars charged for it, and Charles Darwin once said that he received only one thing of value from his alma mater and that was the stimulation which came to him as a result of her disapproval of his work.

School days being over, young Ephraim lost much of his liberty, for he had to help prepare more land for cultivation as a necessity for the upkeep of a growing family, and every foot of tillable ground had to be carved out of the dense forest. Trees were at first barked to kill their foliage; the next year these trees were felled and rolled into piles to be burned. This was backbreaking labor in which farm-hand neighbors usually took part. Thus log-rollings were made easier by reciprocal effort. But though Ephraim was large and powerful for his years, the monotony of this drudgery made him look forward to the Sunday rest. First, however, the chores about the place had to be done, but soon he managed his escape from manual labor to the Sunday school. After Sunday school was over the class was transferred to seats before the pulpit, where they "rested" for two long hours in a hard pew as the minister carried the elders through a long discussion of some theological subject. Then came the doxology, and they could enjoy a respite until the evening sermon called them back to the same hard benches.

Several years before Ephraim was born a Dr. Thomas Walker of Virginia made an excursion along the Appalachian escarpment extending from the eastern boundary of Kentucky through Tennessee and Alabama, and discovered a breach in the chain of mountains, which he named Cumberland Gap after the Earl of Cumberland, at that time a hero of the pioneers. Near here he also discovered a deep meandering stream which he named the Cumberland River and which was to provide a means of water transportation for many future Kentucky immigrants. Through the now famous Cumberland Gap, Walker later led a band of pioneers into Kentucky. Returning to Virginia, these adventurers told stories of the beauty of this new country, the plentiful game to be found, and the ease with which this new land could be colonized. It is interesting to know that with the Walker expedition was a man appearing for the first time as a historical character. This was Daniel Boone, an Indian-fighter who was to prove a great help to the new colony by keeping the Indians under control. Soon a stream of immigrants was passing through the Cumberland Gap on the way to Kentucky, but the final colonization of this area did not occur until after the Revolutionary War. At about this time Ephraim McDowell's father packed up his entire belongings, disposed of his Virginia holdings, and made his way into the hills of Kentucky. He settled in Danville and helped to make this dismal village in the wilderness the first capital of Kentucky. Here Ephraim spent the years of his early manhood. For a time he went to a school in Bardstown, Kentucky, but he never progressed to the extent that he could write clear English. The McDowell home was then the same as those of the residents of the immediate neighborhood. In the construction of these homes, logs were hewn on two sides and dovetailed at the corners of the buildings. The spaces between were filled with moss and clay. I have a thorough acquaintance with this kind of dwelling, for I lived in a similar house as a young doctor in an early settlement in East Texas. Many of my patients' ancestors had the distinction of having passed through Cumberland Gap on their way westward. They, like the McDowell family, were of as pure a British strain, I have often thought, as any people to be found in America.

In Danville, Ephraim McDowell hung out his first shingle and he soon became a prosperous surgeon. Later he built a small mansion near the present site of Centre College, of which he was one of the founders and which he endowed. It was at Centre College that I took a part of my premedical training, and it was here that I gathered much of the information which appears in this sketch.

In 1799 Ephraim McDowell was called to the home, fifty miles distant, of Mrs. Thomas Crawford, who had been the subject of an obscure illness for many months. The doctors in attendance had first assured her that she would soon again become a mother. Months passed and the event looked forward to had not occurred. At last it dawned upon the neighbors that the local physicians must be mistaken in their diagnosis. Soon the name of Dr. McDowell, then the best-known surgeon in Kentucky, was mentioned, and neighbors marveled that the husband allowed the condition to continue with no apparent plan to correct the malady, if possible. Finally some friend had the courage to tell Crawford that he believed his wife was nearing her grave and without assistance she would soon be there. Crawford replied that he had long sought to have medical help for his wife, but Mrs. Crawford deferred because she shrunk from injuring the feelings of the local doctors who had been kind to her and because she was awaiting an answer to months of prayer, which she felt would ultimately come. Mrs. Crawford's consent having finally been obtained, Dr. McDowell in a few days stood at her bedside.

McDowell explained to the anxious relatives and the neighboring women present that Mrs. Crawford was suffering from a large ovarian tumor. He told them that the medical profession had never dared to open a pelvis for the purpose of removing such growths, as it was universally believed that no woman could survive the ordeal. He even mentioned that he had been taught in Edinburgh that pelvic tumors should be let alone and that only such steps should be taken as to make the patient as comfortable as possible until the end came. It is possible that the ovary operation done upon the female hog witnessed by him as a boy might have occurred to him at this time. He knew that the animals under the knife of German sow-gelders (spayers) lived, and he believed that an operation done upon a human being might not always be attended by fatal results. He explained all this to Mrs. Crawford, and she is said to have replied, "Dr. McDowell, I know there can only be one ending unless this is done. I wish to go back to Danville with you. Please operate upon me for my husband's and children's sake." For the next hour McDowell sat in deep thought, contemplating the possible disastrous consequences of the operation and attempting to remember the anatomical details of the pelvis which would have a bearing on the case. Then he arose, went over to the husband who sat beside his wife and said, "Mrs. Crawford, if it is your wish and also your husband's wish I will take you back to Danville within three days." On December 20, 1809, Dr. McDowell and Mrs. Crawford drew up before the much-talked-of residence which McDowell used as a hospital in operative cases. They had made the entire trip on horseback.

This episode, which so nearly ended in a tragedy and which might have thrown the progress of surgery back a hundred years, occurred on Christmas morning. McDowell proceeded to operate on Mrs. Crawford, even though he knew it was considered murder to open the pelvis of a human being. On this winter morning the pastor of Dr. McDowell's church is said to have denounced him from the pulpit, and after the service a part of the congregation repaired to McDowell's home and stood, or sat in their saddles, in a threatening attitude in front of a window of the operating room. One of the members of the congregation appeared with a rifle in his hand. Others with the same intent of making an example of the doctor, should Mrs. Crawford not withstand the procedure, had fortified themselves with ropes and prepared improvised hangman's nooses. Just eighty-seven years later we students used to peer over the front fence and take note of the tree limb in the yard where tradition says the end of a rope had already been thrown while the operation was being performed inside the house.

Mrs. Crawford withstood the operation well, recovered, and returned to her family, while Dr. Ephraim McDowell, instead of being branded a criminal, was at once proclaimed as a world hero and a great surgeon.

In 1895 I, as a student, had been permitted to examine the room in which this world-transforming operation had been done. In my early practice of medicine among the more prosperous pioneers of Texas I have seen counterparts of this famous room. On one side was a fireplace. Its proportions were huge. On one end the cooking was done the year round, and there were shovels and tongs and pans with long handles and a crane on which swung a huge kettle. But the other side of this fireplace was swept clean in summer and used for heating only in the winter. There was a smooth surface on one of the side walls, the so-called jamb of the fireplace, where the kitchen utensils were sharpened. Beside this fireplace there usually was a spinning wheel. As a fledgling doctor I remember hearing often the whirling sound of a similar spindle as the busy housewife paced back and forth, interminably spinning the yarn which would go into socks for the men and knitted jackets for the women. In the room in which this famous operation occurred I found many articles which had been the property of Ephraim McDowell. The bottles on the fireplace were lettered in gold and in some of them there were the remnants of the drugs which they originally contained. I was soon to learn to distinguish the properties of the contents of each bottle, for the student at that time learned properties of drugs and how to make various preparations, though not so much about what pharmaceutical houses with their secret formulas had to offer. In one corner of this room was a pair of saddlebags and a small case of instruments, and under a large window was a table said to have been the actual one on which Mrs. Crawford lay during the short hour which served to transform surgery throughout the world.

According to Fielding H. Garrison, McDowell later performed the operation for the removal of fibroid tumors of the ovaries twenty-two times without a death. His simple technique as used in the operation upon Mrs. Crawford was later described by him as follows:

"When the external wound was made. . . ," he stated, "the intestines rushed out and we saw that so completely was the abdomen filled with the tumor that they could not be replaced till the massive lesion was removed. . . . We then turned the patient upon her left side to permit the blood to escape before we closed the abdominal wall with continued sutures, leaving out the ligatures which surrounded the fallopian tube, then we applied the usual dressings."

This phenomenal surgical procedure of Ephraim McDowell,

made at a time when nothing was known regarding the laws of asepsis, paved the way for various types of major surgery all over the world, though no one ever attained McDowell's consistent success in saving patients' lives. The reason for this is not known, but it is believed by many that McDowell, who often wrote about the necessity of clean linen and clean dressings, must have stumbled onto a quicker way of getting dried blood off his instruments by boiling, and because of this accidental sterilization of instruments and the clean linen he insisted on having, he did a more nearly sterile operation than any of his colleagues.

It runs true to the pattern of the history of medical innovations that McDowell's work in removing pelvic tumors was opposed by America's greatest obstetrician of the time, Charles D. Meigs of Philadelphia. Dr. Washington Atlee had just published the account of an ovariotomy when Dr. Meigs wrote that such an operation could not possibly be justified by any amount of success. Meigs made an attempt at that time to have a law passed in Pennsylvania which would prohibit the operation of ovariotomy. In Paris the operation of ovariotomy was not much more favorably received, for in 1856-57 the Paris Academy of Medicine fought to have the operation proscribed in France. It may be said that this operation except in the hands of McDowell was attended by a high mortality, until the days of Lister when antiseptic surgery, soon to be followed by aseptic surgery, made the operation of ovariotomy comparatively safe.

Though McDowell saved others, he was powerless to save himself from an abdominal infection. In 1830 he was seized by a severe pain in his right lower abdomen. Summoning a physician, he explained that he had just eaten heartily of strawberries and that he felt sure he had swallowed a poisonous insect. McDowell directed his own treatment. He and the world at that time had no knowledge of infection of the vermiform appendix, and it never occurred to him to have an operation performed. Soon he succumbed to what we now believe was a general peritonitis, the result of a ruptured appendix. In such an instance, a simple incision and the insertion of a drain might have saved his life.

In 1946 I was called to Centre College, Danville, Kentucky, on an important mission, and Dr. Robert McMullen, the president of the college, took me to the old McDowell home, now much changed, and I noted that the tree which we students so often had discussed was still standing, together with its protruding limb which once was prepared for a hangman's noose.

27.

Crawford W. Long and Ether Anesthesia

Anesthesia was not unknown to the ancients and even to primitive man. In its earliest periods the human race became familiar with crude methods of surgery. This frequently was demonstrated by the explorers of the past who found in newly discovered countries people, often in the crudest state of savagery, who had considerable knowledge of the healing art, who set broken bones, applied pressure for the control of hemorrhage, and administered certain herbs for the purpose of producing unconsciousness of various degrees.

S. J. Morans, in his book, *Along the Andes and Down the Amazon,* calls attention to the intricately trephined skulls of an ancient Peruvian race, great numbers of which have been found. Some of these skulls were examined in 1873 by Dr. Paul Broca, the localizer of the convolution which bears his name, and it was pointed out by him that they belonged to a neolithic race existing ten or twelve thousand years ago. I had the privilege of examining one of these skulls, which was exhibited at the convention of the International College of Surgeons in Vienna in 1948. The operations upon these skulls seem to have been done by scraping with sharp flint, a tedious process which must have occupied hours. Descendants of these same people are today using, often to the point of unconsciousness, the juice of the Erythroxylum coca, which has always grown abundantly in this region, and Morans relates a case he observed in which a modern chewer of coca leaves, while under the influence of the drug, had his foot cut off without manifesting the slightest evidence of pain. It is quite probable, then, that the operation done by the Peruvians was actually performed under anesthesia and that the anesthetic used was derived from the coca plant.

While the records of the past on the use of drugs to relieve pain and produce unconsciousness are scanty and uncertain, there are many accounts in ancient literature which point conclusively to medicine so used. Mandrake is mentioned by Pliny and Celsus, and in the writings of Moses we find Rachel seeking to procure this drug from Leah, probably, as suggested by Garrison, for use as an analgesic in labor. The use of mandrake was noted by Shakespeare in *Romeo and Juliet,* together with the suggestion that madness follows its ingestion:

> Shrieks like mandrakes' torn out of the earth
> That living mortals hearing them run mad.

And again, when used as an anesthetic, in *Anthony and Cleopatra*:

> Give me to drink mandragora [mandrake]
> That I might sleep out this great gap of time
> My Anthony is away.

The use of mandrake as an anesthetic may be found in the work of Michael Scott, 1768, who prescribed mandrake and henbane, equal parts, mixed with water, thus: "When you want to saw or cut a man dip a rag in this and put it to his nostrils. He will soon sleep so deep that you may do with him what you wish."

Indian hemp is thought to have been used by the ancient Egyptians as an anesthetic. On departing this life, the deceased was embalmed and placed in the tomb to await the tribunal of another world, and with him were deposited formulas for all possible exigencies occurring after the great tribunal. Here were placed numberless objects which are now known to have been talismans to ward off disease, curious symbols to promote good luck, and formulas for exorcisms against evil spirits, together with leaves of the hemp plant, supposedly to dull his consciousness should the ordeal before Osiris be unfavorable.

There is every reason to believe that the Greeks were familiar with the anesthetic properties of certain drugs long before the fatal draught of hemlock was handed to Socrates, for in the *Odyssey* Homer tells us of a sorrow-easing drug which Helen procured to be cast into the wine drunk by Ulysses. Some passages in the *Arabian Nights,* says Sir Richard Burton, point to the use of anesthetics, and he adds that drugs to produce unconsciousness during surgical operations were in use throughout the East for centuries before ether or chloroform became the fashion in the civilized West. This claim seems to be borne out by the supposed fact that Hao-Tho, a Chinese physician who lived fifteen hundred years ago, used cannabis Indica to produce insensibility during the performance of surgical operations.

It is a matter of wonder that such a boon to humanity as anesthetics were, even in their crude state, could ever have been forgotten. That from operations performed with the subject in dreamless sleep the race should drift into the terrifying surgery of the Middle Ages, when the relentless surgeon worked amid shrieks and screams, where the operating room was a hell and its memory a nightmare, is beyond our comprehension. But we have already noted that for one hundred years prior to and several hundred years following the burning of the Alexandria library science gradually retrogressed. During this period a knowledge of anesthesia was lost and remained so until one day an unknown country doctor in an obscure village in Georgia regrasped the old secret which was again to bless the world, but the world was long to refuse him credit.

On a November day in 1841, Crawford Williamson Long, a young man fresh from a Philadelphia medical college, hung out a shingle in the little village of Jefferson, Georgia. Jefferson was then a crossroad far from a railway; its nearest hospital was at

New Orleans, four hundred miles away. A distinct advantage is afforded by such a beginning, for the young physician thus placed must depend upon his wits or fail ingloriously. J. Marion Sims, Ephraim McDowell, John Wyeth, and John Y. Bassett, illustrious physicians of the southland, were thus favored. In their younger years all of these men were familiar with the application of blisters, occasional phlebotomies, endless delving into well-worn saddlebags, and the simple surgery of the community where extreme necessity demanded it. There were no medical centers then into which they could thrust their difficult cases and in doing so be robbed of their initiative. They had to be equal to all emergencies, the versatility thus acquired paving their way, step by step, for future leadership in both thought and progress. The climb to the top of the ladder never begins at the middle rung.

During the first year of Long's practice an itinerant lecturer arrived in the community and told his auditors strange stories about the exhilaration that might be obtained from a peculiar preparation known as "laughing gas." Some persons who had attended the lecture applied to the young physician for a sample of this gas. Not having the means of preparing nitrous oxide, Long suggested that the same results might be obtained from sulfuric ether, a quantity of which he had in his possession. A number of young men who inhaled this drug in Long's office received bruises which were unaccompanied by pain. The discovery was the result of the accidental observation of this fact, and because of this, it has been contended, it was robbed of its luster. But Long's idea that if a small amount of ether would prevent the pain arising from a contusion, a larger amount would produce unconsciousness of such a degree as to make of surgery a painless process, was a logical deduction arrived at only after a true process of philosophic reasoning, and for this the world must always give him credit.

In 1842 Long performed the first surgical operation under anesthesia ever done in modern times. A description of this operation can be given in no better words than those used by the great discoverer in an essay published in the *Southern Medical and Surgical Journal,* December, 1849. "The first patient to whom I administered ether in a surgical operation," Long states in this paper, "was Mr. James M. Venable, who then resided within two miles of Jefferson and at present lives in Cobb County, Georgia.

"Mr. Venable consulted me on several occasions in regard to the propriety of removing two small tumors situated on the back part of his neck, but would postpone, from time to time, having the operation performed from dread of pain. At length I mentioned to him the fact of my receiving bruises while under the influence of vapor of ether without suffering, and as I knew him to be fond of and accustomed to inhale ether, I suggested to him the probability that the operation might be performed without pain, and proposed operating on him while under the influence. He consented to have one tumor removed and the operation was performed the same evening. The ether was given to Mr. Venable on a towel, and when fully under its influence I extirpated the tumor. It was encysted and about half an inch in diameter. The patient continued to inhale ether during the time of the operation and, when informed it was over, seemed incredulous until the tumor was shown him. He gave no evidence of suffering during the operation and assured me after it was over, that he did not experience the least degree of pain from the performance. This operation was performed on the 30th of March, eighteen hundred and forty-two."

Within the next three years Long operated upon several patients under the influence of ether anesthesia, two of these operations being amputations of toes and fingers, and though he made no attempt to conceal his discovery, which was known to the medical profession locally, he did not at once publish the facts relating to it. At a later time, when further research and repeated operations under anesthesia should make his report sufficiently comprehensive to obtain recognition, he meant to do this. Unfortunately, the report was still in its making when in 1849 W. T. Morton, a dentist of Boston, petitioned Congress for a grant of money as a reward for his discovery of ether anesthesia. This petition awakened what has been since known as the ether controversy, a bitter contest occupying Congress for years and one in which Long at first took no part.

By a Congressional investigation which came about as a result of this controversy the following facts were brought out: That in 1844 Horace Wells, a dentist of Hartford, Connecticut, extracted teeth without pain from patients under the influence of nitrous oxide gas and that following a fatal case of anesthesia, Wells committed suicide. That in 1846 W. T. Morton, a dentist of Boston, at the instigation of Dr. D. C. T. Jackson, performed a painless extraction of a tooth, with the patient under the influence of sulfuric ether. It was proved during this investigation that Morton sought to keep his discovery a secret by applying for and obtaining a patent for "Letheon" a preparation composed of sulfuric ether and a number of ingredients added for the purpose of disguising it. Fortunately for a suffering world, the drug is incapable of concealment and the patent became valueless. Failing in the courts to establish protection, he then made application to Congress for a grant of money to repay him for the blessing he claimed to have conferred upon humanity. Immediately, Jackson and the friends of the late Wells opposed Morton's claim of priority in anesthesia. A committee was then appointed which, be it recorded to their credit, brought in a report on February 28, 1849, which closes with the following paragraph: "He [Morton] was the first to suggest and urge a patent [for ether] and that within twenty-four hours after the discovery is brought to his knowledge he employed a patent solicitor to subdue the 'old and exploded prejudices' of his co-partner, and to hasten the consummation of the enterprise. He anxiously seeks means to prevent the recognition of the agent by changing its odor. Had he succeeded in this wicked attempt his brightest anticipation would have been realized. But failing in his scheme to speculate in the suffering of mankind which, in our judgement, is ten times more culpable than the speculation in the necessities of life, he memorializes the Congress of the United States to make good from the National Treasury what he failed to extort from the

National sufferings." Acting upon this report, Congress refused to have the government mulcted in Morton's favor.

The same evidence presented to this committee had previously been reviewed by the French Academy of Science, which on January 31, 1849, awarded to Doctor Charles T. Jackson its Cross of the Legion of Honor, in commemoration of the discovery of ether anesthesia. In the following extract from an essay appearing in the *Boston Medical and Surgical Journal* during the year 1861, Doctor Jackson gives us the most magnanimous example in medical literature. In this article Jackson set forth the claim that the honor which the French Academy had conferred upon him twelve years before belonged rightfully to Long. "At the request of the Honorable M. Dawson, United States senator from Georgia," he writes, "on March eighth, eighteen hundred and fifty-four, I called upon Dr. C. W. Long, of Athens, Georgia, while on my way to the Dahlonega gold mines, and examined Dr. Long's evidence on which his claims to the first practical operation with ether in surgery were founded, and wrote, as requested, to Mr. Dawson, who was then in the U.S. Senate, all I learned on the subject. From documents shown me by Dr. Long, it appears that he employed sulphuric ether as an anaesthetic agent:

"1st, March 30th, 1842, when he extirpated a small glandular tumor from the neck of Jas. M. Venable, a boy in Jefferson, Ga. now dead.

"2nd, July 3rd, 1842, in the amputation of the toe of a negro boy belonging to Mrs. Hemphill, of Jackson, Georgia.

"3rd, September 9th, 1843, in extirpating a tumor from the head of Mary Vincent, of Jackson, Georgia.

"4th, January 8th, 1845, in the amputation of a finger of a negro boy belonging to Ralph Bailey of Jackson, Georgia. Copies of the letters and depositions proving these operations were all shown me by Dr. Long. I have waited, expecting Dr. Long to publish his statements and evidence in full, and therefore have not before published what I learned from him. He is a very modest retiring man, and not disposed to bring his claims before any but a medical or scientific tribunal. Had he written me in season I would have presented his claims to the Academy of Science of France but he allowed his case to go by default, and the academy knew no more of claims to the practical use of ether in surgical operations than I did."

It is a remarkable fact that, in spite of this evidence given the world by Jackson, the credit for the discovery of anesthesia was, for many years, to go to Morton. This was due to the powerful influence of two men, Dr. John Collins Warren, and Dr. Henry J. Bigelow, both of whom had performed operations with ether administered by Morton and through whose writings, widely read in both America and Europe, the discovery became known. Whether or not anticipation of honor for themselves, if the world could be brought to accept their surgery as the first done under the influence of ether, had anything to do with the conclusions of these men we do not know, but at least it was very human, under the circumstances, to champion the cause of Morton. Their claim gained much additional strength through the writings of Oliver Wendell Holmes, who proposed the term "anesthesia" and who accredited to Morton the honor of first administering ether. Thus were the rights of the modest Georgia physician buried under a mass of superior influence and almost forgotten, but later his case was reopened by his friends and the evidence, freed from its entanglement of prejudice, was reviewed with the only possible conclusion: Long discovered ether anesthesia.

In 1896 Dr. Hugh H. Young of Johns Hopkins Hospital read a paper on anesthesia before the Johns Hopkins Historical Society in which a complete review of the documentary evidence bearing on the ether controversy was made and in which he gave Long the credit for the discovery of ether anesthesia. In 1912 the University of Pennsylvania, after an investigation similar to that made at Johns Hopkins, celebrated the seventieth anniversary of ether anesthesia and struck a bronze medal in commemoration of its originator, Dr. Crawford W. Long. Dr. George Foy of Dublin, in his book, *Life of Crawford Williamson Long, Dis-*

coverer of General Anaesthesia, established proofs of Long's claim and forever closed the ether controversy in Great Britain. *The American Text Book of Surgery* now gives Long credit for his great discovery, and so does nearly every authoritative work on anesthesia that has appeared throughout the world during the last decade.

The heated ether controversy, waged on both sides of the Atlantic, was of long life; but by 1927 Long's claim received unusual recognition by the unveiling of his statue in the National Statuary Hall in Washington, D.C. In March of 1926 the American Medical Association convened at Washington, D.C., where one of its officers delivered an oration in which full credit was placed where credit rightfully belonged, and Long was acknowledged as the discoverer of ether anesthesia. In commemoration of medical discoveries of the past, wreaths were placed on the statues of Benjamin Rush, Walter Reed, and W. C. Gorgas. Afterward, the company returned to the unveiled statue of Crawford Williamson Long, and Dr. Charles Mayo with appropriate remarks placed a wreath on the statue. As a final tribute, the Association of Anaesthetists of the United States and Canada placed upon the front of the statue a beautiful floral tribute. Thus was the controversy ended.

By a strange stroke of circumstance I had an infinitesimal part in the production of the monument which now reposes in the Washington Statuary Hall in commemoration of Long's discovery. The son of Dr. Long, Edward Crawford Long, after coming to Texas during his early years, occupied a position with the city of San Antonio, which employment continued throughout the remainder of his life. I met Mr. Long as a patient in my examination room many years ago. Later his daughter and his wife also became my patients. In 1920 Mr. Long had a number of full-length photographs made and presented me with one of them. When the time came that the artist was commissioned to produce the monument of Dr. Long, it was found that, while a pencil sketch existed, no photograph of him could be found. The family, remembering the photograph of the son given me years before, asked me if I would lend it to them for the sculptor to use as a substitute likeness in preparing the monument. I was, of course, glad to do this and the photograph was in due time returned to me. I still have it filed as one of my prized possessions, and it is believed that it is the only one now in existence.

Long died at Athens, Georgia, June 14, 1878. It is to be regretted that the laurels of discovery were withheld from him during his lifetime, but we are grateful for the fact that the great arbiter, time, has at last meted out final justice and has left to his memory the honor of having been the originator of practical anesthesia.

28.

Credé and the Fight Against Venereal Blindness

Carl Franz Credé, a man of French parentage living in Leipzig, deserves the credit of all mankind because of his untiring work in the Charity Hospital of Leipzig in 1884, which culminated during his lifetime in the rescue from blindness of more than a million children throughout the world. Credé had known for several years that gonorrheal involvement of the eyes of an infant was invariably caused by a specific germ, the gonococcus, discovered by Neisser in 1879. He believed that the poison was transmitted to the child's eyes by the secretions of the mother at the time of birth. It usually appeared about the third or fourth day, manifesting itself by a suffusion of the mucous membrane with blood. Later the lids became swollen so that the eye could not be seen. The discharge from between the lids, which was at first slight and of a watery character, soon became yellow, then creamy and tenacious. Ulcerations occurred in the cornea, which, if extensive, led to blindness by the formation of scar tissue.

Credé observed that this disease was no respecter of persons. The rich, the poor, the college graduate and illiterate vendor were alike susceptible to its ravages. Lying under the veneer of decorous society in his own city were thousands of cases of chronic gonorrhea veiled by ignorance. With social conditions as they were,

Credé felt that some type of preventive measures should be used in every newly born baby's eyes.

Credé was professor of obstetrics in the University of Leipzig and had the right to employ any means that might save the eyes of the large number of infants born under his care. He tried almost every promising drug in the German pharmacopoeia, discarding one after the other as soon as it had failed to free the young infants' eyes from the infectious bacillus which was destined in many instances to cause the child to leave the hospital blinded for life. Many times it had occurred to him to use a solution of nitrate of silver, but he hesitated each time, fearing that, because of its caustic nature, it would destroy a human eye, diseased or otherwise. Finally, in a most desperate case, with all other hope gone, he determined to use the silver drops in an infant's eyes, not as a prophylactic but as a treatment. He was astonished to learn next morning that the child's eyes were improved. Then it occurred to him that nitrate of silver solution might have a preventive action against Neisser's bacillus, if used in the eyes of all infants born of gonorrheal mothers. He was astonished by the results which he obtained, for none of these children developed ophthalmias. For a period of six years, from 1854 to 1860, he continued to use the silver drops before he was thoroughly convinced that he had discovered a preventive for the fatal ophthalmias occurring in the infants of gonorrheal mothers. He was then editor of the *Monatsschrift für Geburtskunde,* and through the medium of this organ gave his discovery to the world. Immediately his prophylactic treatment "caught on," and soon both he and his method became famous.

Credé never expected that his method would be of concern to anybody but obstetricians. He could not anticipate a time when the public, so long asleep, would awaken, or when the press and the pulpit would ever give up their reticence and turn their attention to sex reforms, or that it would be considered proper to teach hygienic truths to young men and women. This problem is now being solved through education. Laws are useless unless the sentiment of the people is behind them, and sentiment in the

United States is behind Credé's discovery for the prevention of blindness, to the extent that a law has been promulgated for the protection of infants against ophthalmias. Credé's method has now become a routine procedure by all attending physicians of obstetrical cases.

The ever-present problem of social diseases had long been recognized as the greatest menace to society. One of the first to call to the attention of the world the disastrous effects of venereal diseases was William Edward Lecky, who in his *History of European Morals* expressed this truth: "In the eyes of every physician, and indeed in the eyes of most Continental writers who have adverted to the subject no other feature of English life appears so infamous as the fact that an epidemic, which is one of the most dreadful now existing among mankind, which communicated itself from the guilty husband to the innocent wife, and even transmits its taint to her offspring, and which the experience of other nations conclusively proves may be vastly diminished, should be suffered to rage unchecked."

There has been a great improvement in the situation since Lecky wrote, and it is impossible now accurately to estimate the number of children that have been ruined by this social stigma, but statistics of from fifty to sixty years ago showed that these diseases were then responsible for thirty per cent of all the world's blindness and for eighty per cent of the blindness then seen in children under two years old. Nor was this all the tragedy. Many infected children were then growing up to become dependent upon society, to burden the poorhouses, and to fill the asylums for the blind.

Now what was responsible for this alarming condition of affairs? So far as the United States is concerned this example of national depravity was largely the result of ignorance, an ignorance fostered by a reticence which put all sex matters under the ban of silence. We had long refused to look sex questions fairly in the face and still were paying terrific dividends in blind children, as well as household tragedies and blighted lives with their attendant misery and despair.

Abroad, the fear of mentioning sex matters in print was even more pronounced than it was in America. In England after the advent of Victoria to the throne, June 20, 1837, a senseless prudery spread over the nation and took hold of much of the continent of Europe, as a result of which Lecky went through a long period of persecution.

In Norway, Henrik Johan Ibsen fared even worse. In 1877, when his *Ghosts* was timidly put on the market and later withdrawn, Ibsen was subject to storms of criticism which made him seek retirement for many months. His *Ghosts* illustrated the awful consequence of venereal disease as he had observed it in Norway. These ghosts which he so graphically depicted were really the image of a father's sins, gruesome phantoms which followed his offspring through life, which put their indelible stamp upon him, ruined his life, and brought him to an untimely grave. These ghosts of society as seen in Scandinavia by Ibsen were leaving behind them thousands of blind and wizened children, along with household tragedies.

This antagonism abroad was due to the fact that society had always rebelled against the publication of anything which interfered with its conventions. Newspaper articles and books which had touched upon sex subjects had nearly always been put under the ban of censorship. Authors who had escaped the censorship of the press had found, almost invariably, that the sentiment of the public was against them. Zola, the fearless Frenchman, made an attack on the evils of French society in a novel which referred to sex questions, but it cost him a seat in the French Academy and awakened an antagonism towards him which eventually made it necessary for him to take refuge for a time in England.

Brieux's *Les Avaries* did for a time an incalculable amount of good where it succeeded in getting by the censors, though it still remained under censorship in several countries. Björnson, who later was awarded the Nobel Prize in literature, while directing attention to Scandinavian social conditions with their corruption and prudish hypocrisy, was silenced by the most scathing criticism.

Humanity has never invited reform. Innovations of thinking have always been viewed with much concern the world over. All great movements for the betterment of the race have had their martyrs. Spinoza's philosophy, which if accepted by his race would have meant reform, led to his excommunication. And we cannot forget that a desire to reform mankind brought the flames to the feet of Savonarola and put the hemlock in the hands of Socrates.

During this early period on this side of the Atlantic a number of physicians wrote articles for the lay press on the subject of *ophthalmia neonatorum*, but the plain facts, as a rule, were handled with a timidity amounting to prudery and had been veiled in a way which lay readers did not understand. No one had the courage to state plainly that these ophthalmias in infants were the direct result of gonorrheal invasions of the genital tract of the mother, which had been transmitted to the child during the process of birth. In the past the medical profession in America as elsewhere had been governed by traditions and ethics which made its members very reticent about teaching sex questions to the public. It will be noticed that where questions relative to sex matters have been discussed in print, the truths have usually been obscured behind technical phrases entirely unfamiliar to lay readers.

In vindication of the American medical profession, it must be said, however, that doctors in the United States were the first to have awakened to the realization that the moral conditions of the world with their attendant physical ills justified them in throwing to the winds their much-cherished prudery and attacking sex evils as they attacked other evils. Americans were among the first people to sense that truths regarding sex questions had been veiled so long behind elusive hints that we were still reaping as a result of this obscuring of facts our share of the world's misery. The first to leave popular convention and to put into print a series of facts on the relation of sex questions to disease, with which the public was entirely unfamiliar, was William L. Howard, who startled America by the following assertion: "There is more venereal disease among the virtuous wives of our country than among the prostitutes. This terrible condition of affairs," he stated in the *Journal of the American Medical Association*," is due to the fact that from 75 to 95 per cent of the male population of our cities have gonorrhea sometime in their lives. Not more than 10 per cent of these were ever cured."

Following the very limited expressions of the press, the medical profession in America began to take stock of itself. At about this time a report of Miller of Pittsburgh demonstrated the effectiveness of Credé's method in the prevention of venereal blindness in children. It contained the assertion that in 1,262 births occurring during the preceding seven years in the various hospitals of the city the nitrate of silver solution of Credé was used in the infants' eyes as a routine, and among these not a single case of *ophthalmia neonatorum* developed. In the Sloan Maternity Hospital in New York all babies' eyes had been treated with the silver solution for six years, and with a total of 4,660 births there had not been a single case of this disease. In the face of such evidence it appeared criminal to neglect the use of this drug in the eyes of all newborn babies, regardless of circumstances.

At about this time Dr. Thomas Woodruff of Chicago began to sense that in order to control a pestilence the beginning was the place to begin, and he advocated compulsory examination of contracting parties before marriage.

Dr. Price Morrow was responsible for the statement that seventy-five per cent of the women who were treated for venereal disease in the various hospitals of New York City were innocent wives who had contracted the gonorrhea from their husbands. Well-qualified surgeons in every city of the country were asserting that the largest per cent of the pelvic operations performed upon women and the greatest number of repeated involuntary abortions were due to this disease. They also called attention to the fact that when a man with a venereal disease leads a bride to the altar the Rubicon of health and happiness for her is crossed forever. She is transformed from a sweet, innocent girl to a loathsome creature before the honeymoon is passed, "and her foul disease," as Dr. Howard Kelly of Baltimore so graphically put it, "makes her innocent wifehood a source of pain and misery, often rendering motherhood impossible; or makes the child, if indeed one ever sees the light, a wizened monster, more fit for the grave than for the sweet happy human relationship."

Following these revelations, several states demanded that the nitrate of silver solution should be used in the eyes of all newborn babies. Illinois then placed upon its statutes the following law: "Should any mid-wife or nurse having charge of an infant in this state notice that one or both eyes of such infant are inflamed or reddened at any time within two weeks after its birth, it should be the duty of such mid-wife or nurse having charge of such infant to report the fact in writing within six hours to the health officer or some legally qualified practitioner of medicine of the city, town or district in which the parents of the infant reside."

Some time later a bill was placed before the legislature of Kansas providing for the free distribution of nitrate of silver drops to all physicians and midwives within the borders of the state. The bill passed the lower house after much heated discussion and was carried to the Senate. Here the senators of that great commonwealth killed it, thus commemorating themselves as stupendous paragons of stupidity, a stupidity destined to rob hundreds of children of their right to vision.

Maud Glasgow and Her Crusade Against Venereal Disease in America

Despite this reversal of opinion in Kansas, the fight against the blinding of children originated by Credé apparently was about won. It remained only for the energetic work of Dr. Maud Glasgow of New York City to electrify the world. Before an international congress looking to the welfare of the young infant, Dr. Glasgow declared, "Influenced by education the world will come to recognize that a sexual intemperance which murders infants born and unborn, which destroys the procreative capacity in both sexes, which breaks up homes, which leads to divorce, which destroys efficiency, and shortens the expectation of life, cannot be tolerated." These words immediately became a slogan with her co-workers and before many weeks had encircled the world. There were already in this country a large number of societies which had been organized with a view to correcting this crime against the newborn child. At about this time the American Federation of Sex Hygiene presented resolutions to the House of Delegates of the American Medical Association in behalf of the helpless child. These resolutions were drawn up not because a controversy existed among the medical profession, but for the express purpose of removing from young men's minds the long-harbored belief that sexual indulgence for the unmarried male was necessary to health. "It was from the beginning," says Dr. Maud Glasgow, "routed in injustice and founded on male domination. It is the asserted will of the slave owner and cannot stand in an age of growing recognition of equal rights."

The moral fiber of the nation has been improved since women have enjoyed the franchise. From the efforts of a number of Chicago women who demanded that children of ten and twelve should not be locked up with hardened criminals was born the juvenile court. Again women had begun at the beginning. Now juvenile courts all over the country are keeping children out of the jails, the greatest vice schools to be found.

The children's playground movement is essentially a woman's movement. From every city of any size in the country the playgrounds are taking dirty, stunted children out of squalid streets and alleys, where they become veritable prodigies in crime and vice, and are teaching them how to play wholesomely.

Women have always been more proficient than men in handling questions of a moral nature which have a direct relation to juvenile delinquency. As an illustration, a number of women in New York City had introduced before the New York State Legislature a bill known as the Mercantile Employers' Bill. This bill was intended to regulate the employment of women and children in the mercantile establishments throughout the state. The bill passed the Assembly, but when it reached the Senate this body appointed the "Rheinhard Commission" to investigate conditions among women and children in New York City. The commission reported to the Senate that they had found many children of eleven and twelve years of age at wrapping tables and cash desks. They unearthed a system of fines in a number of stores, which in many cases took away the amount of a girl's weekly earnings. Now what did such a state of affairs amount to in the case of the underpaid working girl of a great city with her rent unpaid? Simply that she, in many instances, had to sell herself or be put out in the street. This bill finally passed the Senate, and it stands today as the greatest factor in the state of New York for protecting women from venereal disease.

The influence of women in civic, economic, and moral affairs which regulate the delinquency of the young girl and thus govern venereal disease, has had its full value only since women have enjoyed equal political rights. That the moral tone of several foreign countries has improved since women were granted the right to vote is suggested by the establishment of hospitals in Finland and Sweden for the treatment of venereal diseases.

Carl Franz Credé, working in the Charity Hospital at Leipzig before the time of women's suffrage, could never have dreamed of the far-reaching social effects of his discovery of the method of preventing gonorrheal blindness in children.

29.

Semmelweis and the Conquest of Childbed Fever

For hundreds of years superstition distorted the sentiment which is now associated with the function of motherhood. Labor during this period was but the primeval curse resting upon woman with a heavy hand. The prospective mother, it was believed, was about to give the world a new creature cursed with original sin, and to afford her relief from pain at such a time would be to thwart the designs of Providence itself.

Looking down on the now beautiful Princes Street of Edinburgh, Scotland, is Castle Hill. Here in 1591 a crime was committed which illustrates the old-time psychology. Up this hill, one bleak morning, was forcibly dragged Eufame MacLayne, a lady of rank and refinement. A few minutes before, she had clung desperately to her twin babies, but these had been torn from her by the crown bailiff. At the summit a stake had been driven in the ground and around it wood had been piled. As she knelt, chains were wrapped around her body and in less than an hour ashes was all that remained of Eufame MacLayne. This execution was not the result of mob violence, for the victim had been tried by due process of law and had been convicted. Evidence was advanced which proved that she had employed a midwife, "one Agnes Sampson to administer unto her a certain medicine for the relief of pain in childbirth contrary to divine law and in contempt of the crown."

Eufame MacLayne's fate had been sealed by precedent. Convention had made it an insult to the Deity to assist a woman in labor. This was a crime which always drew the extreme penalty in medieval Europe. In 1521 Viethes, a Hamburg physician, was arrested for attempting to mitigate the pains of labor. By nature Viethes was generous and kind, and his patient, a frail woman, begged for relief. Her entreaties reached the heart of this good man and he complied with her request. Immediately the wheels of the law began to turn and a conviction was soon obtained for the crown. A few weeks later an unusual light shone one night over Hamburg. They were burning Dr. Viethes.

For thousands of years antagonism to new ideas choked every independent thought, barred all scientific progress, and made of the ages past one long night of heartache and suffering. The most hurtful habit of the human mind is this tendency to cling to traditions which have withstood the moss, rust, and decay of the past. We seem to hold to our old thoughts with a veneration which is as infallible as it is inexplicable. This unhappy mental faculty makes the mind inaccessible to plain reason and leads towards intolerance.

But did not this spirit die with the Middle Ages, you ask? Well, not just that. Peter Cooper, the first man to dream of a free school system, was vilified and denounced as an anarchist. William Morris was arrested for advocating that property should be shared equally between capital and labor, and it will be remembered further that William Morris represented not labor, but capital. Walt Whitman was denounced for straying away from the beaten paths of thought and saw his *Leaves of Grass* excluded from the mails. Simpson, who first used chloroform in obstetrics, was ostracised; Thoreau was imprisoned for certain original ideas regarding taxation; and Theodore Parker was excluded from his church for taking too active an interest in oppressed humanity. The transcendental experiment at Brook Farm entered into by Emerson, Hawthorne, Charles Dana, and George

William Curtis met with public censure. Had it occurred a few years earlier, its originators would have been confronted with the fate of many of those who in the past ventured into new fields.

One afternoon in 1845 Ignatz Philipp Semmelweis, a young Hungarian physician, was on his way to Vienna to take up the advanced study of obstetrics. This youth was destined to be the instrument by which much of the traditional rubbish relative to obstetrics was to be cleared away. In its place was to be put one of the greatest single achievements of modern medicine.

Poverty had come to Semmelweis as a family inheritance. This was a distinct advantage, for it sharpened his wits and increased his diligence. Poverty stimulates patience and perseverence and often makes success inevitable. Thousands of men, by virtue of this rather inconvenient asset, have attained their goal—a goal that affluence would have put forever beyond their reach. Very few kronen were in the pocket of young Semmelweis that day in his stuffy third-class compartment, but he carried with him a clear head, a generous heart, and above all, a vision; he was to be of some service to the world.

At the Allgemeines Krankenhaus, Semmelweis proved to be an earnest student, and before his second month had passed we find him first assistant to Skoda and Rokitansky. Favored by nature with a happy faculty of keeping his eyes open, he could not long fail to notice the deplorable unsanitary condition of his ward. No better breeding places could have been found for surgical sepsis than were provided, at this time, by the great hospital at Vienna. New cases were frequently put into the unchanged beds of patients who had died from disease. Dressings from wounds were dropped upon the floors or were kicked out of sight under beds and tables, and soiled linen was thrown about promiscuously for the ward scullion to remove at her convenience. Unscreened windows gave admission to swarms of flies, and the general atmosphere of the place was one of untidiness and filth.

The first ward in which Semmelweis worked was notorious for its mortality in puerperal cases. In a very few days every tenth child born in this ward was left motherless. Every day the tinkling of the little chapel bell announced that the deadly childbed fever had done its work. Semmelweis observed these cases with keen interest and pondered, with a tinge of melancholy, over the apparently hopeless clinical picture which they presented. The patient entered the ward in good health, hopeful, and nerved for the ordeal. Labor progressed and the child was born. The mother slept, or lay awake, picturing the future of the young baby nestling at her breast. Suddenly she became chilly, her teeth chattered, and a sense of distress presented itself in the uterine region and increased until the pain became unbearable. Soon she was compelled to lie upon her back with her knees drawn up to relieve a rigid abdomen. The hopefulness disappeared, for already she had read the verdict in the faces of her attendants. Her pain subsided but her nails were blue and her pulse had become thready. An attendant leaning over her detected upon her breath a septic odor like that of new-mown hay. Gradually she sank, soon someone carried an orphan child away from the first ward, and again the tolling chapel bell told of an obstetrical failure.

At this time a great many theories were current regarding the etiology of this disease. It was attributed by some to excessive modesty occasioned by being confined in the presence of men, by others to bad ventilation, to bad water, to improper food, and to disordered psychic states. By the older and more devout physicians it was thought to be the result of the Edenic curse, as evidenced by the writings of Meigs of Philadelphia, one of the greatest obstetricians of his time, who attributed the mortality in puerperal cases to the "justification of Providence; a judgment instituted to remind us of the sin committed by the mother of the race."

Semmelweis, with his depression deepening, because of the apparent hopelessness of the situation, sought to institute some form of treatment to reduce the death rate in his ward, only to be told bluntly that childbed fever, if not providential, was at least an implacable decree of nature that would never be made to respond to medical treatment.

Not to be lulled into apathy by the current opinions relative to the etiology, pathology, and treatment of the disease, Semmelweis applied for permission to perform autopsies upon his fatal cases. Midnight often found him in the deadhouse dissecting, observing, pondering. The pelvis and abdomen of each deceased patient examined presented evidence of a general peritonitis. The uterus was often bathed in pus, the *dépôt laiteux* or milky deposit, as it was called, a fluid believed by the old authors to be carried from the mammary glands to the womb by metastasis. And here it is interesting to remember that our term "milk leg" arose with this erroneous idea that in certain cases the milk may be vicariously carried throughout the body and may find lodgment in the legs.

Semmelweis continued to perform his post-mortems, but the pictures presented did little more than add to his bewilderment; the real cause of this mortality escaped him entirely. One day while overworked, nervous, and discouraged, he left the hospital for Venice, determining to give up for all times his investigations relative to the illusive cause of puerperal fever. Returning to Vienna a few weeks later, he found his colleagues beginning an autopsy on the body of Kolletschka, a fellow doctor who had just died from septicemia as the result of a wound received in the dissecting room. As he stood over the body of his former associate and heard the history of the case recited, Semmelweis noticed that the pathologic picture was identical with those of his fatal puerpera of the first ward. Immediately he began to suspect that these too might have been due to infection carried to the mother from the dissecting room. He remembered that in the first ward the mortality was high and the students came there daily after finishing their dissections and made examinations of the women with hands bearing all sorts of contamination from the deadhouse. Reasoning along these lines, he remembered that in the second ward the mortality was low. This ward was reserved for the instruction of midwives who made no dissections. Were not the students from the deadhouse poisoning the women in his ward and were not these women dying of septicemia?

Semmelweis immediately adopted the expedient of having all his students wash their hands with a solution of chloride of calcium. In the next year the mortality of the first clinic sank from 9.99 per cent to 3.6 per cent. This was sufficient argument to transform a theory into a fact; it made the evidence complete.

As soon as Semmelweis announced his discovery, orthodox obstetricians immediately opposed his innovation and denounced him. This was inevitable and its effect was salutary. Opposition always spurs to greater effort and very few men have ever gained their objective without it. In this case it provided the stimulation necessary to the preparation of his book, *The Cause, Concept, and Prophylaxis of Puerperal Fever,* a work which one day was to revolutionize the science of obstetrics.

Semmelweis' book was written while he was professor of obstetrics at the University of Budapest and was published in 1861. By a strange coincidence Oliver Wendell Holmes at about the same time called attention to the contagiousness of puerperal fever in an essay "On the Contagiousness of Childbed Fever," but his efforts had ended with this essay, which was unsupported by clinical evidence. It remained for Semmelweis to supply the proof. *The Cause, Concept, and Prophylaxis of Puerperal Fever* was not well received. As usual it interfered with the conventional methods then in vogue and disturbed traditional ideas. Soon the initial intolerance to Semmelweis and his contagion theory assumed the proportions of a persecution. In Austria he was bitterly attacked by Scanzoni and Carl Braun, and leading obstetricians throughout the world vied with each other in abusing, ridiculing, and denouncing him and characterizing his theory as an absurd imposition. The antagonism to the sepsis theory is well set forth by the following extracts from the textbook of Charles D. Meigs, the noted Philadelphia obstetrician.

"I prefer to attribute them (cases of puerperal sepsis) to accident or Providence of which I can form a conception," says Meigs, "rather than to a contagion of which I cannot form any clear idea, at least as to this particular malady. . . .

"In a crowded lying-in hospital there are many servants and pupils, and physicians and other officers. There are also many unmarried women, as, for example, the sisters of Charity, who wait on the sick. Often times the lying-in wards are nigh to fever wards or wards for the wounded. How is it that this contagion, which destroys like the most violent poison even in the duration of only eight hours—how is it I ask that other human beings, females and males, are never even suspected to be in danger? .... I repeat, that the epidemic cause of childbed fever cannot affect other than women pregnant or lying-in; it must therefore be a feeble cause—else it would produce disease in unmarried women and girls as well as males."

The stigma which his work created goaded Semmelweis to reply in "Open Letters to Sundry Professors of Obstetrics." In these letters vituperation was repaid with denunciation. He charged that obstetricians, by following the old and dirty methods, were guilty of the crime of murder, and entreated the medical profession no longer to submit women to execution to uphold an outworn theory.

During the early part of 1865 violent controversy played havoc with the sensitive nature of Semmelweis. Brooding over the injustice of the attacks upon him, he became insane. Physical disease set in, and one night in November he died, a martyr to the cause to which he had devoted his life.

The seed sown by Semmelweis lay for years on fallow ground. But it began to take root with Pasteur's discovery of the role played by microorganisms in the production of fermentation. From a knowledge of fermentation to the study of putrefaction in wounds was only a step and soon this step was taken by the immortal surgeon, Joseph Lister. When Lister saw his principles of antiseptic surgery accepted by the scientific world, he magnanimously proclaimed Semmelweis as his forerunner. Thus was the bitter controversy ended.

In Budapest rises a monument to the memory of the father of scientific obstetrics, erected by the women of the world as a token of their devotion and gratitude, and nearby under a mossy slab rests the body of the great obstetrician. To this spot pilgrims from many lands have gone and have poured out their adulation over his tomb, without thinking, perhaps, how much a single sentence of this appreciation would have meant to the great and tender man before death, which rights all wrongs and heals all heartaches, laid upon him its heavy hand.

30.

The Development of Dentistry

Primitive dentistry, so far as we know, was practiced first by the neolithic men of Europe and northern Africa. Men of this New Stone Age seldom had caries in the structure of the teeth, this fact applying to the young as well as to those of the more advanced years. All, however, appear to have been victims of alveolar (jaw) abscesses, and the pain these infections occasioned called for removal of their aching teeth. These they were relieved of by the primitive dentist, who applied to the apex of the tooth a spearhead or arrowhead and, with a stone fragment, this improvised punch was given a light tap which drove the tooth sidewise into the mouth. The reason for our belief in this kind of extraction is that there is found a similar pattern to all teeth thus removed. An observation of the inner walls of the jaws where teeth are seen to be missing usually reveals a necrosis of bone at the base of the tooth, and the inner wall of the jaw opposite the removed tooth shows that it had invariably been pushed inward as a result of this crude type of surgery. The destruction of the lingual or inner wall of the jaw opposite the removed tooth is so uniform a condition that it points at once to the probability of this method of extraction. Coming down to later prehistoric times, we find that extracted teeth had been lifted out by probelike instruments, examples of which are on display in the various museums of Europe and Egypt. This is indicated by the various degrees of injury seen in the bony structures surrounding the teeth when these skulls were found, which, it may be noted, all bear a striking resemblance to each other. This is particularly the case in skulls taken from the ancient Etruscan ruins and tumuli in various parts of Italy, in which many fine specimens have been found of bronze and silver work as well as of surgical instruments. The Etruscans, whose power reached its height in the sixth century B.C., buried their dead in these carefully prepared receptacles. Though their language is lost to us, we can now, by these resurrected instruments and appliances, determine the attention which they gave to their sick and ailing.

It is a singular fact that instruments of much the same design as those found in Etruscan burial places near Rome are to be seen in the Athens Museum, and anthropologists give as the reason for this that during Homeric times, before they migrated to Italy, the Etruscans were an adjoining race to the Greeks in Asia Minor. Both the Homeric Greek and the Etruscan were skilled in silver carving, and their surgical instruments and objects of craftsmanship are surprisingly alike. Both peoples extracted teeth by pushing under the ailing member a sharp bronze elevator with a projection on one side which acted as a fulcrum in elevating the tooth.

During medieval times in Europe dentistry had not yet made much progress, consisting solely of extracting teeth. This operation was in the hands of itinerants who not only removed teeth but perpetrated all manner of impostures upon the unsuspecting public, such as claiming to extract stones from the scalps of their patients as a cure for epilepsy and migraine.

Later Dentistry

A century and a quarter ago the situation of the world in relation to the mouth and teeth was not calculated to advance the profession of dentistry as we now know it. It may be said that before the year 1839 the dentists of the United States received their training only at the hands of other dentists who acted as preceptors, and in European countries little thought was given to the preparation of young men for the profession of dentistry. Until this time, the medical colleges of the United States, as of all countries, failed to see the importance of caring for diseased conditions of the mouth and teeth. Attempts had been made to have chairs established in the various medical colleges of the country for the purpose of providing a foundation not only for the study of the teeth but also of the mechanical means of improving conditions of the mouth. These all ended in failure because the colleges could not see the importance of such a step. In Baltimore Dr. Horace Hayden, after much opposition, during the years of 1837-38 succeeded in giving a course of dental instruction to the students of the University of Maryland, and in 1839, finding so little co-operation among the medical profession, Hayden established the Baltimore College of Dental Surgery. This was the first dental school to be founded in the world, and it proved to be such a popular venture that in 1845 the Ohio College of Dentistry was founded in Cincinnati, this being followed in Philadelphia in 1856 by the establishment of the Pennsylvania College of Dental Surgery and, in 1863, the Philadelphia Dental College. Harvard College, seeing the success of these first schools of dentistry, soon after this time established in Boston its own school, the Harvard Dental College.

Several of the states in 1868 passed laws regarding registration in dentistry as a requisite to taking up the practice of the dental profession, but not until 1900 did all the states require a license of those who wished to practice dentistry. It will be seen by this that the United States gave origin to the profession of dentistry as we now know it, and this lead of American dentists has not lost any ground since it was first acquired, as nearly all countries in the world now have dentists of American training who are leaders in this profession. At this time there are few dentists in the United States who have not had at least one year in preliminary college work and three years devoted to practical study and to training on the various steps of mechanical dentistry. The dental courses have now been extended to four years in most of the better schools.

Because of the great advance made in treatment of diseases of the mouth and teeth, the United States may also be regarded as the founder of the science of oral hygiene as an important department of the profession of dentistry.

31.

Joseph Lister and Antiseptic Surgery

Joseph Lister is mentioned by medical historians as one of the great trio of surgeons (Hunter, Simpson, and Lister) born in the British Isles, who in a few years carried around the world the fame of Great Britain as the mother of surgery. Lister was a member of the Society of Friends, a sect formerly despised, to which William Penn also had belonged and which for a century or more had met with severe persecution in England. Lister got his early education in one of the schools of the Quakers. His religion, however, may be viewed as having been the groundwork for his later fame. The success he acquired, he later vowed to his associates, was largely due to the fact that he had been guided throughout his career by the "inner light." To his calumniators he had never replied unless "moved by the spirit," which he felt had held him in sway by "nonresistance," a recognized attribute of all Quakers. These restrictions on the human desire to reply to all adversaries in kind no doubt carried him through many troubled periods when his new methods of surgery were receiving criticism and often contempt throughout the scientific world.

During the early years of Joseph Lister's residence in Edinburgh the Crimean War was in progress. The frightful effect seen in soldiers who had lost their lives in actual combat, to say nothing of the tremendous number of those who had been destroyed by surgical diseases after the fighting was over, was exercising both surgeons and laymen. The hospitals of Europe were filled with patients who had taken part in the disastrous battles of their time. This was an incentive for noncombatants to hope to find some way in which these terrible results of warfare, as seen by them in the hospitals, could be mitigated. Nothing thus far had come of their efforts, and a fatalism gradually grew up during this period among the surgeons of Europe, to the effect that such results of warfare were permitted by Providence. This belief, resulting from passages in the Scriptures which, it was observed, were not followed by messages prophetic of improvement in warfare in the future, filled the minds of all with gloom. Lister, however, felt dissent at these conclusions and fully believed that some method could be arrived at which would save those suffering from deadly compound fractures and which would protect wounds of the arms and legs from the then almost certain complication of hospital gangrene, a condition which in nearly all instances meant the patient's death, either soon after the injury or, more often, following a lingering illness.

Sir Hector C. Cameron, a former pupil of Lister in Edinburgh in a comment on this trying period in Lister's life, said that "the grief and mental worry arising from such experiences, often repeated, produced in Lister's mind a discontent with things as they were and thus seemed to many of us . . . in strange contrast to the resignation with which some of his colleagues viewed similar experiences."

When Joseph Lister came upon the surgical scene and announced to his colleagues that a leg with a compound fracture had healed completely without having to submit the patient to the usual amputation to save his life from gangrene, all those who did not already know of this incident were astonished. In all the terrible wars of Europe, such legs had become infected from without and had to be removed. This operation, while successful in a majority of instances, under the old methods of treatment often served to end the patient's life. It is not a wonder that Lister's auditors were skeptical. At that time nothing was known of aseptic surgery, which means methods to keep germs out of wounds. The best operating rooms throughout Europe and America were equipped with stands on which the surgeon hung his operating cloak after the operation was done. This cloak was more or less standard equipment, and onto its broad lapels the surgeon placed his needles and ligatures which were to be used in the operation. The hospitals also provided a rack upon which the instruments which had been used in a former operation could be flushed with water to remove the blood. Here they remained until they became dry, and then a ward scullion carefully polished them. Instruments were expensive, and he knew it was his duty to prevent rusting. The polishing was accomplished by the use of rags brought from the wards. Often these were torn and soiled sheets and pillowcases taken from beds upon which patients had died. The operation of cleaning taken care of, the instruments, bright and shiny but laden with germs, were ready to be used in the next operation.

It had occurred to no one at the time that these same instruments to be used on the next case were more deadly to the life of the patient than was the disease which the surgeon was to attempt to cure. The surgeon and his associates, when no pus cavities were to be opened or when no large spurting vessels were to be severed and tied off or sealed with red-hot irons, often dispensed with the surgeon's cloak entirely, its primary purpose being to protect the surgeon's clothing from stains. This is evidenced by the vast number of paintings scattered throughout the art galleries in Europe and America which depict the surgeon working in his street clothes. Such a scene is also represented in a daguerreotype taken in the Massachusetts General Hospital, representing what was then thought to be the first operation done under ether anesthesia. Here the surgeon, Dr. John Warren, and his assistants and the various interested onlookers are all seen wearing the elongated street coats of the period. In a painting of Lister doing his first operation under a spray of carbolic acid, the artist represents him as wearing street clothes. The expectant surgeons and attendants are depicted also as wearing everyday attire. Climbing out of a rut which robbed thousands of infected patients of their lives has been a slow and painful process even to those who may have taken part in it.

Lister Applies Carbolic-Acid Spray to Wounds and Originates Antiseptic Surgery

The idea of using a carbolic-acid spray was forced upon Lister because of the great number of patients who died in the Glasgow hospital where he worked. These deaths, he had become to suspect, came from infection from without. At first it was his opinion that life destroyers responsible for these disastrous results were swarming in the air. The use of carbolic-acid spray which he adopted at this time was originated with the intent of destroying this menace to human life. There is an old English expression that ideas come out of the atmosphere, but no chance guided Lister to the great idea which has since saved millions of lives and entirely revolutionized surgery. It was a direct result of sound reasoning. A colleague, while consulting him, mentioned the fact that in his home town of Carlisle the formerly stinking atmosphere of the place had been entirely cleared up by a command of the city council that a solution of carbolic acid be used in the privies and cesspools. It immediately occurred to Lister that germs had caused the odors in Carlisle and that these had been in the air. Being familiar with Pasteur's work on fermentation and reasoning over the thought which Pasteur had expressed in his paper, "Spontaneous Germination," in 1862, he determined to use carbolic acid as a spray in the air surrounding the operating table of his patients. On August 12, 1865, in a case of compound fracture, he proceeded to spray the fracture as well as the air in his operating room with a weak solution of phenol (carbolic acid), and it did not take him long to decide from the excellence of his results in this case that his method was effective. He termed this new procedure "antiseptic surgery." In his first article relative to this subject, published in 1867, he called attention to his method, the title of his paper being "On the Antiseptic Principle in the Practice of Surgery." Immediately he was covered with a cloud of ridicule and scorn by his contemporaries which would have crushed a weaker man, and here his religious training stood him well in hand, for realizing that "a soft answer turneth away wrath," he in reply took the pains to explain to his critics that his results were not contrary to nature. His accusers were still relentless, but, regardless of this, he proceeded with his studies uncomplainingly and continued to do antiseptic surgery.

For his dressings Lister now began to use oiled silk but soon adopted instead a porous gauze. As a spray he experimented with cyanide of mercury and zinc and found these as effective and much less caustic than the carbolic acid. He now applied his principle of antiseptic surgery to excision of the leg at the knee joint, the result of which was published in 1878, to operations on the breast, published in 1881, to fractures of the patella (kneecap), published in 1883, and later to all manner of surgical conditions with unusually favorable results.

Since the days of Lister antiseptic surgery "against infection from the air" has given way to aseptic surgery, a method of preventing sepsis from the surgeon's hands, clothing, and equipment from getting into wounds. The principle first originated by Lister, that sepsis coming from without could be prevented by the surgeon, has stood the test of time and has now entirely revolutionized surgery everywhere.

Getting tired of the abuse heaped upon him in Glasgow, Lister removed to London and accepted the chair of surgery in King's College, where the former vindictive atmosphere of that institution seems to have entirely cleared away as the fame of his methods became known and later were adopted by all surgeons. Here he worked for the remainder of his life.

Lister is to be remembered as a man who always proceeded carefully in the operating room and one who was ever free from any form of ostentation, which his Quaker religion forbade. However, he was anxious to give merit where merit was due and this he did wholeheartedly. At a Louis Pasteur jubilee in 1892 Lister paid a lasting tribute to this great scientist and gladly accorded to him the part he had played in guiding his early surgical steps into more fruitful channels. F. H. Garrison, the leading medical historian of English-speaking countries, said of him in 1914, "The character of Lister was one of rare nobility. As the Quaker is the puritan transposed into a softer and more grateful key, so his nature had these elements of sweetness which proverbially can come out of strength . . . and no praise of him is more touching than that of the Scottish clergyman who standing at his bier delivered one of the greatest orations ever to be directed to the activities of any man of medicine, as seen by this conclusion. 'That such a man endowed with God's gift of genius should rise to lofty heights and achieve great things was inevitable.'"

Lister before his death was made a peer by the British Crown and thus goes down in history as Baron Lister. This was the greatest honor which could be bestowed upon him by his country. From his patients, it was observed, he had always received friendship, and one such patient, the poet Henley, has given us the following lines in his memory:

> His brow is large and placid and his eye
> Is deep and bright with steady looks that still.
> Soft lines of tranquil thought his face fulfill—
> His face at once benign and proud and shy. . . .
> If envy scout, if ignorance deny
> His faultless patience, his unyielding will,
> Beautiful gentleness and splendid skill
> Innumerable gratitudes reply.

32.

Fame of the Vienna School

The Vienna School became what it was only because of the startling scientific innovations which sprang into being in Vienna and which served to carry the name of these new achievements around the world. It will be seen then that the Vienna School was not an organized institution but rather it represented a general recognition of the scientists of Vienna who brought into being so many medical and surgical accomplishments. That this great educational center had succeeded in thus establishing itself was a fact recognized for more than three centuries, and Vienna continued to maintain its standard of excellence during a greater part of these years, or until a period when great social and political upheavals had almost shut off the areas from which Vienna's student bodies had been garnered. The former pupils of the Vienna School were now scattered over all the scientific world and so emulated their great teachers that the loss of Vienna as the leading world medical center was to a degree compensated for by the many teaching centers established elsewhere, particularly in England and the United States. Besides a large number of gifted workers who helped to make Vienna great as a medical center, three noted though self-effacing teachers, like the unknown architects of some of the great cathedrals of Europe, were content to give their lives in service with no thought of reward. These men were Josef Hyrtl, Carl Ludwig, and Theodor Billroth.

Josef Hyrtl

One of the great names to add favor to the Vienna School was that of Josef Hyrtl. This illustrious teacher of anatomy is considered to be the most persistent investigator on the subject of regional and topographical anatomy since the days of Andreas Vesalius. He was educated at the University of Prague and at the age of twenty-six became professor of anatomy at this institution. He removed to Vienna in 1844, where he continued until shortly before his death to be one of the most gifted teachers on any scientific subject to be found in all of Europe. It is said that his fame as a teacher drew such a large number of students from all over the world that Vienna, during his lifetime, became the chief rendezvous of young students of all nations who sought to excel as surgeons or as teachers of anatomy. In 1847 Hyrtl published his first work on topographical anatomy, and in 1860 his *Manual Guide for Dissection* was given to the world. This work contained many new and novel features, including models of the human ear which are still considered unsurpassed in excellence. According to Garrison, the recognized dean of medical history, he "was the first to demonstrate the 'blood' circulation of the suprarenal capsule and the origin of the coronary arteries and he made a large collection of hearts devoid of blood supply."

Hyrtl resigned from the University of Vienna in 1874 in order, as he said, to avoid the embarrassment of being pensioned, as he would have been at the age of seventy. He retired to his country home, where he wrote three volumes, one on the subject of Hebraic terminology and another on Arabic anatomic terminology, as well as a work on German anatomical expressions. This caused him to be looked upon as the greatest medical author of the century.

His last years were not happy ones, as it is said these years were clouded by attacks of pessimism and despondency. He died in 1894.

Carl Ludwig

One of the most famous leaders of the Vienna group was Carl Ludwig. Born in Witzenhausen, Hesse, in 1816, Ludwig became a professor of anatomy in Marburg, his alma mater, soon after graduating in 1840, but later he moved to Zurich and established a practice. In 1849 he was attracted to Vienna, where he accepted the chair of physiology and zoology. It is said of him by Garrison that he "was probably the greatest teacher of physiology who ever lived." His pupils came from all countries, and nearly all the great physiology teachers of the world at the time of his death had been trained by him. Strange to say, most of the important discoveries he made were published under the names of his pupils. His object in this was to leave behind him at his death investigators in physiology who would be better fitted to carry out his work by having thus prepared and presented their own subjects in their own way, but it is noteworthy that their work was always carefully gone over by Ludwig before it was sent to the Saxon Academy of Science or other like scientific institutions, where much of Ludwig's work is still on record. These student essays, when reviewed after his death, were seen to cover the whole field of physiology except that of the physiology of the brain, a subject he considered to be the most important and difficult and, therefore, had left it for the last. But Ludwig lost his health about this time, and returned to Leipzig where he died with his contemplated work unfinished. Ludwig probably did as much as any other of his colleagues to establish the name of Vienna as a great medical and surgical center. He, more than any other teacher who ever lived, laid the groundwork of the science of physiology as it is understood and taught today. Ludwig died in 1895.

Theodor Billroth

Of the large number of surgeons who left their imprint on the work done in Vienna in the latter part of the nineteenth century none stands out more clearly than Theodor Billroth. He will always be remembered as the European pioneer of abdominal surgery, and though he never saw Ephraim McDowell, his great American predecessor who first invaded with success the closed cavities of the body, he was guided by his example until his death.

Following the example of Lord Lister, Billroth gave much attention to the treatment of wounds before he launched on a career of visceral surgery. Returning from Berlin to Vienna in 1867, he gave his almost complete attention to diseases of the esophagus and larynx, and in 1873 he was the first surgeon to successfully excise the complete larynx. The previous year he had made an excision of the esophagus, the patient recovering. This encouraged him to perform during the next several years a large number of resections of the stomach and intestines in cases of cancer, with such a high degree of success that this type of surgery was taken up by British and American surgeons who further developed the technique and paved the way for gastrointestinal surgery as it is done today. Billroth left to the world a work on surgical pathology and therapeutics which is still considered to be a classic.

Billroth was a teacher of note, and during the last years of his life he taught many surgeons who later became famous in the technique of his end-to-end anastomosis, and thus paved the way for such great surgeons as John B. Murphy of Chicago, renowned for his "Murphy's Button." Billroth was a man of charming personality who endeared himself to his students to such a degree that soon after his death in 1894 money was raised by subscription, chiefly by his ex-students, for the erection of a monument which stands on the grounds of the Allgemeines Krankenhaus in Vienna in commemoration of this great discoverer of many surgical techniques.

The later Vienna school continued to exert its influence over foreign medicine until the beginning of the present century. This is notably exemplified in the work of Robert Baroney, the first to suspect and to demonstrate the truth of the fact that a direct relationship exists between the labyrinth of the ear and human equilibrium, and today there is not an aviation school in existence that does not profit by what that modest investigator did. In Vienna, Killian succeeded in suspending a patient in order to look down his homemade bronchoscope. He thus became the first to view in a living human being the bifurcation of the bronchial trachea into the right and left bronchi. In Vienna for over half a century worked Prof. Adam Politzer. He it was who first determined that much of the world's deafness was due to the lack of ventilation of the middle-ear cavity and discovered a method of equalizing intertympanic air, thus doing more for the deaf than anyone had ever done before and thereby laying the foundation upon which has been built otology as it is practiced today. It was also in this great center that Prof. Ernst Fuchs carried on his studies. He was the co-discoverer of the part played by uveal pigment in the production of sympathetic ophthalmitis. I as a young man knew all of these innovators, and that fact has served as a valuable inspiration to me through a long life of medical practice.

Coming down to the present, there now is associated with the teaching staff of the University of Vienna one who it is no figure of speech to refer to as belonging not to Vienna alone nor to Austria, for Prof. Hans Finsterer is now claimed by the entire world as one who possibly has done as much to solve nature's secrets of the upper abdomen as anyone now living, and last but never least, are Professors Felix Mandel and Schönbauer, who today head the list in great achievements and whose work is known in every country in the world.

33.

Walter Reed and W. C. Gorgas and the Control of Yellow Fever and Malaria

Yellow fever had been prevalent in the South and along the Atlantic seaboard for over one hundred years before Walter Reed, who discovered its cause, was born. It appeared every summer. It had broken out as far north as Portland, Maine. Portsmouth, New Hampshire, also had the disease, as did Boston, Providence, and New Haven. But in this latitude the deaths had been fewer. Further south, in Baltimore, Charleston, and Savannah the disease occurred sporadically every year. In 1793 yellow fever broke out in Philadelphia and New York. In Philadelphia in that year it killed more than 4,000 out of a population of 56,000. In 1798 it killed 3,500 more in Philadelphia. In New York in 1795 it killed 732 people. It recurred in New York in 1798, when 2,086 died of it, and again in 1803, when 606 residents succumbed to its ravages. But in New Orleans the disease was at its worst and threatened to depopulate the city.

Benjamin Rush with his co-workers, Drs. Currie and Pinkhard, had struggled bravely against the disease, and although their efforts were directed at times into wrong channels they at least fought the idea that yellow fever could be carried by fomites, or articles used by former yellow-fever patients, from one city to another. It remained for Walter Reed to establish the fact forever that, in this particular at least, the contentions of our American pioneer physicians of a century before were correct.

But Walter Reed had this in his favor in arriving at the true cause of yellow fever: During his studies of this disease Dr. Reed had the results of the work of Dr. Ronald Ross of the Indian Health Service, who had established that malaria could be transmitted to the domestic chicken by the bite of a mosquito. Walter Reed also had another advantage over all others who had studied yellow fever. He had behind him the authority of the United States Army.

Yellow fever was then sporadic among the inhabitants of Cuba, and a number of the personnel of the United States Army had already come down with the disease. Reed had selected an ideal site for his experiments into the cause of yellow fever. An extract from Reed's medical record, August 10, 1901, contains the following paragraph: "Any location selected, provided it should be one mile from such a centre of infection and surrounded by proper safeguards, would be just as free from the occurrence of yellow fever as if it were located ten miles from such a town. My own experience on the Island of Cuba had already taught me that yellow fever could be easily kept out of a military garrison, although prevailing in epidemic form in a town less than one mile distant. For this reason it was not considered advisable to establish our experimental sanitary station at a greater distance than one mile from Quemados, Cuba. Thus Camp Lazear could easily be reached by the members of the Board and was conveniently located as regards its basis of supplies." "It was now proposed," he wrote at about this time, "to attempt the infection of non-immune individuals in three different ways, namely, first, by the bites of mosquitoes which had previously bitten cases of yellow fever; second, by the injection of blood taken during the early stages from the general circulation of those suffering the disease; and third, by exposure to the most intimate contact with fomites." The first experiment was conducted upon the person of an army private by the name of John R. Kissinger, of Ohio, who courageously volunteered for the experiment, as well as another volunteer, John J. Moran, also of Ohio. On December 5, five mosquitoes were selected, two of which had bitten a yellow-fever patient fifteen days before, one of which had bitten a yellow-fever patient nineteen days before, and two that had been contaminated in the same manner twenty-two days before. In a station thoroughly screened so that no contamination could come from the outside, Kissinger developed at the end of three days and nine and a half hours a well-developed case of yellow fever. During the following week four other cases had developed in a second army camp through inoculation by mosquitoes previously contaminated by yellow-fever patients. The mosquitoes in question were those of the *stegomyia fasciata,* and thus it was proven conclusively that this mosquito was the carrier of yellow fever.

In a frame house at Camp Lazear volunteers were enlisted for the experiment to determine whether or not fomites, such as articles of clothing and bedding which had been used by yellow-fever patients who had died of the disease, could carry the infection of yellow fever to others. This camp house was double-screened and similar to the one used in the first experiment, so that no mosquitoes could possibly enter from the outside. The volunteers slept and lived there during the period of the experiment. Reed next called for volunteers who were non-immune to occupy the camp. Three responded, and after a period of quarantine to dispel any possibility of their having obtained the disease in any other way, they were accepted for the experiment. After this the non-immunes for a period of five days not only slept on the mattresses upon which yellow-fever patients had died but actually wore the clothing that had been worn by these victims. In a room artificially heated to the temperature most favorable to the development of yellow fever, these non-immunes lived for five days, but none of them developed yellow fever. This and other series of experiments following the same careful technique were sufficient to prove to the world that the cause of yellow fever had been scientifically determined and that contagion was due to the stegomyia mosquito and could never be contracted by actual contact with the yellow-fever patient.

The fight on yellow fever has been more successful than that conducted to clear the world of malaria, chiefly because of the fact that the stegomyia mosquito is a domesticated insect that breeds in rain barrels around human habitations and is more easily destroyed than is the anopheles, the carrier of malaria, which breeds in cesspools, rivers, and small streams. But, as proven by Walter Reed and W. C. Gorgas, both are subject to easy extermination. Yellow fever and malaria, once the greatest destroyers of human lives in warm climates, are now little feared by those who understand them and who, by adopting proper scientific methods, are able to protect themselves.

Gorgas and His Fight to Control Malaria

When Dr. W. C. Gorgas went to the Canal Zone of Panama in May, 1905, he found a number of small cities and towns which, because of their swampy locations and the carelessness of their people, were the most unhealthful spots in the world. Stagnant pools of water lay in the streets of the towns and the yards of the inhabitants. Uncleanliness and disregard for the purity of the water supply were fixed habits. To make the situation more unfavorable, a distrust of the Americans, who appeared to be interfering with long-established customs of the inhabitants, was evident everywhere.

Gorgas had a complete knowledge of the sanitation failures of those who attempted years before to cut de Lesseps' canal across the Isthmus of Panama. He well understood that the tremendous mortality which ended in the ultimate failure of this project was largely due to the refusal of men to undertake work which almost inevitably meant death. He therefore was conscious of the fact that he must clean up the area and thus protect the workers, or disease, in the same manner as before, would take its grim toll, and the project would fail ingloriously.

In the particular locality in which the canal was to be cut

Gorgas realized that malaria was his greatest enemy. But as a student of epidemics and sanitation, he had the advantage, as did Walter Reed, of the conclusive findings which Dr. Ronald Ross had made in India. He knew that the anopheles mosquito caused malaria. Ronald Ross had also proven that malarial fever was due to minute organisms in the blood. While Ross should have credit for his discovery of the part the mosquito played in causing malaria, there can be no doubt that W. C. Gorgas' practical application of the theory that the anopheles mosquito carried malaria was to prove that the disease could be combatted and eradicated. For this Gorgas deserves full credit.

Gorgas began his fight on malaria by draining all the swamps infested by the anopheles mosquito over the entire area of the Canal Zone. In the first year he had cut two million feet of ditches. Along these ditches all the low places which harbored stagnant water and thus caused the breeding of mosquitoes were entirely filled in. The undergrowth which would prevent the sunlight from drying out the surface of the land was also cleared away. In addition to this he soon learned that weeds and grass sheltered mosquitoes, and within a year he was able to report to his chief that he had eradicated and burned 29,000,000 square yards of grass and weeds.

Farther in the interior, receptacles were set up on the margins of all streams, which continuously spread over the surfaces of the water, drop by drop, a thin mixture of crude and refined oils. This coating floated for miles with the streams, thus bathing with oil their surfaces and finding its way into all hidden crevices. The larvae of the mosquito must come up to the surface of the water to breathe, and in doing so on streams thus treated their breathing apparatus becomes filled with oil instead of oxygen. As soon as this occurs the process of breathing is arrested, the larvae fall to the floor of the stream and die, and soon the mosquito in such areas is eradicated.

Having accomplished the destruction of the mosquito in the rural areas, Gorgas now turned his attention to Panama City and

Colon. Here the drainage was not only bad but old cans, jugs, and other receptacles were found filled with water and laden with mosquito larvae. Serious objections were encountered by his workers in upsetting and removing such breeding places. To the most obstinate of these Gorgas made a personal appeal, and his friendly manner and reasonable explanations made it possible for the work to continue everywhere, and soon the two largest cities of the Canal Zone, as well as the rural areas, were at last almost free from mosquitoes.

But other important work had to be accomplished. Gorgas found mosquitoes infesting the homes of the people. By a system which provided free mosquito netting to the inhabitants and instructions for its use, results were soon obtained, and the process of mosquito eradication was so complete that even before the canal was finished the Canal Zone was considered to be one of the most healthful places in America.

Today it is recognized that a finished Panama Canal has been due almost entirely to mosquito control. The area adjacent to the canal was once one of the most deadly spots in the known world. Yet the staff of the finished canal, through which millions of members of ship crews and passengers have passed for years, has not recorded a single case of malaria directly traceable to infection from this area. This alone is a sufficient monument to the labor and the persistence of one of the world's greatest sanitarians.

34.

Discovery of the X Ray

This great diagnostic and therapeutic agent, the unknown or X ray, came into existence as a result of accident coupled with long periods of experimentation and deduction by Wilhelm Konrad Röntgen of the University of Würzburg. One evening in 1893, after a trying day with his classes, while sitting and relaxing at his desk in his laboratory Professor Röntgen picked up a vacuum tube which had been given him by a friend. This device was not new; it had been experimented with by numerous curious persons long before it fell into Röntgen's hands. To one of the tube's two metal plates he attached a 110-volt direct current. He then turned off the light in his laboratory, thus leaving the room in total darkness. The fragile contrivance was encased in a wooden box for protection. Without removing it from its container and while observing its soft glow as he turned the switch off and on, Röntgen was startled to see a light on the opposite side of the room. By the merest chance this faint light had fallen on a sensitized curtain which he had used in demonstrating a series of experiments to his students. Röntgen, greatly puzzled, once more turned the switch, and the light on the curtain disappeared. With the switch on again, the light was there as before. Now excited by what appeared to him as a strange phenomenon, he placed his hand behind the box to better center it on the screen, and what he beheld so astounded him that for a few minutes he could not go on with the experiment. Then he again placed his hand on the back of the box and convinced himself that what he had seen was no illusion, for the bones of his hand were pictured on the sensitized screen. To convince himself that it was in reality his own hand that he saw, he moved his hand in many positions and the shadows of each movement were faithfully depicted on the screen. Röntgen was so overcome with the knowledge that he was witnessing that which had never been seen before, a part of a living skeleton, that he remained in his laboratory for several hours, repeating the strange experiment and contemplating its possible tremendous importance to the scientific world. For a period of two years, Röntgen said nothing to his colleagues about his startling discovery, experimenting all the while with various types of sensitized plates prepared so that by a photographic process the impressions created on the screen could be put into permanent form. Then he exhibited all his apparatus, along with his pictures, before his scientific society.

"What kind of a device would you call this?" asked one of his scientific friends present.

"I call it an X ray," said Röntgen.

"Then you don't know what kind of a ray it is," replied his interrogator. "And you found it by accident?"

"Yes," said Röntgen, "it was the result of an accident."

These words of the great discoverer were used many times by his jealous confreres to belittle his invention. But have not accidental observations resulted in many of the world's greatest scientific achievements? From the casual observation of a lamp swinging in a cathedral in Pisa came the pendulum, which has evolved into the intricately delicate modern timepiece. By the merest accident a distant church spire seems enlarged when seen through two reading lenses of different strength. From this came the telescope that now brings countless worlds within our view. A teakettle forcibly ejects a stopper from its spout, and as a result of the observation of this trivial incident the world resounds with the hum of steam-powered industry. By chance a diminutive canal is noticed in the fang of a serpent. From this observation has come the hypodermic needle and the development of intravenous therapy. Illustrations of this kind could be multiplied indefinitely. Nothing of importance has ever been said or ever can be said to lessen the value of this great chance invention or detract from the luster of its great inventor.

Conclusion

The field of the historian is to delineate facts of world interest; yet it is difficult to decide in what period a medical historian should bring his narrative to a close. Facts that occur in modern life will undoubtedly be considered as history a few years hence and will be ably described by some future medical writers. With the ending of Chapter 34 it seems to me that we have come to times which are entirely modern. While it is true that the sciences of pediatrics, preventive medicine, psychiatry, dermatology, and radiology have come into existence since the period devoted to this final chapter, the intelligent readers of lay periodicals of today have acquired a remarkably true grasp of these new branches of medicine and have rather a sound knowledge of such lately discovered substances as hormones, vitamins, penicillin, insulin, and other remedial substances. The understanding public of today has such a working knowledge of the subject of dietetics and of danger signals, such as acute abdominal pain, that they have to be considered as being partly responsible for the great increase in longevity which has occurred during recent years in both Europe and America. And this social consciousness of the means to promote health and prevent disease is, I believe, destined to live and grow in the average citizen, to the immense profit of present and future generations.

As our meandering journey is brought to a close the reader may have arrived at the correct conclusion that, while medicine today is the product of the experiences of thoughtful men through thousands of years, it is far from an exact science. Much has already been done by the development of science in the laboratory, but more important work lies ahead in thousands of laboratory experiments yet to be made and by the administration of newly discovered remedies to the sick. Tremendous results have already been accomplished by the personal investigation of medical men who have risked their lives for the benefit of humanity. Experimenters have injected their own bodies with the extracts taken from cancer and from other diseased human tissue, as well as with secretions known to be infectious. We note the example of Doctor Jesse William Lazear, a physician in the United States Army, who permitted himself to be bitten by mosquitoes which had been taken from a room where yellow-fever patients had been confined, and who died as the result of his sacrifice. Countless other medical men have imperiled their lives in the study of diseases, and as a result of their labors the great epidemics of the world have been brought under control.

While medical science today, even in the light of its tremendous life- and health-saving accomplishments, may be considered as only in its infancy, let us consider what would happen if the achievements of the men whose lives have been here reviewed were to be suddenly blotted out. Should this occur, of the millions in all civilized countries who would lose their lives as a result of the return of the plagues, the inhabitants of crowded cities would be the first to succumb. In metropolitan areas no knowledge would exist as to how to prevent contamination of milk and drinking-water supplies. Children by the thousands would succumb to intestinal infections before they were a year old, as they did a hundred or more years ago. Typhoid fever, also carried through the medium of infected milk and drinking water, would immediately begin to take its toll. Asiatic cholera, another disease conveyed by infected water and milk, which once ravaged all the civilized world, killing thousands at each outbreak as it did on three occasions in this country, would again become rampant. The blight of smallpox would be resumed with its tremendous death rate, accompanied by the horrible scarring of faces and blinding of eyes similar to the epidemics which occurred before Edward Jenner made his discovery of how to hold it in check. Leprosy, now almost under complete control but of which there still are foci of infection, even in this country, would soon multiply its numbers by thousands. Countless victims of this loathsome disease would be banished to remote areas, even to the solitude of graveyards, where as the living dead they would spend the remainder of their lives as they once did in nearly all European countries. Syphilis would again afflict the innocent as well as the guilty and transmit itself to millions of unborn children, this being followed by epidemics similar to those to which whole European armies succumbed following the return of Columbus and his infected sailors from their first voyage to America. The return of these diseases and many others not mentioned here would, without modern controls, be sufficient to slowly rid the world of great numbers of its inhabitants. These infections, even in most remote sections, would make the destruction now feared by A-bombs and H-bombs dwindle into insignificance.

The possible results depicted here of the withdrawal of all the scientific methods of preserving life are in no sense a fancy sketch. Such conditions as are here mentioned existed throughout centuries of history and populations were thereby kept in check, until the great army of scientific men, only a few of whom could be mentioned in a volume of this size, gave the world valuable lessons in the control of the spread of disease. A grateful people should ever remember the deeds of these innovators, who have transformed an ancient superstition into a scientific means of protecting human life.

Acknowledgments

Adventures of Robinson Crusoe: Daniel Defoe, M. A. Donohue & Co., Chicago, 1922.

Akhnaton, Pharaoh of Egypt: Arthur Weigall, G. P. Putnam's Sons, New York, 1923.

American Antiquities: H. H. Bancroft, Bancroft Co., New York, n.d.

Among the San Blas Indians of Panama: Leon S. De Smidt, Troy, N.Y., 1948.

Andes and the Amazon, The: C. R. Enock, Fisher Unwin, London, 1907.

Arab Medicine and Surgery: M. W. H. Simpson, Oxford University Press, 1922.

Arabian Medicine: E. G. Brown, Macmillan Co., New York, 1921.

Astrology in Medicine: C. A. Mercier, Macmillan Co., New York, 1914.

"Babylonian Caduceus, The": F. H. Garrison, *Military Surgeon,* 1919.

Brotherhood of the Sea, The: K. Chatterton, Longmans, Green & Co., London, 1927.

Buccaneers of America: John Esquemeling, London, 1684.

Captain Cook's Voyages: Lt. Charles R. Low, A. L. Burt Co., New York, n.d.

Christopher Columbus: Washington Irving, A. L. Burt Co., New York, 1902.

Chronological History of Ancient Egypt: Orlando P. Schmidt, George C. Shaw, Cincinnati, 1900.

"Coat of Arms of the Medical Corps, U.S.A.": Col. C. C. McCulloch, *Military Surgeon,* August 1917.

Commentaries on the Laws of England: Sir William Blackstone, Cooley's edition, London, n.d.

Crawford W. Long: Frances Long Taylor, P. B. Hoeber, New York, 1928.

Crucibles: Bernard Jaffe, Tudor Publishing Co., New York, 1934.

Cruising Voyage Around the World, A: Woodes Rogers, Andrew Bell, London, 1718.

Crusades, The: Harold Lamb, Garden City Publishing Co., New York, 1930.

Defoe: James Sutherland, J. B. Lippincott Co., Philadelphia, 1938.

Ebers Papyrus: Cyril P. Brown, Appleton, New York, 1931.

Egypt in Transition: Sidney Low, Macmillan Co., New York, 1914.

Elements of Therapeutics and Materia Medica: N. Chapman, M.D., M. Carey & Sons, Philadelphia, 1821.

Elizabethan Seamen in the XVth Century: Scribner, New York, 1895.

Elizabethan Seamen to America: Richard Hakluyt, La Rue & Co., London, 1880.

Epidemics of the Middle Ages: J. F. C. Hecker, M.D., George Woodfall and Son, London, 1884.

Essays on the History of Medicine: Karl Sudhoff, Medical Life Press, New York, 1926.

First Book of Maccabees, The: Sidney Tedesche, Harper & Brothers, New York, 1950.

Going Down from Jerusalem: Norman Duncan, Harper & Brothers, New York, 1909.

Golden Bough, The: J. G. Frazer, Macmillan Co., New York, 1911.

Great Doctors, The: H. E. Sigerist, Norton and Co., New York, 1933.

Greek Biology and Greek Medicine: C. J. Singer, Oxford University Press, New York and London, 1922.

Guide to the Antiquities of Upper Egypt, A: Arthur E. P. Weigall, Macmillan Co., New York, 1910.

Hammurabi Code, The: Chilperic Edwards, Watts & Co., London, 1921.

Healing Gods of Ancient Civilization: W. A. Jayne, Yale University Press, New Haven, 1925.

Hellenism and Christianity: Gerald Friedlander, P. Vallentine & Sons, London, 1912.

Herodotus, The History of: Tudor Publishing Co., New York, 1932.

Hippocrates, The Works of: Francis Adams, Sydenham Society, London, 1849, 2 vols.

Historical Relations of Medicine and Surgery to the End of the Sixteenth Century: T. C. Allbutt, Macmillan Co., New York, 1905.

History of Medicine: F. H. Garrison, W. B. Saunders Co., Philadelphia, 1913.

History of the Buccaneers: James Burney, Swan Sonnenschein, London, 1891.

History of the Jews: Translated by William Whiston, A. L. Burt Co., New York, n.d.

Human Origins: George G. McCurdy, D. Appleton Co., London, 1926, 2 vols.

Jews, The: James K. Hosmer, G. P. Putnam's Sons, New York, 1913.

Kings and Gods of Egypt: Alexandre Moret, G. P. Putnam's Sons, New York, 1912.

Koran, The: Translated by George Sale, A. L. Burt Co., New York, n.d.

Last of the Heretics, The: A. S. Crapsey, Alfred A. Knopf, New York, 1924.

Life and Times of Ambrose Paré: Francis R. Packard, P. B. Hoeber, 1931.

Life of Cesare Borgia, The: Rafael Sabatini, Brentano's, New York, n.d.

Life of Francis Drake, The: A. E. W. Mason, Doubleday, Doran & Co., New York, 1942.

Life of Paracelsus, The: Anna M. Stoddart, J. Murray, London, 1894.

London Dispensatory, The: N. Culpepper, London, 1649.

Magellan: Arthur Sturges Hildebrand, Harcourt, Brace and Co., New York, 1924.

Makers of Florence, The: Mrs. Oliphant, Macmillan Co., New York, n.d.

Martyrs of Science, The: Sir David Brewster, J. C. Hotten, London, 1870.

Medical Leaders from Hippocrates to Osler: S. W. Lambert and G. M. Goodwin, Bobbs Merrill, Indianapolis, 1929.

Medicine in the Bible: C. J. Brim, The Froben Press, New York, 1936.

Medicine—Its Contribution to Civilization: Edward B. Vedder, Williams Wilkes Co., Baltimore, 1929.

Medicine, Magic and Religion: W. H. R. Rivers, Harcourt, Brace and Co., New York, 1924.

"Medieval Hospitals": Ely Sparkman, *Dublin Review,* 1903.

Medieval Italy: H. B. Cotterill, Frederick A. Stokes Co., New York, n.d.

Medieval Medicine: J. J. Walsh, Macmillan Co., New York, 1920.

Medieval Mind, The: H. O. Taylor, Macmillan Co., New York, 1927.

Mohammed and the Rise of Islam: D. S. Margoliouth, G. P. Putnam's Sons, New York, 1905.

Modern Sons of the Pharaohs: S. H. Leeder, Hodder and Stoughton, New York, 1918.

Moors in Spain, The: Stanley Lane-Poole, G. P. Putnam's Sons, New York, 1911.

Nemesis of Nations, The: W. R. Paterson, E. P. Dutton & Co., New York, 1917.

New Voyage and Description of the Isthmus of America, A: Lionel Wafer, James Knapton, London, 1704.

Nova Francia: Translated by P. Erondelle, Harper & Brothers, New York and London, 1928.

Religious Life in Ancient Egypt: Sir Flinders Petrie, Houghton Mifflin Co., Boston, 1924.

Romance of the Spanish Main, The: N. J. Davidson, Seeley, Service & Co., London, 1916.

Sacred Writings: Edited by Charles W. Eliot, P. F. Collier & Son, New York, 1909, 2 vols.

Saracens, The: Arthur Gilman, G. P. Putnam's Sons, New York, 1908.

Sixty Centuries of Health and Physick: S. G. B. Stubbs and E. W. Bligh, P. B. Hoeber, New York, 1931.

Stories from the Thousand and One Nights: Translated by Edward William Lane, P. F. Collier & Sons, New York, 1909.

Story of Medicine in the Middle Ages, The: David Riesman, M.D., P. B. Hoeber, New York, 1935.

Superstition in Medicine: J. L. Sallinger, Funk and Wagnalls, New York, 1905.

Tragedies of the Medici: Edgcumbe Staley, Brentano's, New York, n.d.

Westminster Abbey: Helen Marshall Pratt, Duffield & Co., New York, 1914.

William Dampier: Clennell Wilkinson, John Lane the Bodley Head, London, 1929.

World Encompassed, The: Francis Drake, Hakluyt Society, London, n.d.

Index

ABOUT THE AUTHOR

Donald T. Atkinson is a physician who for forty years has specialized in diseases of the eye. He received much of his technical training abroad, having studied the eye in The Royal London Ophthalmic Hospital and the University of Vienna. He holds a postgraduate degree from the latter institution. He is a member of the American Medical Association and a fellow of the American College of Surgeons, the International College of Surgeons, Geneva, Switzerland, and the Royal Academy of Medicine in Ireland. In 1947 he was awarded a medal of merit from the University of Florence, Italy, for his original researches, as well as a life membership in the National Surgical Society of Italy. He is the author of two textbooks on the subject of the eye, published by Lea & Febiger, Philadelphia. On the subjects treated in this book, Dr. Atkinson has done research on all five continents and has personally investigated almost every incident mentioned. He has long been an illustrator of scientific books and in this capacity has made illustrations for, and otherwise collaborated with, many educators and surgeons in both Europe and America. He is married and lives on Huebner Road in San Antonio, Texas.